CATACLYSM

CATACLYSM

SECRETS OF THE HORN OF AFRICA

ZEYNAB ALI

To order additional copies of this book, contact:
Xlibris
1-888-795-4274
www.Xlibris.com
Orders@Xlibris.com
730187

This book is dedicated to the many innocent lives lost due to senseless wars and conflicts throughout the globe, as well as those inflicted by violence within the status quo. Surely, Allah will indeed bring forth justice.

CONTENTS

PART 2: SURVIVING SOMALIA: OUR JOURNEY TO AMERICA

List of Acronyms

AIAI al Itihaad al Islamiya

AMISOM African Union Mission In Somalia

AQ Al- Qaeda

ARS Alliance for the Re-liberation of Somalia

AU African Union

CDBG Community Development Block Grant

DRA Department of Refugee Affairs

EU European Union

FGM Female Genital Mutilation

GOK Government of Kenya

IB International Baccalaureate

ICT Information and Communication Technologies

IED Improvised Explosive Devices

IGAD Intergovernmental Authority on Development

INS Instant Network Schools

IOM International Organization for Migration

ISWA Interim South West Administration

KRCS Kenya Red Cross Society

MMSA Milwaukee Math & Science Academy

MPS Milwaukee Public Schools

NISA National Intelligence and Security Agency

NGO Nongovernmental Organization

NRC Norwegian Refugee Council

OAU Organization of African Unity

OCHA Office for the Coordination of Humanitarian Affairs

RRA Rahanweyn Resistance Army

SDM Somali Democratic Movement

SFG Somali Federal Government

SGBV Sexual and Gender Based Violence

SNA Somali National Alliance

SNF Somali National Front

SNM Somali National Movement

SPM Somali Patriotic Movement

SRRC Somali Restoration and Reconciliation Committee

SSDF Somali Salvation Democratic Front

SWDO Somali Women Democratic Organization

TFG Transitional Federal Government

TNA Transitional National Assembly

TNC Transitional National Charter

TNG Transitional National Government

UIC Union of Islamic Courts

UN United Nations

UNHCR United Nations High Commissioner for Refugees

UNITAF Unified Task Force

USC United Somali Congress

WFP World Food Programme

PART 1

OVERVIEW

The Horn of Africa

The Horn of Africa is the region of eastern Africa. It is the easternmost extension of the African continent. The region consists of eight countries with an estimated total population of about 226.9 million in 2012 and a total area of 5,209,975 square kilometers. The countries of the region include: Djibouti, Eritrea, Ethiopia, Kenya, Somalia, Sudan, South Sudan, and Uganda, and they are all members of a regional integration, the Intergovernmental Authority for Development (IGAD), although Eritrea's membership in the regional body has been suspended since 2007. The countries have been associated with their long history. Part of the Horn of Africa region is also known as the Somali peninsula; this term is typically used when referring to lands of Somalia and eastern Ethiopia. Two of the youngest countries of the region, Eritrea and South Sudan, were formed through secessions from Ethiopia in 1993 and from Sudan in 2011, respectively. Somaliland has also declared its independence from Somalia, but it has not yet gained international recognition as an independent state.

In recent years, the region contains one of the deadliest conflicts in the world. Each of the countries of the Horn—especially Somalia, Ethiopia, Eritrea, Djibouti, and Sudan—suffer from prolonged political conflict, emerging from local and national affront, identity politics, and regional in-state rivalries. The region also faces an increasing amount of environmental ignominious, which caused many humanitarian disasters, including periodic droughts and famines. Likewise, without significant changes in the political system, the region is more likely to remain one of the deadliest places in the global system.

According to researcher Klaus von Grebmer, despite the fact that agriculture is the most popular field in all the countries of the region, most of them suffer from chronic food shortages, undernourishment, and periodic famines. An IGAD official in 2010 described the region as "the most critically food insecure region of the world." The 2010 Global Hunger Index, for example, rates hunger severity of the countries of the region from "extremely alarming" (Eritrea) to "alarming" (Djibouti, Ethiopia, and Sudan) and "serious" (Kenya and Uganda) (Von Grebmer et al., 2010).

As reported, every country in the region has experienced at least one civil war during the post-independence period. In most cases they have fought numerous civil wars. Some of the civil wars in the Horn are closely linked with state conflicts, and the substate participants who fight against the state mostly serve as proxies of other states. The countries of the Greater Horn have engaged in what authors Lionel Cliffe and Phillip White (2002: 54) call "mutual intervention" in each other's domestic conflicts. Some regimes support insurgencies in a neighboring country either because of ethnic ties with the rebelling groups or because such groups undermine regimes they have poor relations with. This book is primarily about one of the countries in the Horn of Africa—Somalia. Of all the countries in the Horn of Africa, Somalia remains the most deadly of them all. Somalia is currently a war zone and remains exceedingly dangerous for traveling and sightseeing due to the terrorist group al-Shabaab. As reported by Kidane Mengisteab, the author of *The Horn of Africa*, despite the conflict Somalia is improving (Mengisteab, 2014). Throughout the book, I'll speak about the history of the country, which briefly explains how the conflict began as well as the country's current state.

Location

According to the US State Department, the Republic of Somalia was constituted on July 1, 1960, which consisted former British Somaliland (north) and former Italian Somalia (south). The country has an approximate landmass of 246,331 square miles (638,000 square kilometers). It is a bit bigger than the United Kingdom (242,900 square miles). It is nearly smaller than the state of Texas (268,601 square miles). Somalia is bordered to the northwest by Djibouti; to the northeast, the Somali Peninsula projects into the Arabian Sea. The entire north is bordered by the Gulf of Aden with Yemen on the other side of the sea, and the entire eastern shores are prominently circumscribed by the Indian Ocean. The virulent seas—the Gulf of Aden, the Arabian Sea, and Indian Ocean—have provided a rich source of seafood, serving since ancient times as a main route for a profitable international commerce linking up the East African societies with the Middle East, India, China, Europe, and the rest of the world.

The capital is Mogadishu, which in 1987 had a population of one million, followed by the other major towns of Hargeisa with four hundred thousand and Kismayo with two hundred thousand (U.S. Department of State, 2015).

Somalia is principally deserted. There is a monsoon in the northeast from December to February, with moderate temperatures in the north but very hot in the south. Between monsoons it is generally very hot and humid. Somalia is divided into three main topographic regions. The northern region is somewhat mountainous with high plateaus ranging from nine hundred meters (2,953 feet) above sea level to peaks at 2,450 meters (8,038 feet) above sea level in the northeast. The second region extends south and west to the Shebelle River and hosts a plateau elevated to a maximum of 685 meters (2,247 feet) above sea level. The third region lies between the Jubba and Shebelle rivers and is a low agricultural land that also extends into a low pasture land lying southwest of the Jubba River toward the Kenyan border.

The Jubba region is a fertile agricultural land mass stretching between the Kenyan border to the west and the Indian Ocean to the east. Unlike the Shebelle River, which usually dries up from January to March, the Jubba River is permanent and is capable of irrigating about 150,000 hectares (370,500 acres) of land. Land, particularly farmland is one of the most important possessions in the river valley. Farmland, known locally as *dhooboy* (muddy land), is the most arable land in Somalia.

Another source of water for farming is rainfall, which is scarce in some seasons.

Most of the Jubba River valley receives about twenty-four inches of rain per year. There are two rainy seasons in this region that corresponds with the river's high points, which, combined with water from the Jubba River, allows farmers to grow crops throughout the year. Most farmers in the region practice a mixed farming system, as rain-fed land mainly provides sorghum and beans. As a result, farmers tend to exploit the recession of river flooding from the adjoining *dhesheeg*, or depression, along the Jubba River. This makes the Bantu-occupied areas of the Jubba River valley extremely productive—and valuable—and thus the backbone of agricultural production for national and international markets in southern Somalia.

Geography

According to Negussay Ayele, author of *The Horn of Africa: Revolutionary Developments and Western Reactions*, "history and geography are somewhat connected in this region." In Somalia, geography holds the key to a better understanding of the people's history, culture, technology, economy, politics, and national characteristics, as well as its pace and challenges of development.

Somalia's landscape, consisting mainly of highlands, plateau, and both flat and surging plains, contrasts at different points in accordance with the country's varying seasonal climates and vegetation zones. In this East African region you'll find some of the oldest rocks on the continent, dating back to the Mesozoic era (age of dinosaurs 250 million years ago). The timeless age of these prehistoric rocks stands today as a solid reminder that Africa is the oldest continent in the world. The rocks also preserve fossils that can be studied to appreciate how nature, humans, fauna, and environment have interacted across different millennia in the evolution of culture in this part of Africa.

From the northern shores of the Gulf of Aden, the lounging terrain is dominated by blanketed and surging Karkaar Mountains running from the northeast tip of the Horn of Africa to the northwest border regions with Djibouti. Approximately, the entire northern region is defined by three terrains: the coastal *Guban* (scrub land), the mountainous *Golis*, and the central plateau *Haud,* a very extensive zone stretching from Northern Somalia through the Ogaden as far as Mudug and upper Shabelle areas of southern Somalia along the Ethiopian-Somalia borders.

Squeezed in between the coastal plains of Gulf of Aden and the mountains is the Guban, a lower stretch of territory whose name originated from its desert environment and translates to "burned by a network of dry riverbeds, ridges, and knolls. The crisscrossing broad and shallow watercourses form beds of dry sand except in rainy seasons when they are filled with rainwater. This makes the Guban seasonally useful during the short rainy season that runs from May to June when travelers flock to the area to cool off, farm, and graze their animals.

Farther south, a small range of highlands called the *Ogo* or *Oogs* leads to the Golis zone. This means the area in the north has two mountain ranges (the Golis and the Ogo). At its highest peak at Shimber Berris, the Golis Mountains reaches up to nine thousand feet (2,743.2 meters) high. The Ogo gradually slopes eastward toward the Indian Ocean.

The Haud, extending from three corners—the city of Hargeisa (northwest), the Doollo plains (west), and the Nugaal valley (east) is a broad, undulating terrain that provides some of the best arable and grazing lands. The attraction of the Haud for grazers is further enhanced by natural depressions that temporarily become lakes during the rainy season.

In the southern region of the country are two rivers, the Shebelle and the Jubba, both of which originate in Ethiopia, running in the southeastward direction toward the Indian Ocean. The sections of the land that are not cultivated assist in the abundance of wildlife. Shebelle River and Jubba River are cooperatively the country's heartland. They provide the waters for the irrigation of crops; however, the amount of water depends greatly on the amount of rainfall brought by the two rainy seasons starting from around March to April. Altogether, there are four seasons, comprising two wet seasons and two dry seasons. The seasons run simultaneously in the following order: April–June, July–September, October–November, and December–March. In the midst of extreme climate, most parts of the lands obtain no more than 19.7 inches (500 milliliters) of rainfall per year. With the exceptions of the coastal areas, certain highlands in the north and the southwest and some crucial parts of the lowlands in the north gain as little as 1.97–5.91 inches (50–150 milliliters) of rainfall annually. While the monsoon winds bring seasonal rains to the Sahel and the Sudan, they tend to lose their moisture upon getting to Djibouti and Somalia.

The first period of the rainy season, known as the *gu*, roughly begins in March to April, lasting through June to July. As inhabitants of the cold regions of North America and Europe yearn for the summer season, so do Somalis long for the *gu* or the "long rains," as it is often called. The *gu* season is usually a huge relief for people, animals, and plants after the four months of dryness that follow it. During this period, there is plenty of water, milk, meat, and food. The land, reprieved from four months of harsh dryness, usually comes alive with celebrations, rituals, and recreational activities such as singing, poetry, and dancing.

High temperatures (ranging from twenty to forty degrees Celsius, and averaging thirty degrees Celsius) coupled with the monsoon winds cause rapid evaporation of rainwater that has a negative impact on the recharging and level of groundwater. Rainfall is relatively low—most of Somalia gets less than 500 millimeters of rain annually. Along the coast of the Gulf of Aden, the annual rainfall has been measured at 100 millimeters; the same applies to enclaves in the northeastern region. Around 500 millimeters annual rainfall is more common in the Kismayo area in the south extending along the coast into Kenya along the coast, an area which is characterized by humid savanna in the inter-riverine area between Jubba and Shabelle and also in a few mountainous places in the north around Erigavo and Sheikh and in the area stretching from Gebiley to Jijiga.

According to Somali scholar Abdi Ismail Samatar, the level of rainfall in Somalia and in the Ethiopian Highlands determines the seasonal availability of water resources, including the water level of the Shabelle and the Juba, the occasional appearance of seasonal rivers such as the *Tug Jerer* and *Tug Fafan* and temporary lakes in the Haud in southeastern Ethiopia, the productivity of wells, and the amount of water storage in artificial water basins.

It is probable that about five thousand geniuses of vascular plants with lignified (i.e., converted into wood) tissues for conducting water are found in the entire Horn region. Out of this variety, at least 2,500, or 55 percent, are native to the region. In Somalia, most of these plants are concentrated in the "garden" area around the Jubba and Shebelle Rivers. Some of the popular indigenous plants include the acacia trees, aloe plants, and other vegetation such as juniper trees. The most popular, however, remain the boswellia tree, from which frankincense is tapped, and the commiphora tree, which produces myrrh resin. The ancient Egyptians processed myrrh from the region for high-grade incense used in religious festivals and rites. The common understanding today is that the Egyptians referred to the area known today as Somalia as the famed Land of Punt from which they received their steady supplies of myrrh and frankincense (Samatar, 1989: p. 16).

As reported by author Raphael Chijioke Njoku, the Somali people live in the easternmost part of continental Africa, known as the Horn of Africa, bordering the Gulf of Aden and the Indian Ocean. The area stretches about 250 kilometers south and 1,250 kilometers north of the equator, roughly between the forty-first and the fifty-first degree of eastern longitude. The coastline runs along the Red Sea in the north and continues southward along the Indian Ocean to approximately the Tana River, which forms the southwestern limit of Somali population (Njoku, 2013).

In total, the Somali coastline is a little more than three thousand kilometers long. To the West the branches of the Ethiopian highlands form the limit of Somali expansion. The Somali-inhabited area in the Horn comprises about nine hundred thousand square kilometers, of which 637,600 square kilometers makeup the Somalia state territory, as it existed from July 1, 1960 to the end of January 1991. The remaining Somali-inhabited areas form parts of Djibouti, Ethiopia, and Kenya, which have borders with Somalia of 58 kilometers, 1,626 kilometers, and 682 kilometers, respectively (Njoku, 2013).

Society

Although there are no reliable statistical sources today, the Somali population is estimated at about 7.5 million people. Of that figure, the entire Bantu population in southern Somalia is estimated at about six hundred thousand, and those with strong East African identification estimated at a fraction of that number. The Bantu people are ethnically and culturally distinct from the Somali nomads and the coastal people, who generally contempt agriculture and value a tribal lineage system that does not include the Bantu.

The Bantu peoples seen as having predominant Negroid physical features are distinct from that of the Somali nomads and give them a unique identity. Among the physical features used to differentiate the nomads from the Bantu is hair texture—*jareer* (kinky hair for the Bantu people) and *jilec* (soft hair for the non-Bantus or Somalis). People with such features are subjected to a variety of discriminatory treatments. They are often excluded from political, economic, and educational advancement. The Bantu, therefore, have had to settle for the lowest and most undignified occupations.

Some Bantu populations still maintain the tribal identities of their ancestral country of origin. However, unlike the nomadic Somalis, who consider clan affiliation and tribal identification sacred and critical to survival, most Bantu people identify themselves by their place of residence, which for those with strong cultural ties to Tanzania, often corresponds to their ceremonial kin grouping. The Bantu slated for resettlement in the United States, therefore, place much less emphasis on Somali clan and tribal affiliations than do the non-Bantu Somalis who have been resettled in the United States. Other Bantu who lived in the vicinity of nomadic Somali clans (particularly those residing outside of the lower Jubba River valley) integrated into the Somali nomadic clan system, which provided the Bantu with protection and a sense of identity with the nomads.

Excluded from mainstream Somali society, many Bantu have retained ancestral social structures. For many of the Bantu from the lower Jubba River valley, this means that their East African tribe of origin is the main form of social organization. For these Bantu, smaller units of social organization are broken down according to matrilineal kin groupings, which are often compared with ceremonial dance groupings. Bantu village and community composition normally follows the Bantu's East African tribal and kin groupings.

Many Bantu from the middle Jubba River valley lost their East African language and culture. These Bantu have attempted to integrate, usually as inferior members, into a local dominant Somali clan social structure. Like the Bantu from the lower Jubba River valley, the Bantu from the middle Jubba River valley also regard their village as an important form of social organization. Although Bantu with strong cultural and linguistic links to southeast Africa have been known to level sarcasm against those who attempted to assimilate into the dominant Somali clan culture and language, there is no real hostility between them. In fact, the war and refugee experience have worked to strengthen relationships between the various Bantu subgroups in some cases.

Modern Somalia is made up of 85 percent ethnic Somalis, and the rest are small-minority Bantu, Bravenese, Bajuni, Rerhamar, Eyle, Ogadenis, etc. The major languages of the people include Somali, the primary language; and Arabic, the language of Islam, which is also one of the four languages in official use. The other official languages are Italian and English. In a sense, Somali society was formed as a nation of migrants, but because of the prevalence of the Somali language as both a unifying factor and a mark of ethnicity, it is assumed by foreigners that the nation had a greater level of national homogeneity than most other African countries. It should not, however, be overlooked that although the ancestors of the Somali came from the Ethiopian Highlands, they were, over time, joined by diverse elements from the Cushitic race, Bantus, Arabs, and a couple of Indians, and Lebanese.

Sources have revealed that the present inhabitants of the country have an ancient history. This understanding is contrary to previous theories that have tried to place the Somali homeland in the area surrounding the Red

Sea's western coast or even in southern Arabia. For instance, writing in 1912, Ralph E. Drake-Brockman, a British colonial scholar, had speculated that the Somali are a "Hamito-Semitic race" and that their birth could be traced to 696 CE, when one obscure Arab visitor named Darod was shipwrecked on the Majerteen coast. Such speculations are common in the old colonial historiography as the Europeans attempted to attribute every element of cultural achievement found in Africa to outside migrants.

The new light shed on African history by vital archaeological materials indicates that the modern ancestors of Somalia known to medieval Arab visitors as "Berbere" had settled on the Horn of Africa by 100 CE. The oral tradition claims that the early Somali settlers were part of the Cushitic race, and that they originally came from the Ethiopian Highlands and its surrounding areas. The Somalis are most closely related to the Oromo of Ethiopia and the Afars (Danakili) of Djibouti. If we rely on the linguistic evidence, it suggests a migration from southern Ethiopia no later than the fifth century CE.

The Arab population of modern Somalia was latter migrants, some of whom, through their participation in the seaborne trade across the Red Sea, via the Aden Sea, and the Indian Ocean, began to establish permanent settlements in Somalia. By the eighth century, the population of traders from Arabia and Persia had grown remarkably in the coastal cities of Somalia. A good number of the traders' connections on the Indian Ocean and the Red Sea. Particularly, cities like Zeila (Zeyla), Mogadishu, and their immediate neighborhoods were swollen by Arab Muslims. Over time, the settlers made Islam the dominant faith in the region. Zeila, once a walled commercial city called Seylac, was popular for its coffee and slave markets; hence it was a favorite destination for foreign merchants and visitors.

Somalis consider themselves as sharing a common ancestor, Somaal, a mythical father figure (Putnam and Noor, 1999). Somalis, the dominant ethnic group in Somalia, make up 85 percent of the population, and share a uniform language, religion, and culture. In fact Somalia has been characterized as one of the most ethnically and culturally homogenous countries in Africa. Several minority groups in current-day Somalia are Arabs, Southeast Asians, and the Bantus, who were brought from southeastern Africa to Somalia as slaves (Putnam and Noor, 1999). An estimated six hundred thousand Bantus lived in Somalia before the civil war, and although some Bantus integrated into Somali society, others maintained their ancestral culture, languages, and sense of southeast African identity. These Bantus, in particular, have been marginalized and persecuted in Somalia, and because of this historical subjugation, may have quite distinct needs from ethnic Somalis (Lehman and Eno, 2003).

The universal language in Somalia is Somali, a Cushitic language shared by people of Eastern Africa. Somali includes distinct regional variations. The two main variants, *Af Maay* (Af My) spoken by the Somali Bantus and *Af Maxaa* (Af Mahaa) spoken by the Somalis, were the official languages of Somalia until 1972 when the government determined that *Af Maxaa* would serve as the official written language. The two languages are similar in written form.

The civil war that ravaged the country since the mid-1980s, counted a large number of people killed. As the majority of the population is Muslim, Arabic is the second most commonly spoken language. The formally educated in Somalia may also speak French, Italian, English, Russian, or Swahili. After 1972, however, when Somali became the official language of government and instruction, young people had little exposure to other languages; therefore, those who are currently at least middle-aged and educated are more likely than their younger counterparts to be proficient in English, Italian, Arabic, or Russian.

Competence with speech is highly valued among Somalis. Additionally, Somalis tend to appreciate oral communication above all other art forms. The Somali language has a long and rich tradition of proverbs and idioms, which are passed down through generations and embellished by the individual speaker. Everyday Somali speech often includes these expressions, and some Somalis, finding English lacking in these terms, may translate and use Somali expressions (Putnam and Noor, 1999). Somali speakers may also use humor based on puns and wordplay to counter criticism, "save face," or disentangle themselves from uncomfortable or embarrassing situations (Samatar, 1993). In Somali society, one's abilities as a leader, warrior, or suitor may depend largely on the ability to speak articulately and with humor.

Naming convention among Somalis does not include the use of surnames; instead, Somalis typically use three names, their given name and their father's and grandfather's given names. These names can be used interchangeably. Additionally, most Somali names signify birth time, birth order, or physical characteristics. For example, first children are often called either Faduma or Mohammed, and male twins are frequently named

Hassan and Hussein. Many Somalis have nicknames that are used in public (Putnam and Noor, 1999). Health care workers can inquire about a person's nickname and verify whether this name should be used. Lastly, women do not change their names at marriage (Lewis, 1996). The common way to greet a person is to say *asalamu alaykum* (peace be with you) and, when greeters are of the same gender, to shake hands. (The Islamic tradition that women and men do not touch each other is observed.) Upon departing, the appropriate phrase is *nabad gelyo* (good-bye). Elders are often given respect by being addressed as aunt or uncle, even if they are strangers (Lewis, 1996).

As previously mentioned, determining the population of Somalia has long been a difficult task. According to the February 1975 population census, the population of Somalia was 3,253,024 (excluding adjustment for undercounting), while the February 1986 census recorded it at 7,114,431, implying a doubling of the population over the decade. According to the United Nations (UN) estimates, the midyear population in 2000 as 7,253,137. All such estimates were derived by extrapolating from official censuses taken in 1975 and 1986 by the Somali government. Such estimates are complicated by the large number of nomads and by refugee movements in a country that has been racked by war and famine for a decade.

Nearly 50 percent of the population is nomadic, moving mainly in the central and northern areas, where drought is an ever-present threat. Almost all the nomadic clans are acclimatized to grazing on both sides of the border with Ethiopia. About 28 percent of the population is settled farmers, mostly in the southern areas between the Jubba and Shebelle rivers. The population profile was estimated in 2000 as 44 percent in the 0-14 years age group, 53 percent between 15 and 64 years, and 3 percent in the 65 years and over age group.

Before the 1991 civil conflict, population density averaged twelve people per square kilometer (thirty-one per square mile) but was unevenly distributed. The areas of greatest rural density were the settled zones adjacent to the Jubba and Shebelle rivers, a few places between them, and several small areas in the northern highlands. The most lightly populated zones were in northeastern and central Somalia, but there were some other sparsely populated areas in the far southwest along the Kenyan border.

Somalia's entire coastlines, the longest in Africa, measure about 1,800 miles from the lava fields of the neighboring northwestern country of Djibouti to the southernmost parts bordering Kenya. To the west, Somalia shares indecisive and frequently violent contested boundaries with Ethiopia. This disunity which began in the colonial became eradicable and is a serious concern for the British on the independence of Somaliland.

In the meantime, Somali predominates the languages. Several dialects: common Somali most widely used, coastal Somali spoken on the Benadir Coast; central Somali spoken in the inter-riverine area. English and Italian used by relatively small proportion (less than 10 percent) of urban population. Somali and Italian used at university level; Somali used at all school levels below university. Arabic used in religious contexts. Indigenous languages include various dialects of Afar and Boni. An overwhelming majority of nationals are ethnic Somalis; and two agricultural clan-families (Digil and Rahanwayn). In 1991 centralized state disintegrated into its constituent lineages and clans.

In 1991 modern public education was offered free at all levels, nationally owned educational facilities closed after the collapse of the Somali state, school attendance grew rapidly in settled areas in 1970s primary education extended to nomadic children in early 1980s. Literacy campaigns resulted in substantial increases in 1970s but less than government's estimate of 60 percent, with relapse among nomads by 1977; United Nations estimate shows 24 percent literacy rate in 1990.

Improvement in the numbers of health care personnel and facilities during 1970s was offset by civil war, refugee burden, and failure to expand services beyond urban areas; weak modern medical infrastructure deteriorated dramatically after the 1991 collapse of the central government. There exists a high incidence of pulmonary tuberculosis, malaria, tetanus, parasitic and venereal infections, leprosy, and a variety of skin and eye ailments; relatively low incidence of human immunodeficiency virus (HIV) less than 1 percent; general health was severely affected by widespread malnutrition and famine in 1992 (United Nations, 2015).

Islam in Somalia

It is evident that Somalia maintained commercial and cultural contacts with the ancient world, especially with Egyptians, southern Arabians, and other West Asian groups. Pre-Islamic Arabia and Persia established a very active trade in Somalia.

Islam found its way to Somalia from the religion's very beginning. In fact, many Somalis claim that their ancestors were converted to Islam before Islam even reached Madina, Islam's first capital city. Somalia has played a unique role in the history of Islamic Africa: As the only country in the whole continent whose population is virtually all Muslim, all Somali Muslims are considered Sunni.

One might expect, therefore, that in Somalia the effort to build a unified, harmonious nation would be more successful than in other African nations in which religious and partisan differences hinder social integration. Furthermore, there is a strong belief that Somalia's ancestors descended from the family of the Prophet Muhammad (peace and blessings be upon him), so that all Somalis belong to the Hashimite stock of the Qurayshi clan. Against, this would seem to be another factor bound to boost Somalia's sense of common nationhood, unlike the other African nations, in which tribalism and clannism remain major obstacles to unity.

Islam is professed to be both *Deen* (religion) and *Dawla* (state). Islam is presented as an all-encompassing system of beliefs and ideas in which the realms of ethics and politics are intimately related to a system of supreme, all-embracing morality. Although theoretically all the resources of Islamic culture were open to Somali Muslims, not all were available, because of the means and ways by and in which Islam spread to Somalia.

Despite the centrality of Islam in Somali life, very little is known about the manner and forms of its diffusion in the countryside, partly because Somalia remained an oral society whose languages were never put into a written form. Moreover, scholars have not exhausted and explored sources on Somali history and culture in a comprehensive way.

Early sources confirm a South Arabian presence along the Somali coast. Somali-Arab connections of the pre-Islamic period were manifested primarily in trade relations, although some historians believe that constant Arab visits and migrations cultivated strong cultural ties with the Somali people, including marriages. It was, however, with the rise of Islam in Arabia during the seventh century A.D. that the Arab impact became pronounced. This was natural. Islam is a universal religion that strongly urges its adherents to spread and preach Islam all over the world, which requires travel and migration.

Concerning the early Arab Muslim migrations to Somalia, there are three possible scenarios to consider: *fath* ("conquest"), *hijrah* ("voluntary or forced migration"), and *tijarah* ("trade and commerce"). Concerning the first scenario, "conquest," it is necessary to understand the nature and causes of Islamic conquest. The early adherents of Islam were looking for political stability and the betterment of their economic situation. They were surrounded by powerful empires that threaten their existence. Therefore, the early waves of Islamic "conquests" were defensive, purely reactive efforts at warding off perceived threats. However, Somalis, unlike the Persians, the Romans, or even the Arab chiefs, neither posed a threat to the Muslim community in Arabia nor offered any economic potential to be exploited. So Somalia as a whole cannot properly be regarded as part of an aggressive Islamic conquest.

Nevertheless, Arab sources indicate that parts of Somalia fell into the hands of Umayyad conquerors during the Caliphate of Abdul Malik Ibn Marwan (685–705). The caliph sent a Muslim army led by Syrian General Musa Ibn Umar al-Khath'ami to conquer both Mogadishu and the neighboring East African city-state of Kilwa. The directives given to Musa Ibn Umar were identical to those given to any other Muslim conqueror: to secure the taxation of *al-Kharaj*, to teach the Qur'an, and to safeguard the security of the country and assure its loyalty to the Islamic state in Damascus. *Kitab al-Zunuj* confirms that the Umayyads controlled parts of Somalia until their downfall.

Thus it is clear that while the Muslims did not conquer the whole Somali peninsula, they did claim authority over significant parts of southern Somalia, known to the Arabs as *Bilad al-Zinj* (the land of the blacks), which extends from Mogadishu to Kilwa in East Africa. This region provided the Arabs adequate economic resources. Moreover, the region was politically volatile, as it was a refuge and safe haven for the disputing claimants to the Islamic throne in Madina, Damascus, and Baghdad.

Islam advocates migration, one of the most effective factors in the spread of Islam throughout the world. The early Muslim migrants to Somalia, mainly from Yemen, Hadramaut, Uman, and Persia, were initially motivated by the desire to spread Islam overseas; but since the economic and climatic conditions of the migrant's homeland were poor and harsh, they were also motivated by the desire to strike it rich in a land of opportunity. Furthermore, the emergence of Islam itself in Mecca and the establishment of the Islamic state in Madina generated tremendous tension between the followers of Islam and the pagan Arabs. Hence, newly converted Muslims victimized by severe persecution were advised by the Prophet Muhammad to migrate.

The Muslim migration grew tremendously from the rise of Islam to the tenth century A.D. According to authoritative Arab sources, there were eight major waves of Arab and Persian settlements in Somalia. Inscriptions on some tombstones found along the coastal regions of southern Somalia are vivid evidence of the presence of Islam in Somalia during the few centuries of the Islamic era. Sharif 'Aidarus in his book *Bughyat al-Amal* offers ample evidence to show the arrival of many Arab tribes in Mogadishu, such as the Makhzumis.

Medieval Muslim writers, as well as Benadiri oral tradition and genealogical claims, report the presence of Persian Muslims on the Benadir coast. In Mogadishu, inside the *Mihrab* niche of the Arba' Rukun Mosque, there is an inscription showing the name of the person who founded the mosque and the date of construction (Khusrow Ibn Muhammad al-Shirazi, in the year 667 A.H. / 1268-69 A.D.). One of the ancient quarters of Mogadishu became not only predominantly populated by the Persians but was also given a Persian name, *Shingani*, a Nishapurian place name in Farsi. The *Shanshiya* tribe in present-day Somalia derives its name from a very prosperous district in Iran.

To understand more about the Persian presence in Somalia, one must emphasize the Shi'a elements in contemporary Somali Islam. Somalis follow the Sunni school of law; however, unlike the rest of the Sunni Muslims, they regard the household of the Prophet Muhammad with special honor, particularly the fourth Caliph Ali and his wife Fatima, the daughter of the Prophet. In fact, the veneration of Fatima developed into a cult. Southern Somali women hold regular memorial ceremonies chanting poems on her deeds "Abaay Sitidey" or "Abaay Nabiyey," the latter referring to Fatima as the Prophet of womenfolk.

Arab historians of the time described southern Somalia as predominantly Sunni Muslim. Ibn Sa'id al-Maghribi (d. 1286) declared that by his time the majority of Somalis had become Muslims, particularly those of the coastal region of Benadir. He calls Mogadishu the city of Islam, *Dar al-Islam.*

Commercial and religious activities in the southern Somali regions were conducted both by Somalis and by the Muslim migrant communities in their early stages, but eventually those activities were dominated by the Somalis. Al-Hamawi (d. 1229), in his *Mu'jam*, describes Somalis as black to distinguish them from the migrant Asian communities. Mogadishu, he writes, "was predominantly populated by foreigners and not blacks." According to al-Hamawi, Somalis provided for the inter-regional trade considerable quantities of ivory and hides of what he called "strange animals," such as giraffes, rhinoceroses, and leopards "not found elsewhere in the world.

In the Northern Somali coast, though more adjacent to the center of Islamic activity, the situation was quite different. Unlike southern Somali society, most of the present Northern Somalia clans claim to be the descendants of Arab ancestors. However, it is hard to find evidence to support any Arabic or Islamic legacies; the Arab presence in the region seems to have been small and insignificant.

Despite the Somali belief that Islam was introduced in the northern region of Somalia as early as the time of the Prophet Muhammad, we lack evidence to support the claim. Four factors illustrate the nonappeal of the northern region of Somaliland for Muslim migration. First is the region's proximity to the headquarters of the Islamic State. Fugitive Muslim migrants, concerned about their future security, would not risk settling in neighboring areas such as Somaliland. They drew this lesson from the first Muslim migration to Abyssinia (now Ethiopia), in which pagan Meccans sent to Abyssinia a punitive mission led by 'Amr Ibn al-'As to claim the repatriation of those expatriates. Secondly, there were few urban centers to attract Muslim migrants. Even today, Northern Somali nomadism would not have been conductive to the development of such an infrastructure. The nomadic life remained the predominant culture in the region throughout its history.

The nomads roved behind their flocks, looking for pasture and water and conducting their affairs through tribal customary law. Islamic culture is generally urban, but Somalia had relatively few towns and cities. Thus, where no town existed, Islam could not penetrate. Thirdly, the lack of natural harbors and the frequent violent cyclones made the journey to that part of Africa very dangerous. Al-Mas'udi on one of his travels to East Africa reported the sea storms, particularly toward the approaches of Cape Guardafui. The fourth reason why migrants were not attracted to the northern region of Somaliland was the lack of viable economic resources.

Somalia, with the exception of the inter-river regions, consists largely of dry savannah plains. The rainfall is inadequate, as one goes north of the Shabelle River. It is also hot throughout the year, though seasonal winds have a moderating effect in localized mountain areas. Away from the well sites and rain basins, the land appears to lack human habitation. Frequent droughts and famine became part and parcel of Somalia pastoral life.

This harsh environment, therefore, is not conductive to attract any foreign migration, even the Arab Muslims. The Arabs were migrating from a similar environment to that of Somaliland and were looking to enhance their economic life, as well as better and more pleasant climatic conditions. Thus, the Northern Somalis' claim that they are "more Arab" remains enigmatic, perhaps more accurately "puzzling," according to Dr. Hersi, who concluded: "The groups who claim descent from Arab ancestors had the least signs of Arab habitation in the whole of the Somali coast.

Islamization and *arabization* were twin processes in the spread of Islam beyond the Arabian Peninsula. Arabs, indeed, succeeded in Islamizing as well as *arabizing* certain areas of what is now known as the Islamic world, such as the North African region. Whereas, in certain other areas, the Arabs succeeded only in *islamizing*, as is the case with the rest of Islamic Africa, Central Asia, India, and Southeast Asia. However, Islam in Somalia was introduced not just by the Arabs; southwest Asians participated substantially in the process, and eventually in Somalia's role in spreading Islam into its interior, as well as into neighboring African societies.

Modern archaeological excavations have identified several historical sites along the coast of the peninsula. Most of them were located on the southern coast. Early Arabic inscriptions on tombs, religious sites, and royal houses are common in the cities along the Benadir coast. The Italian and French, as well as German colonial records, often ignored by Somali scholarship, indicate the existence of ancient towns and markets along the Jubba and Shabelle valleys. It was in these areas where the bulk of Muslim migrants found safe haven that *islamization* occurred.

In certain areas of the south, the immigrants (Arabs, Persians, Indians, and other southwest Asians) came from different racial backgrounds. This reflects on their activities with regard to the *islamization* process. The earliest waves of Arab migration go back to the runaways of the Riddah apostasy wars, mainly of Umani groups. The leaders of the group were reported to be from the *Julanda* tribe, and they settled in places along what Muslim geographers of the time call the *Zanj* coast, later known as the Benadir Coast. They were pushed to the hinterland by a Shi'ite group, the Zaidis, running away from the Umayyad persecution.

In general, societies with structured governments were most likely to adopt and absorb Islam into their systems. The oral tradition in the *Doi* belt of Somalia suggests the existence of powerful pagan dynasties in the region, like *Ghedi Baabow, Dubka Baalow, Feyle Arow, Barambara,* and others. The headquarters of these dynasties were mainly located on the tops of mountains, like *Bur Hakaba, Bur Haybe, Bur Gerwiine, Gelway,* and others. Such dynasties found in Islam a means of protecting their political power. Through proselytization, the place as well as given names of pagan historic sites were renamed in the *islamization* process. Even pagan sites became Islamic.

North of the *Doi* region and up to southern Ethiopia are the Bay and *Harqan* territories, dominated by the *Asharaf cult*, which is a mixture of Islamic mysticism and local customary traditional *Heer*. The early Sharifs, accommodating local customs and coordinating with the local political authority, gradually succeeded in converting the people and helping them make a new socioeconomic order. The Ashrafs encouraged the warlike people of *Reewin* to come to peace, which is an Islamic ideal, and settle their disputes in an Islamic way. They counseled the clan authorities to forget their pre-Islamic lineages and join the wider Islamic identity. Boundaries were drawn between major clans, with grazing and water resources clearly defined. They also established public grazing and wells and *Wars* (artificial water reservoir) with rules and regulations inspired by the Islamic law that also accommodates aspects of the local customs of the *Heer*.

To the Somali nomadic groups of the Peninsula, the situation was quite different. The nomadic organization was based on nested groups of egalitarian lineages assumed to descend from a common ancestor Samale. The relationship between each lineage rested on segmental opposition, that is, lineages were either supported by or opposed to one another based on their degree of relatedness. This ideal, though often more honored in the breach, produced the ethnographic cliché often cited by anthropologists. This egalitarian situation inhabited the development of a subverted hierarchal structure necessary to establish political authority and led to what Dr. Hersi described as "a state of chiefdom where central political authority meant nothing, as indeed it does not even to this day."

Due to the harshness of the environment and the poverty of economic resources in the nomadic regions of Somalia, the Muslim migration was small and insignificant. Unlike the southern regions of the peninsula whose oral sources provide sufficient evidence on the arrival and activities of early Muslim migration, there is little reliable evidence relating to the nomadic societies, and what is offered is dubious and mythical stories of a few mysterious individuals.

There are two figures in the oral tradition of the northern nomadic groups of Somalia that are related to the early arrival of Muslim migrants. The first one is Sheikh Abdurahman Ibn Isma'il al-Jabarti and the second is Sheikh Ishaq Ibn Ahmed al-'Alawi. They both married local women and produced two of the larger clans in the north, the Darood and Issaq clans.

Like the nomadic groups of Somalia, Arabs before Islam were divided and lacked strong leadership and central authority; however, under the banner of Islam they become organized and found leadership in the Prophet Muhammad and his succeeding caliphs.

In relation to the obsession with the Arabic elements in Islamic history on the part of some Somali nomadic clans, who constructed tribal lineage from mythical figures, the question of leadership in Islam and its interpretation could be another issue that might shed some light on the nomadic attraction to aspects of Islamic history, that they might use to enhance their social and political status.

The Prophet of Islam, Muhammad, established in Medina the first centralized Islamic state in which believers formed a single community, an *Umma*. The commitment to the Islamic *Umma* ranked above tribal affiliations, in a new state structure based on an organized religion, Islam. However, immediately after the death of the Prophet, the Medina community disagreed over how to fill the leadership void. The Arab tribes of non-Qurayshi clans articulated their right to the leadership position at the conference of *al-Saqifa*.

After a fiery debate, Abu Bakar—another Qurayshi—was chosen as the successor of the Prophet. This marked the beginning of the end of the Muslim solidarity. As Ibn Hisham eloquently stated: "The position of the Caliph is the issue that causes Muslims to shed the blood of their coreligious people." Because of the above dispute, three of the four orthodox caliphs were murdered, namely Omar, Uthman, and Ali. This power struggle continues among Muslims today.

The impact of this struggle left a tremendous legacy on Islamic political thought throughout the Islamic world. A significant number of Muslim jurists required the Qurayshi descent as one of the prerequisites governing the institution of Caliph. This view, though, was stubbornly advocated by the scholars of Qurayshi origin, such as al-Shafi'i and Ibn Khaldun. Thus, the world of Islam was not free from these crucial distractions. In fact, concerning the non-Arab Muslims, it brought a new dimension to the power struggle. The closer one is to the household of the Prophet of Islam, the greater chance one has to be a leader of a non-Arab Muslim community.

The case of the Somali Arabized clans is, therefore, identical to the *Sadah* of Southeast Asian Muslims, the *Mawlanas* of Islamic India, the *Bani Ma'qils* of Egypt, or the Yemeni tribes in northern Sudan, who each invented their own myth of descent from Prophet Muhammad's tribe, in order to dominate the position of leadership in their respective areas.

The Somalis weren't the only African people who practiced the religion of Islam; however, ancestors of the Bantu in southeast Africa practiced indigenous ceremonies and beliefs prior to their abduction into slavery. Since Muslims are prohibited from owning Muslim slaves, some Bantu freed themselves from slavery by converting to Islam. Over time, many others also converted to Islam. A small number of Bantus who resided in the Dadaab refugee camps recently converted to Christianity. Some Bantus, whether Muslim or Christian, retain animist beliefs, including use of magic, curses, and possession dances.

Islamic influence among the escaped slaves in the Jubba River valley gained momentum after the Bantu leader Nassib Bundo converted to Islam. Although the pre-Islamic traditions and ritual practices were not completely eliminated, most Bantu people in the Jubba River valley had converted to Islam by the beginning of the twentieth century. Unlike some politically motivated Islamic groups, the Bantu people from the Jubba River valley practice Islam and do not mix it with politics for personal or popular gain. The lower Jubba Bantu, with strong linguistic and cultural ties to southeast Africa, place great value on belonging to a ritual group, known as Mviko. Some traditional ceremonies performed by the group are known as Mviko rituals.

Mviko and other Bantu ceremonies that include playing drums and dancing are not considered appropriate Islamic behavior and are forbidden by some local Muslim sheikhs. In pre-civil war Somalia, newly resettled nomads in the Jubba River valley would often disrupt Bantu dance performances. Some Bantu ceremonial dancing in the Dadaab refugee camps was also disrupted—sometimes violently through intimidation and stone throwing—by fundamentalist Muslim Somalis who objected to the perceived sexually exasperating dancing (Jimale, 1995). Although there is some conflict in mixing Islamic Sufi mysticism, which is acceptable to Muslim sheikhs, and the traditional Bantu ritual dances, both seem to coexist in Bantu religious life.

Conversion to Islam by the Bantu communities has served to somewhat reduce hostilities between them and the Somali pastoralists who live in the vicinity of the Jubba River.

With regard to religious practices, the Bantu are among the more liberal Muslims in Somali society. Evidence of this are the ceremonies performed by the Bantu and the roles that women are allowed to play in the community, such as being allowed to work in the fields and, although they dress modestly by American standards, some do not wear the hijab, which Muslim women wear to cover themselves while in public. There is no evidence to link the Bantu with any fundamentalist religious or extremist political group. In fact, some fundamentalists in Somalia dismiss the Bantu's religious saints (Sufis) and Islamic practices as unorthodox.

Like other Islamic groups, the Bantu people celebrate the two major religious occasions, Eid-ul-Fitr, which comes at the end of the holy month of Ramadan, and Eid-ul-Adha, which coincides with the annual pilgrimage to Mecca in Saudi Arabia.

There appeared to be no Christians among the Bantu who first arrived in refugee camps in 1992. By 1996, however, a small number had converted to Christianity in the Ifo refugee camp, which was also home to several hundred Christian Ethiopians. The Christian Bantu stated that they didn't want to belong to a religion (Islam) that could allow atrocities to be perpetrated against them. A 2002 report by the International Organization for Migration (IOM) notes the presence of a Bantu-constructed Christian church in the Ifo refugee camp.

The vast majority of Somalia (about 99 percent) is *Sunni* Muslim. Religious belief is considered one of the uniting factors within Somali society. Even before Islam, relations between Somali and Arabs were intensive, predominantly through trade and commerce. Islam spread to the Horn of Africa at a very early stage. Most early Muslim migrants were looking for a political safe haven and economic opportunities, which they found in the Somali areas on the northern coast along the Gulf of Aden and on the southern Benadir coast. In the *Kitab al Zanj* (The Book of Blacks), referred to southeast Africans by medieval Arabs, has records showing that one of the most extensive waves of Muslim immigration to Somalia took place during the reign of Caliph Abdul Malik Ibn Marwan, which show that the Muslim migration grew tremendously from the rise of Islam to the tenth century AD.

HISTORY OF SOMALIA

Colonial Times

The image of Somalia as a homogenous nation of one people who speak one language, practice one religion, and share one culture has been prevalent in the media as well as in research and literature. Only recently have divisions based on language, religious brotherhoods, and occupation been recognized as significant distinctions in Somali society. Somalia can no longer be represented as a "nation of nomads" or "a pastoral democracy" since the majority of modern Somalis have settled into the relatively sedentary lifestyles of farming or urban dwelling. Additionally, the perception of a homogenous population of cattle-and-camel herders is historically incorrect because it excludes the significant number of farmers who have lived along the banks of Somalia's two major rivers, the Jubba and the Shabelle, for generations. The riverine farmers speak Somali, practice Islam, share Somali cultural values, are legally Somali citizens, and most consider themselves members of Somali clans. Despite outward trappings of being Somali, however, many look different, and so are considered different by Somalis.

Histories of Somalia are liable to two generalizations: one, that the Somali people have always formed one unified nation that was only recently divided by colonialism; second, that Somali clan-based violence is a manifestation of an ancient, primordial tribalism. Researches have shown that these generalizations are inaccurate.

Spread throughout the Horn of Africa, the Somali people are comprised of numerous clans and subclans, a group of people tracing descent from a common ancestor. Traditionally, Somali society has been marked by nomadic-pastoralism in the north and agricultural pastoralism in the south. Lacking a unitary government, the Somali "territory" was divided by the

European colonial powers after the late nineteenth century. Past of the north were administered as British Somaliland, while much of the south became Italian Somalia.

There were stark differences in the colonial economic policies of Italy and Britain, which tended to amplify regional traditions. While Italy developed a comprehensive economic plan for the more agrarian southern Somalia, the largely nomadic British Somaliland remained neglected. This situation produced lasting disparities in wealth and infrastructure. Under this colonial economic order, the clans evolved into political identities tied to economic benefits or disadvantages. Rivalry was inevitable, particularly once the end of colonialism produced the first unified Somali state.

In about AD 700, settlers from Arabia and Persia (Iran) started to establish settlements along the Somali coast. Saylac, northwest of modern Somaliland was a crucial town. Traders from Abyssinia (Ethiopia) used Saylac's harbor to ship goods to Arabia and some countries in Asia. Traders sold animal hides, ostrich feathers, slaves, and ivory. They bought cloth, dates, pottery, weapons, and iron shipped from Arabia and Asia.

Arabs and Persians established the city of Mogadishu around 900. In the early 1000s, an Arab sheikh (chief) named Daarood Jabarti settled in northeastern Somalia and married Dombira Dir, the daughter of the local sheikh. His descendants formed the audacious Darod clan. About two hundred years later, another Arab founded the Isaaq clan. Ultimately, the Somalis began to believe that they were Arab origins. They claimed that they were from Arab ancestry. Arab culture had a huge influence on Somalia. Arab merchants and sailors introduced the religion of Islam, which the Prophet Muhammad spread throughout the Arabian Peninsula during the 600s. Between 1000 to 1300 many Somalis became Muslims. The Arabs also established a way of tracking generations through the father.

After 1200, large numbers of Somalis started moving from north to south. There isn't a direct reason to why that occurred. Some historians believe they were trying to escape a horrendous drought. Others believe that the population was trying to make more room. As the Somalis moved in, they pushed people out of the land. The Somalis forced Oromo herders to leave the land, and they dislocated Bantu farmers from the fertile south. During this period, Mogadishu was an important trading city, famous for its magnificent cotton.

While many people in the Horn of Africa were Muslims, the Ethiopians were Christians. At first they got along very well, but in the early 1400s, a long period of conflict began. Saad-ad-Din was the sultan of the Islamic state of Ifat, located in Saylac. He called for a war against "Christian infidels." (*Infidel* is an insulting name for someone who does not believe in a particular religion, in this case Islam.) His troops invaded Ethiopia, burned Christian churches, and forced the Ethiopians to convert to Islam. Ethiopians then chased the sultan to an island near Saylac and killed him in 1415. After the triumph, the Ethiopian king commanded musicians to write a hymn thanking God for the defeat against the Muslims. The hymn contained the word Somali—perhaps the first time it was used anywhere (Hamilton, 2007).

In 1499, a Portuguese expedition sailed up the coast of Africa. The Portuguese were looking for gold, ivory, slaves, and other resources. Portuguese troops attacked Mogadishu but failed to capture it. They continued attacks along the Somali coast over the next twenty years not being able to gain permanent control over the country (Njoku, 2013). Ifat, which was then called Adal, became a powerful gain in the early 1500s. Saylac became a prosperous port with schools and beautiful mosques. The Muslims became strong enough to take on the Ethiopians again. Their religious and military leader, Ahmed Guray, attracted many followers. He declared jihad, or holy war, on the Ethiopians.

Somali nomads, especially members of the Darod clan, made up a large part of Ahmad Guray's army. They invaded Ethiopia, burning the countryside and killing many citizens. By 1535 Muslim forces controlled most of central Ethiopia and had converted many Ethiopians to Islam. But eventually, a new Ethiopian ruler came to the throne, rearmed the troops, and enlisted the help of the Portuguese to fight the Somalis.

By then the Portuguese controlled key outposts along the east coast of Africa, the Red Sea, the Persian Gulf, and the ocean route between Europe and India. Portuguese troops helped the Ethiopians defeat the Muslim invaders. Ahmed Guray died in battle in 1543.

Portugal was not the only foreign nation interested in the riches of Africa. Other European nations explored and set up colonies in Africa, as well as in the Middle East and Asia. In 1839 the British established a coaling station (to supply coal to ships on their way to the British colony in India) at Aden in Yemen, across the Gulf of Aden from Somalia. The British in Yemen relied on Somalia as a source of meat. Herders brought their sheep to Saylac and Berbera and shipped them across the gulf to the British.

Europeans also explored Somalia itself. French explorer Charles Guillain traveled along the southern coast in 1847. He found Mogadishu in ruins following a famine and an outbreak of plague. In 1854 British explorer Sir Richard Burton visited Saylac and then traveled inland to Harer in Ethiopia. A year later, Burton was camped at Berbera, planning an expedition to the interior. Several hundred Somali fighters, armed with spears, attacked his pack. The Somalis killed or badly wounded several officers and speared Burton in the mouth. He survived and escaped to Aden. The British Royal Geographical Society, which had sponsored the expedition, blamed Burton for the attack. He never returned to Somalia.

Between the seventh and tenth century, Muslim Arabs and Persian settlers established trading posts along Somalia's Gulf of Aden and Indian Ocean coasts; Mogadishu commenced as a trading station. During the fifteenth and sixteenth century, Somali warriors typically joined the armies of the Muslim sultanates in their battles with Christian Ethiopia.

(Somalia: SSS) Although several foreign powers showed interest in it during the nineteenth century, the Somali region never played more than a secondary role for the powers involved in colonial occupation.

It was Egypt, in co-operation with and supported by Great Britain, which first aspired to secure access to the sources of the river Nile. Since one of these sources was located in Ethiopia, at Lake Tana, the Egyptians decided upon a strategy of encirclement (Rubenson, 1991: pp.288-410), and it was in line with this strategy that, in 1869, they occupied the harbor towns of Zeila and Berbera on the Northern Somali coast. From 1875 to 1884, Egyptian rule was established further inland, including the trading center and religious place of learning.

Great Britain had signed a protection treaty with one of the Northern Somali clans as early as 1827 and had taken possession of Aden at about the same time. However, there were no permanent British representatives in the Northern Somali towns of Zeila and Berbera until 1839. The British post on the Somali coast became more interested with the opening of the Suez Canal in 1868. In 1873, Khedive Ismail- an expense that he hoped to recover many times over through exploitation of the hinterland. At that time, British interests did not conflict with the Egyptian presence in the same area (Lewis, 1965). Indeed, in 1877, Britain signed a treaty in

Alexandria, which guaranteed privileged status to British citizens all along the coast, and in the Harar hinterland (Petrides, 1983: p.23).

It was only after the British occupation of Egypt in 1882 and the Mahdist uprising in Anglo-Egyptian-occupied Sudan which the Egyptians withdrew from their Somali territories that a power vacuum was created. This motivated the British and the Ethiopians to claim the territory as being under their jurisdiction. In 1884 and 1886, the British government signed protection treaties with Issa, Gadabuursi, and Isaaq subclans Garxajis, Habr Jaalo, and Habr Awal (Lewis, 1965:p.46), and in July 1887 the Protectorate of British Somaliland was officially inaugurated.

The Ethiopian claim to Somali territory was officially raised by Emperor Menelik in the so-called Circular Letter of 1891 (Rubenson, 1991: pg.316). In the letter, large parts of Somali territory, including the lands of Somali clans who had signed protection treaties with Britain and France, were theoretically included in Ethiopian territory.

The imperialism of Britain, France, and Italy all played a dramatic role in the region during the nineteenth century. Great Britain's concern with the region was essentially to safeguard trade links with its Aden colony (founded 1839), which depended on the meat of sheep from Somalia. The British opportunity came when Egyptian forces, having occupied much of the region in the 1870s, withdrew in 1884 to fight the Mahdi in Sudan. British penetration led to a series of agreements (1884–86) with local tribal leaders and, in 1887, to the establishment of a protectorate. France first acquired a foothold in the area in the 1860s. An Anglo-French agreement of 1888 defined the boundary between the Somali possessions of the two countries.

Italy first asserted its authority in the area in 1889 by creating a small protectorate in the central zone, to which other concessions were later added in the south (territory ceded by the sultan of Zanzibar) and north. In 1925, Jubbaland, or the Trans-Jubba (east of the Jubba [now Jubba] River), was detached from Kenya to become the westernmost part of the Italian colony. In 1936, Italian Somaliland was combined with Somali-speaking districts of Ethiopia to form a province of the newly formed Italian East Africa. During World War II, Italian forces invaded British Somaliland; but the British, operating from Kenya, retook the region in 1941 and went on to conquer Italian Somaliland. Britain ruled the combined regions until 1950, when Italian Somaliland became a UN trust territory under Italian control.

On the other hand, Ethiopia did not control such dominant Somali territories permanently—it made its presence in Jijiga town but not farther south or east (Echete, 1988). But although the Ethiopian presence consisted only of infrequent raids on livestock and intermittent fighting with Somali nomads, nonetheless, Ethiopia's territorial claims conflicted with those not only of Britain but also of France.

The French presence in the region dated back to 1859, when they obtained the cession of the port of Obok. However, it was not until 1881, when a French-Ethiopian trading company was initiated in Obok, that the French made their presence felt (Lewis, 1965: p.41). An increasing Anglo-French rivalry, coupled with the need for a secure stopover seaport on the way to France's new acquisitions in Madagascar and China, made a permanent French presence indispensable. In that sense, a major factor motivating both France and Britain to establish a protectorate or colony in the northern Somali region was their imperialist competitiveness. Finally, in 1888, an Anglo-French agreement was reached which defined the borders between the two protectorates as lying between Zeila and Djibouti.

European Colonization

Between 1491 and 1498, the Portuguese, led by Vasco Da Gama, plotted a course from the western to eastern coast of Africa. The Europeans navigated through the seas reaching modern Tanzania in the south in 1491 and moving northward to the coastal city of Mombasa in Kenya in 1498. During this period, Portugal claimed to be interested in finding a safe passage to harness the profits of the Indian Ocean-borne sea trade.

Later, they were joined by the Dutch, the British, and the French merchants. The Europeans wanted to avoid the high taxes that were levied by the Ottomans, who firmly controlled the shorter route to India via the Mediterranean Sea and the Red Sea channels. The exorbitant tariffs levied by the Ottomans had left the European merchants with high-priced goods that consumers in Europe could hardly afford. Only the nobles desired imported commodities like silk, spices, clothes, and curry to show their wealth and maintain their elite status. An unobstructed access to the Indian Ocean trade became urgent for the merchants to expand the market in Europe for more profit.

Similar to the Spanish exploration in the Americas in the late fifteenth century, Portuguese-led exploration for new routes to India marked the genesis of colonial aggression that ended in the colonization of the entire continent in the late nineteenth century. As the new route to East Africa, the Far East, and China became entrenched, the Europeans made frequent stops off the African coasts, interfering in the local politics of the East African coastal states, including the Somali coasts.

Imperialism as well as the expansions of the American plantation later took place. This brought the coastal enclaves of Africa closely and more vigorously integrated into the new global trade. In this new trade, Africa would serve as an important source of a highly demanded slave labor in the Americas. The Arab-Indian Ocean slave trade had been in existence prior to the European arrival, with every African port turned into a major slave supply route. Most of the slaves were captured from the hinterlands of the contiguous territories known today as the Great Lakes Region, comprising Uganda, Democratic Republic of the Congo, Ethiopia, Rwanda, Burundi, and Tanzania. The Europeans also traded in gold, ivory, ambergris, wax, and spices throughout the sixteenth and seventeenth centuries.

Normally, the Europeans stayed on the coast and used African chiefs and individual traders to acquire their victims. Some African rulers cooperated with the slave merchants because it gave them an opportunity to attack their adversaries, sell them off, and make some profit out of the enemy. The victims of the horrendous trade were not only prisoners of war. In some cases, those sold as slaves were victims of kidnappers. Others were pawns of debt and condemned criminals who had committed acts like murder, incest, and other things considered an abomination in the local culture.

While the trade brought wealth to local merchants, it brought misery to the African victims and their families, disrupting village life, the local manufacturing industries, and the sociopolitical structure. In the Somali region, for instance, slave trading negatively affected existing clan alliances, causing wars and hostages against clans. By the end of the trans-Atlantic slave trade in the first half of the nineteenth century, the local economy of the East African coastal cities had taken a serious downturn because of the overdependence on the hated trade across the sea.

The desire of Britain, France, and Italy to claim territories in Somalia in the late nineteenth century was motivated first by each country's political, diplomatic, military, and nationalistic interests. The material motive was nonetheless a big factor, particularly for economically poor Italy. Somalia's strategic location on the Horn of Africa was magnified through a number of political developments on the global stage during the nineteenth century. First, the opening of the Suez Canal in 1869 increased or rather renewed the European powers' long-standing interests in the region. The major participants in the Berlin Conference on African colonization in 1884–1885—Britain, France, Italy, Portugal, Belgium, and Germany—all arrived at the meeting with clear aims to secure some measure of power and control in Africa.

In regards to Somalia, the equations were complicated by similar designs nursed by Ethiopia and Egypt as internal colonialists. These African powers were determined not to be outplayed by the Europeans in a region particularly considered by the Abyssinian (Ethiopian) emperor as his top priority. As Menelik II (1844–1913), the emperor of Ethiopia, had unequivocally declared in a letter of 1891 addressed to the European powers, "I have no intentions at all of being an indifferent spectator, if the distant powers hold on to the idea of dividing up Africa. For the past fourteen centuries, Ethiopia has been an island of Christians in a sea of pagans." The emperor of Ethiopia was serious in his words, especially with his stated belief that "in the past, the boundary of Ethiopia was the sea." By the late 1800s, the partition and formal colonization of Somalia had been completed on paper. Ethiopia was joined by three foreign powers: Britain, Italy, and France.

In the words of historian Angus Hamilton, the Horn of Africa became the subject of a Triple European Alliance. Egypt's colonial interests in the area suffered an irreparable setback following its entanglement with the Muslim Mahdists in Sudan in 1884. The heavy financial and military costs the revolt placed on the Khedive's army forced Egypt to quickly evacuate the region, thus giving Britain enough reason to step up its presence and establish ultimate control of the territory. Originally, Britain had wanted to commit fewer resources in the Somali Peninsula, using Egypt as a source of vital security in the region.

In the 1880s and 1890s, Britain's major colonial policy in regard to additional territorial acquisition was the defense of its Indian colony. In order to guard their trade and empire, tropical African and Pacific claims were repeatedly sacrificed as pawns in the higher game of imperialism. At the Berlin Conference, the Foreign Office decided that the security dangers facing Britain in Egypt weakened the ability of the country to successfully compete with other European powers in West Africa.

Britain's primary interest in the Somali lands arose from this need to protect its colonial territory of India, and to this end, it intended to secure a steady supply of food—specifically beef—needed by the queen's soldiers stationed in the Yemeni port of Aden. The British first seized the strategic Aden seaport by force in 1839. In 1869, the port of Aden became even more vital for the British navy following the opening of the Suez Canal that year. This meant that the canal would witness more traffic, more trade, and more conflicts.

For the British to successfully protect the route that led to the queen's Indian dominion, Somali meat was needed to feed the army. Prior to 1839, Aden had procured its meat exclusively from its Somali neighbors on the other side of the sea. In other words, what the British needed at the time was simply to strengthen and safeguard this existing supply route. As long as the meat supplies were uninterrupted, the British government did not seriously consider an outright colonization of the territory. This was reminiscent of the Dutch presence and subsequent colonization of the Cape colony in South Africa after initial arrival in 1652. Prior to 1887, the British considered Somalia a secondary concern in relation to Aden. This attitude would change after almost fifty years.

The Somalis welcomed the Egyptians in an apparent show of distaste for what they had perceived as Zanzibari-British collaboration to colonize and exploit the Somali coast. At this point, the British decided that Egypt's presence in the region and the security its forces provided actually helped to maintain British interests in the region. In 1877, the British signed an agreement with the khedive Pasha formerly recognizing Egyptian jurisdiction as far south as Ras Hafun, a small low-lying territory in the Bari (Majerteen) region of northern Somalia. One of the crucial terms of the agreement was that Egypt should not, under any pretext, cede any part of the Somali coast to a foreign power.

But Egypt's hopes for empire in the Somali lands was shattered by the Sudanese anti-Egyptian Mahdist revolt in 1884, which compelled the Egyptians to request British assistance in evacuating their troops trapped on the coast. To fill the vacuum created by Egypt's forced withdrawal, Britain, between 1884 and 1888, concluded several treaties with local rulers of northern Somalia. This marked the beginning of formal British colonization of northern Somalia. For the next fourteen years, the British ruled northern Somalia from their Indian colonial territory using the indirect rule system. Like elsewhere in Africa where the British applied the indirect rule model originally developed in colonial India, the newly appointed Somali traditional official began to assume unusual despotic powers.

Though the French and the British had been fighting for the territorial control of Africa since the eighteenth century, the two countries began fighting for the Horn of Africa as a result of French intrusion into the port of Obock in Afar (Danakil) country in 1862. The French, who had been evicted from Egypt by the British, sought to have a coaling station on the Red Sea to strengthen its naval logistics to their colonies in Indochina.

For nearly two decades, the French did not seek to further consolidate their presence in the Horn region until after the British beat them in establishing claims to Zeila, one of the major port cities in the north. Because of such response, the French expanded the pre-1862 land to include a strip of area on the coast belonging to Somalis who the French mistook as the same as the Afar. This oversight on the part of the French resulted in the creation of a new country, French Somaliland (now known as Djibouti), with the Somalis as half the population.

According to Raphael Chijioke Njoku, "in his study of Italy's colonial policy in the Horn, Said Samatar, one of the doyens of English Somali studies, argues that Italy was amateurish in the conduct of its imperial politics in Africa and that it was careful to stake out a territory without antagonizing its more powerful European competitors." Italy was newly unified as a state in 1861, and thus its cautious approach to colonial acquisition was conditioned by its economic, military, and political fragility rather than the lack of experience and its "reluctance" to colonize. Factors driving Italian colonial moves were both economic and political.

In terms of its economy, the government wanted to use the new colonies in Africa as an emigration outlet for its increased population. Also, the colonies were to provide Italy with a secure market for its manufactured goods. Politically, colonies were wanted by Italy for national pride. Italy needed this in order to be taken seriously by its critics and to attain continental respect. Italy's opportunity was limited in the scramble for African lands.

With parts of Somalia left out of the Conventional Free Trading Area in East Africa, Italy immediately saw an opportunity to grab a territory that not only provided a strategic link with the Eritrean colony, but also shared a border with Ethiopia—a country that had since the fifteenth century caught the imaginations of many Europeans as the legendary land of Prester John—a mythical figure popular among the Europeans. In a letter addressed to Prime Minister Depretis by Macini, an Italian colonial agent, it was revealed that with Eritrea in their hands, Italy would have unhindered access to products from Ethiopia if the Benadir coastal area in the south of Somalia was added to Italian control. In February 1885, the Italians seized control of Massawa in Eritrea, following the withdrawal of Egyptian troops under the fire of the Madhist army.

Italy had engaged in tricky mobilizations to attain control of the Benadir coast proper since 1886, gaining presence in April 1889. But it wasn't until 1893 that the Benadir lands were finally taken from the rule of the Omani rulers of Zanzibar. The new possession enabled Italy in 1893 to lift its flag in Merca (Marka), which lies between Mogadishu and Barawa. This marked the formal establishment of the colony of Italian Somaliland on the Somali Peninsula. The Italians followed their successes with an aggressive participation in the local trade, to the displeasure of Somalis and at the risk of conflict with the Omani rulers.

Under colonial rule, the Europeans tried different styles of controlling in accordance with the colonial power's goals in the colony. Whether direct or indirect rule, it was designed to exploit the colony while making the colonized subjects inferior to the colonizers. In the first two decades of the colonial era, the biggest challenge for each of the imperial powers was to gain firm control of the colony. Because of this, the Europeans achieved limited and often varied successes depending on who was the colonizer, the colonized, and in what sociopolitical environment they operated. In order to understand the dynamics, it is a must to approach it from a geographic standpoint.

In British Somaliland, the colonial order created two "republics": subjects and citizens. The subjects were those in the cities and coastal town like Zeila and Berbera where the colonial influence and authority were frequently exercised. The citizens of British Somaliland were in the hinterlands, where they continued with life as usual with little or no direct contact with the Europeans.

Fortunately, Somali culture and politics remained mostly unrefined in the countryside continued to function as the center of sociopolitical organization, and family hierarchy was the most common social structure. Somali chieftains "formed a well-defined autonomous community with a distinctive way of life, language, and culture." The native people proceeded to live as nomads, maintaining loyalties to their local clan rather than to Queen Victoria's agents who supposedly "owned" them. The colonial subjects were found mostly in the cities.

For the people who lived in the cities, the major attraction was to obtain opportunities to earn a living within the global capitalist economy. The anticipation that the local economy would be developed did not transpire due to several factors including lack of natural resources, the predominantly nomadic population, and of course the Europeans' vested economic interests.

Italian interests in the Horn of Africa including Somalia were not similar to the British. While the British mainly focused on forming a colony, the Italians dissimulated their intentions. The Italians wanted to use Somalia as a source of raw materials for their industries. Thus, the Italian government encouraged Italians to migrate to Somalia to help develop plantations on the Shebelle and Jubba Rivers. The river valleys were favored as the most convenient site of the plantations for irrigation purposes. Italian settlers did not come into the areas in droves because the imperial government lacked the strategy to recruit Italians for supervisory duties in Africa (Hamilton, 2007). The African laborers coerced to work on the plantations were watched by armed guards, and most of the workers were Somalis of Bantu origin. The following is an excerpt from *The History of Somalia, a* book written by Raphael Njoku:

"After landing in 1919, Prince Luigi Amedeo of Savoy, duke of Abruzzi (1873–1933), launched the plantation system in Somalia with the fascist administration of Governor Cesare Maria de Vecchi de Val Cismon (the governor of the Somaliland Protectorate from 1923 to 1928) providing the crucial logistic support. The plantations produced cotton (the first Somali export crop), sugar, and bananas. Although Somali bananas were first exported to Italy in 1927, overall, plantation agriculture attained primary significance in the colony in 1929, after the world cotton market collapsed.

From 1929 to 1936, banana plantations covered more than 3,975 hectares of land. From 1935, the Italian government authorized the Royal Banana Plantation Monopoly (Regia Azienda Monopolio Banane, or RAMB) to take charge of all banana exports as a monopoly. In 1950, when the United Nations (UN) granted Italy the administration of the Somalia trust territory, RAMB was reorganized and renamed the Banana Plantation Monopoly (Azienda Monopolio Banane, or AMB). This was part of the move to resuscitate the moribund Somali economy almost destroyed by the war. The Italian monopoly was a mixed bag of blessings for the local economy. Whereas it made possible the initial penetration by Somali bananas into the Italian market, it also eliminated incentives for Somali producers to become internationally competitive or to seek markets elsewhere.

In comparative terms, the investment in cotton brought fewer dividends than bananas. Although cotton showed some promise in 1929, it experienced serious problems following the 1930 world commodity crisis. The impact was such that exports fell from nearly 1,400 tons in 1929 to just 400 tons by 1937. In the 1950s were years of marginal success but no consistent growth. Matters were complicated by the lack of Somali wage labor for cotton harvesting—a problem that the Italians tried to reconcile without a significant result.

Among all the plantation crops, sugarcane was the most profitable. First, the sugar business was different from the banana and cotton economies because it was produced for domestic consumption under control of the Italo-Somalia Agricultural Society (SAIS), based in Genoa. Launched in 1920, the SAIS estate near Giohar started with a modest size of land under cultivation. In 1950, the output had attained about 80 percent domestic demand with 4,000 tons of harvest. Seven years later, the output had met 100 percent domestic demand of 11,000 tons.

In order to solve the acute labor shortages that beleaguered the plantations, the administration changed from forced labor to paid wages. It also granted some extra incentives to workers in the form of permission to maintain private gardens on some of the irrigated lands. As a result, a relatively permanent workforce developed for the plantations. In 1957, the plantation contributed about 58 percent of total exports, thus creating the postcolonial structure of the Somali economy."

The Somalis: Origins and Settlement

Traditionally, it has been accepted that the Somali people originated from the shores of the Red Sea, expanding southward since the start of the tenth century, driving out the Oromos, who were thought to have been the first Cushitic-speaking occupants of the Horn of Africa. The Oromos in their turn were thought to have pushed the Bantu-speaking peoples farther south from the Jubba River area. This implied that almost all of northern Somalia was occupied by Oromo. Similarly, southern Somalia was said to have been occupied by Bantu-speaking groups with a well-established kingdom known as "Shungwaya" located in Bur Gabo along the Jubba River.

The early history of the Horn of Africa has thus been commonly seen as a result of contacts between Africa and southern Arabia. Support for such history was mainly found in the writings of early Arab individuals who married local Somali women. This union supposedly produced the first ancestors of the current Somali ethnic population. Also, the descendants of these unions were said to have later overwhelmed most of the Horn of Africa region through conquest, migration, and southward expansion.

But the written records suggest the existence of Hawiye clans before the name Somali itself appeared in the written documents. The first appearance of the name Somali in a written historical record was in the victory-claim song of Negash Yeshak (1414–1429) of Ethiopia over the neighboring Islamic Sultanate of Adal. In this, the Somali groups were mentioned as one of the enemy groups of the King. Another document containing Somali elements is found in the Arab chronicle dealing with the jihad wars of Ahmed Gurey.

The Somali groups which are found in this chronicle are the ones that are found in today's northwest Somalia. However, Ibn Said, the fourteenth century Arab geographer, wrote about Merka as being the capital of Hawiye country, which consisted of more than fifty tribal villages. Even though these early records are fragmentary in nature, they at least contradict the suggestion that non-Somali groups occupied the area prior to the alleged Somali conquest from the north. This supported the fact that most of the current Somali clans have occupied and maintained separate geographic locations until recently.

The Somali clans of Hawiye, Dir, Isaaq, and Reewin, for example, inhabited relatively restricted areas. Somali clan politics in the past also indicates a clear segmentation of political authority in the region. There have been regional sultanates, imams, or Malaqs between the sixteenth and the eighteenth centuries, but the Somali people never came under the control of a single political authority until 1960.

Also, the nature of the Arab influence in Somalia has been exaggerated. This doesn't mean that there was no Arab influence or migration to the Horn of Africa shortly after the first century of Islam, but their capacity for dramatically changing the ethnic configuration of the Somali people has been exaggerated, especially in the north. The early Arab immigrants who arrived before the sixteenth century were mainly disjointed individual families who came as a result of economic and political pressures within their homelands. In fact, if there was any recognizable Arab migration and settlement, it was in the south rather than the north.

The northern part of the country has never attracted any sizeable Arab immigrants because of its harsh environment, among other things. Indeed, Mukhtar gives us four convincing reasons as to why the Arab immigrants were not interested in settling anywhere around the Red Sea in large numbers. First, because the runaway Muslim migrants were concerned for their safety and thus would not take the risk of settling in a neighboring area such as that of northern Somalia. Secondly, unlike southern Somalia, there were no significant urban centers to attract these immigrants. Thirdly, the lack of natural harbors and the frequent violent cyclones discouraged Arab immigrants from traveling to that part of Africa. And fourth, the lack of viable economic resources made it unattractive for the Arabs to settle there permanently. Thus, the Somali claim that they are the descendants of immigrant Arabs remains, as Mukhtar accurately characterizes, "enigmatic, perhaps more accurately 'puzzling.'"

Since 1966, however, several scholars have attacked this view, suggesting that the original dispersal point of the Somali-speaking people must be located somewhere between southern Ethiopia and northern Kenya. This view has radically reversed the earlier belief that the Somali-speaking people migrated from north of their present settlements. Nevertheless, these scholars, despite their great contributions to the development of Somali history, neglected the role of the southern Somali clan families in the historical and ethnic development of the Somali-speaking people.

The dominant myth of origin is built upon the Arabian ancestry of the Somali. According to this myth, "ultimately all Somali genealogies go back to Arabian origins, to the Prophet Muhammad's lineage of Quraysh and those of his companions" (I.M. Lewis, 1961 p. 11). There are differing opinions about the actual line of descent from Arabia. One is that the pastoral clan families trace their descent from an ancestor called Samale while the agricultural clan families, the Digil and Mirifle, are descended from a cousin of the Prophet Muhammad, Aqiil Abu Talib. (Lewis claims that the Isaq trace their descent from Aquiil's brother Ali Abu Talib who married the Prophet's daughter Fatima.)

There is a second set of narratives of Somali origin that refers to the story of the man in the tree, the charismatic ancestor who came from Arabia and married a Somali girl, thus founding the patrilineal descent line originating in Arabia. According to Luling (1988) and Mansur (1995), this narrative is rooted in old African mythology and was fitted into the new belief system after the conversion of the Somali to Islam. This interpretation of the myth, then, asserts a historically African origin of the Somali.

Most of the Eastern Cushitic people, the Afar, Borana and Guji Oromo, and the Darod and Hawiye Somali refer to a similar legend, in which a local girl discovers a stranger with extraordinary powers (in the Somali case, the Arab progenitor) in a tree. Only after being promised that both the girl and the man to marry and the submission of the local people—often in the gesture of descending from the tree on the back of a local—does the stranger agree to come down. In the belief system of these groups, some trees are considered sacred. The man in the tree is equated with the man from the sky—god *Waaq*, which in the Oromo language means sky as well as God.

Along with the myth of Arabian descent goes the portrayal of early Somali history as the "story of the great Somali expansion from the North"

(Lewis, 1965). According to this oral tradition, the arrival from Arabia of Sheikh Ismail Jabarti around the tenth or eleventh century, the expansion of his descendants, the Darod and, about two centuries later, the arrival from Arabia of Sheikh Isaaq whose descendants settled west of the Darod, marked the beginning of the southward migration of the Somalis.

According to Lewis, the Somalis moved from the northeast into the Horn, not only occupying empty land but also pushing the Oromo into what is today Ethiopia, and the Zanj population (consisting of Bantu sedentary people along with two rivers) farther South. The question remains where the other Somali clans come from.

The Hawiye are the first Somali clan that was mentioned by an Arab geographer in the thirteenth century. Another oral, traditional speaks of Somali Digil having settled in the Shabelle area even before that time. These accounts, together with the incorporation and transformation of African mythology and customs into the dominant myth of Arab descent of the Somali tend to suggest that oral records of Somali origin to which Lewis refers, may be more mythical than historical. Pastoral Somali oral tradition claims an agnatic descent, exclusively in the male line. It is historical fact that Arab immigrants intermarried with Somali, and several generations later created their own lineages within the Somali clan system.

However, a strict descent from Arabia would imply that at the time of the arrival of the first such immigrants there were no Somalis (men) already inhabiting the area (Schlee, 1994). Historical and linguistic analyses (Kusow, 1995) reveal the origin of the Somali to have been in the southern fertile zone. From there, stimulated by population pressure and facilitated by the introduction of the camel, Somali begin in about the sixth century to move toward the harsh environment of the central, northern, and northeastern regions. According to Kusow, this is when camel pastoralism became widespread in the Somali peninsula. Nomadic migration patterns were established and enabled the population of the vast, hot and dry thorn bush savanna plains.

Over generations, the offspring of early nomads built their own pastoral clan-families. This development was met by the advent of Islam about two centuries later. Somali adopted the Islamic religion and reconciled it with their earlier belief systems. In the process, Somali genealogy was linked to Arabian ancestry representing the superior, dominant culture at the time.

A similar myth is told by author, Janice Hamilton, author of *Somalia In Pictures.*

In the book she states the settlement of Arabs and Persians and how the Somali people may have originated from them. The following is an excerpt from her book:

"Arabs and Persians created the city of Mogadishu around 900. In the early 1000s, an Arab sheik (chief) named Daarood Jabarti settled in northeastern Somalia and married Dombira Dir, the daughter of the local chief. His descendants formed the powerful Darod clan. About two hundred years later, another Arab founded the Isaaq clan. Eventually, the Somalis created a myth about their Arab origins. They said that all Somalis were descended from one Arab ancestry. His name was Samaale or Somaal.

Arab culture had a big impact on Somalia. Arab merchants and sailors introduced the religion of Islam, which the prophet Muhammad had founded on the Arabian Peninsula in the 600s. Between 1000 and 1300, large numbers of Somalis became Muslims (followers of Islam). The Arabs also introduced a system of tracking generations through the father."

Historians now know that the people's rich history and culture dates back to several millennia, although details of that past have remained blurred as a result of the pervasive nomadic mode of production, which hardly supports solid and stable state institutions and the cosmopolitan lifestyle that comes with continuity and adaptation. Nomadic lifestyle was engendered and sustained by both the arid nature of the environment and the characteristic inclement climate. This makes Somalia a rare but fascinating paradox of nature. Although flanked from the north through south by the longest stretch of coastline on the continent, and with two major rivers cutting through the southern parts of the country, most of Somalia is arid land with scorching temperatures year round.

This condition, more than anything else, has made a pastoral lifestyle both endemic and systemic. At present, no indigenous form of writing has been associated with the pastoralists beyond ordinary speculations about the existence of such culture in the ancient past. The Somalis do have a rich culture of oral traditions such as poetry and literature, which makes decoding the details of their historical past no easier. Much of the existing accounts, sometimes encountered in forms of songs, poems, proverbs, legends, and fables—and that speak to genealogies of people, life and living, religion, and wonders of this world—have been adapted over time, as they are handed down from one generation to the next. This is especially with the strong influence of alien cultures, particularly Islam, which have substantially colored the people's memory. While the oral literature are significant as they provide some narratives on the origins and movement of the people and their material cultures, historians must exercise discretion in relying on these accounts. When used along with more credible archaeological, linguistic, and anthropological sources, oral literature provides significant insights into the dark past.

In terms of the Somali genesis, linguistic and cultural studies have linked them to a sublanguage group, the Omo-Tana. This tongue is spoken today in Djibouti, Ethiopia, Somalia, and Kenya. It is speculated that the Omo-Tana, who are also called Sam (after their mythical ancestor Samaale), broke away from the original Cushitic family in the first millennium BCE—that is, the period encompassing 1000-1 BCE. The original homeland of the Sam, or rather their known point of dispersal, has been traced back to the confluence between the Omo and Tana rivers, from which the name Omo-Tana derives. This is the territory running from Lake Turkana in northern Kenya and stretching eastward to the Indian Ocean. It is believed that the ancestors of the Somalis followed the trail of the Tana River to the Indian Ocean coastal shores prior to the first century CE. On the coast, the group, sometimes referred to as the proto-Sam, further broke into two; one of the splinter groups moved farther north, settling in southern Somalia, while the other half (the Boni) remained on the island areas of Kiunga and Lamu Archipelago, close to the northern coasts of Kenya near the border with Somalia.

Subsequent movements in search of pasture land took the Samaale farther to different directions in the north. According to the German linguist Bernd Heine, the migrants had successfully occupied the vast Ogaden plains to the west, as well as traversing the southern shore of the Red Sea by the first century (100) CE.

Other sources of important information on the East African coastal peoples and the seaborne trade in the ancient and premodern era were left by an anonymous ancient Greek sailor, who wrote his *Periplus of the Erythraean Sea* in the first century CE, and Cosmas Indicopleustes ("who sailed to India"), whose book was entitled *The Christian Topography of Cosmas an Egyptian Monk* (547 CE). Both books are rare resource documents depicting eyewitness accounts of the East African coastal city-states, including those located in the territories of modern Somalia.

Apart from the well-known enclaves like Mombasa, some of the ancient city-states like Opone, Mundus, Malao, Mosylon, Sarapion, Tabae, and others were integrated in a profitable trading network drawing merchants from Greece, Egypt, Phoenicia, Persia, Saba, Nabataea, and the Roman Empire. Therefore, one can assert that both the *Periplus* and *The Christian Topography*, in 547 CE were the very few books that first documented the importance of Somali coastal trading cities. Both sources agree that a good number of the cities were located in the northern region of Somalia, and this has been supported by contemporary archaeological research.

The available sources reveal that the ancient Somali traders employed a locally made ship called the *beden* to transport their cargo from one port to the other. After the Roman conquest of the kingdom of Nabata in 25 BCE and their subsequent naval deployment to Aden to curb piracy, Arab merchants, upset by the Roman military presence in the region, resolved to censor Indian traders from trading in the free port cities of the Arabian Peninsula.

The embargo was intended also as a punishment for Somali merchants who reaped huge profits from cinnamon brought by Indian merchants. As one of the best-guarded secrets of the Red Sea trade, the Romans and the Greeks had long been misled by Somali traders to believe that the Somali Peninsula, which was free from Roman control, continued as usual, with the Somali enjoying some advantages.

One of the major episodes that dominated the course of history on the coastal areas of East Africa in the medieval era was the presence of Arabs and their new religion of Islam. Islam was founded by the Prophet Muhammad in 610 CE, in the month of Ramadan (the ninth or holy month of fasting) when the Prophet of Allah first received a series of revelations that led to the rise of the new creed. Its vantage position on the Horn of Africa with access to the contiguous seas placed the Somali people in constant interactions with Arab and Persian traders and immigrants.

Some of the migrants began to take up permanent residence in the coastal cities as the international commercial exchanges expanded and became more profitable. By the ninth century CE, these Arabs and Persians had either created or contributed to the development of new trading enclaves, which continued to flourish even as they were caught up with the Age of Islamic expansion when the new ideas and belief systems infiltrated into the area and gradually became a definitive ideological force.

In reality, the history of Islam on the Horn of Africa goes back to the early days of the new religion. According to Ethiopian sources, the first Muslims to enter the African continent in 615 CE were the Prophet

Muhammad's immediate family, and other companions comprising a total of eighty-three families. The migration (*hijra*) from the Arabian Peninsula was prompted by an eruption of persecution against followers of the new religion whose ideology seriously threatened the pre-existing belief system and its elite class. Islam's five "pillars," which comprise its core precepts and were in opposition to the status quo, included: (1) *shahadah*, profession of the belief that Allah is the one and only God, and Muhammad was his last messenger; (2) *salat*, praying five times a day; (3) *zakat*, almsgiving; (4) *sawm*, abstinence from food and water from sunrise to sunset during the month of Ramadan, which comes in the ninth month in the lunar calendar year; and (5) the *hajj*, making a pilgrimage to the Holy Land in Makkah (located in Saudi Arabia) at least once in one's lifetime. However, the injunction on pilgrimage is conditional to the physical and financial ability of the believer to make the journey, which is usually observed in the twelfth month of the lunar calendar.

Landing safely on the African side of the Red Sea, the Arab Muslims sought protection in the Christian kingdom of Aksum or Axum (modern Ethiopia). One of the cities (then under the jurisdiction of King Ashama ibn Abjar, the powerful Axumite ruler) the refugees settled in Zeila (Zeyla), which is now part of modern Somalia. Aksum's rulers provided the Muslims with shelter and hospitality as long as it took for the situation in Arabia to improve, thus enabling Prophet Muhammad and his party to make the return trip back to Arabia in 628 CE. Between this period and the death of the Great Prophet of Allah in 632 CE, other individual Muslims crossed the Red Sea into Africa for personal reasons other than evangelism.

They preached the new religion to the Africans but never tried to force it on them. Seven years after the death of Muhammad, however, the age of militant Islam commenced when armed Muslim Arabs marched across the Red Sea from the area where Aksum was located into the African continent in 639 CE. A strong passion to expand and consolidate the tenets of the new faith to all corners of the globe informed the Muslims' program of violence. The invaders' idea was to first "win the political kingdom and the religious would be added." Within a decade, the Muslims not only seized total political control of the Arabian Peninsula but also extended the political borders of Islam across the Red Sea from Nubian lands into the Byzantine territory of Egypt.

The period from 1150 to 1250 represents a milestone in Islam's role in reshaping the evolution of Somali history. Much of the history of this period was described by Yaqut al-Hamawi, the twelfth-century, Syrian-born historian who visited the region. According to Hamawi, Berbers, described as "dark skinned" and considered ancestors of modern Somalis, inhabited the Mogadishu areas.

On the Somali Peninsula, Mogadishu became one of the most important centers of the new religion and its subsequent expansion to North Africa and along the East African coastal area. Around this time, Somali traders ran commercial expeditions three thousand miles down to Mozambique, where they successfully established a colony to extract gold from the rich mines in Sofala. According to Arab and Somali chronicles, in about 1403, the small trading city of Adal in the southern Somali region of the Gulf of Aden was established by the newly converted African Muslim merchants as one of the fastest-growing Muslim coastal trading enclaves.

Inland, the new religion brought significant influence to bear on the nature and organization of the indigenous clan systems and the political grouping of the Somali people. In the fourteenth century, for instance, the Ajuuraan clan established a dynasty, which soon commenced control of the coastal cities and a lucrative trade across the sea. At this point, much of the Somali people were spiritually unified by Pan-Islamism, which became virulent especially among the inhabitants of northern Somalia. Somalia became integrated in the spiritual commonwealth of Muslims and by association, part of the global army of mujahideens united in resistance against the Christian Crusaders.

Slavery and the Somali Bantus

The term "Bantu" is used as a label for over three hundred ethnic groups in Africa. These groups make up a significant part of the population of nearly all African countries south of the Sahara. Among the well-known groups are the Swahili, located throughout eastern Africa especially in Kenya, and the Zulu, predominantly in South Africa. Because of the various groups of Bantu, the Bantu are known more as a language group rather than a distinct ethnic group. The people that comprise this group are placed there because they share a common language family and similar social customs. Though they belong to a variety of different tribes, the Bantu refugees in the United States typically refer to themselves as the Bantu.

Throughout the years, the Somali government has declared that Somalia is a homogenous country, when in reality Somalia is actually comprised of various different groups. The Somali population is estimated at about 7.5 million people, of those, the Somali Bantu population is estimated at about six hundred thousand.

The Somali Bantu belong to three distinct groups:

1) Those who are indigenous to Somalia
2) Those who were brought to Somalia as slaves but integrated into Somali society
3) Those who were brought to Somalia as slaves but maintained their ancestral culture and languages

The first settlers of Somali Bantu came to Somalia centuries ago during what was recognized as one of Africa's major migrations. During this time, it is said that Bantu-speaking peoples trekked eastward from the west and central Africa where a large portion of them settled in the sub-Sahara region.

The second group of Somali Bantu came during the eighteenth and nineteenth centuries and is predominantly descended from six African tribes: the Yao, Makua, Nyanja, Ngidono, Zigua, and Zaramo. The sultan of Oman, Sayyid Said, whose sovereignty extended from northern Mozambique to southern Somalia, regularly abducted Africans from those areas and forced them into the slave trade. During this time period, Arab slavers captured and shipped thousands of Bantu men, women, and children via Zanzibar's slave market. Although many of these slaves were sold to European merchants, some slaves were sold to Africans, Somalia included.

One famous theory among many of the Somali Bantu is that their ancestors were actually tricked into slavery. In the late 1830s, there were several years of drought in Tanzania that resulted in widespread starvation. Many Africans, in the hope of averting their families' untimely demise, accepted promises of wage labor in a distant land. When promises of a better life failed to entice them anymore, the Arab slave traders, and their African accomplices, used brute force. Those that were enticed or forced from their homes were sold as slaves once they landed in Somalia.

Slavery left out of Somalia slowly. In 1895, forty-five slaves were freed by the Italian colonial authority under the administration of the chartered company, V. Filonardi. Massive emancipation only began, however, after the antislavery activist Robecchi Bricchetti informed the Italian public about the slave trade in Somalia and the indifferent attitude of the Italian colonial government. Slavery then lasted until early in the twentieth century when it was abolished by the Italian colonial authority in accordance with the Belgium protocol. There were some inland groups, however, who were not freed until the 1930s.

Though slavery was abolished in the early part of the twentieth century, in the mid-1930s, the Italian colonial authority introduced coerced labor laws and the conscription of the freed slaves in the agricultural industry. The newly freed Bantu were expected to work as farm laborers on over one hundred plantations owned by the Italian colonial government. The Bantu were forced to abandon their own farms to live in government established villages around the Italian plantations. Over time, some Bantu were able to migrate to large Somali cities where they found jobs as manual laborers and sometimes, semiskilled tradesmen.

Life didn't get any easier after slavery in Somalia. Though they have been living in Somalia for over two centuries, the Somali Bantu are in many ways, viewed and treated as foreigners. While those that arrived during the early migrations are, by this time, integrated into Somali society, those that arrived via slavery have a difficult life. They lived in mud-plaster huts and most have never been in a town or seen a building taller than two stories. Excluded from mainstream society, many Bantu have retained their ancestral social structure. For many, this means that their East African tribe of origin is the main form of social organization.

While some Bantu who've lost their language and culture have attempted to integrate into the dominant Somali clan social structure, they are viewed as inferior members. The Bantu are subjected to discrimination and are often excluded from political, economic, and educational advancement. Several physical features are used as means to distinguish between who are persecuted and who aren't—the Bantu have darker skin and heavy features while the Somali have sharply angular faces.

Many Bantu say that life became more difficult for them after Somalia became independent from colonial rule in 1960. Though the Somali government made declarations in the 1970s that tribalism should be abolished, discrimination against the Bantu continued, and from the 1970s until the early 1980s, the Somali government forcibly conscripted Bantu into the military.

Civil war broke out in Somalia following the 1991 overthrow of dictator Mohamed Siad Barre's regime, having horrific results for the population and the Bantu people in particular. As society broke down between 1991 and 1992, the agricultural market began to cease normal operations. Because the Bantu were the backbone of the agricultural production in southern Somalia, they had large stocks of food on their property.

As hunger increased, food grew increasingly more valuable among the population and among bandits and rogue militias. Because the Bantu were excluded from the traditional Somali clan protection network, bandits were able to attack the Bantu, stealing food stocks, as well as robbing, raping, and murdering Bantu farmers.

As the civil war progressed, more and more devastation was put upon the Bantu. In October of 1992, the Bantu began to flee in large groups for refugee camps located in Kenya's northeastern province. By January 1994, an estimated ten thousand Bantu were living in these camps, known collectively as Dadaab. Many more traveled by sea to camps in Mozambique. In light of the persecution that the Somali Bantu would face if they returned home, the UNHCR began making attempts to resettle them. Initially, the Bantu sought resettlement to Tanzania and Mozambique, their countries of origin who later refused to resettle them. In late 2002 and early 2003, nearly 12,000 Somali Bantu were approved by the United States for resettlement in the largest resettlement program ever undertaken out of Africa.

Industrialization in the eighteenth century increased the demand for harsh labor around the world. Although slavery in east Africa predates the Sultan of Zanzibar, widespread plantation and industrial slave operations in the early nineteenth century increased the need for labor. To take advantage of this business opportunity, the Sultan of Oman (Sayyid Barkesh) relocated his seat on power from Oman to the east African island of Zanzibar in 1840. The sultan's sovereignty extended from northern Mozambique to southern Somalia. Africans from these areas were abducted into the slave trade. Tanzania, which now includes Zanzibar, was particularly terrorized by the slave trade. A majority of the Somali Bantu refugees, who were originally from Tanzania applied for resettlement to the United States. Bantu refugees with ancestral origins in northern Tanzania, primarily the Wazigua and Zaramo, similarly describe how their ancestors were transported by sea from the Tanzanian port city of Bagamoyo to Southern Somalia. Although many slaves were sold to European buyers with destinations beyond Africa, some slaves were sold to Africans to work on plantations on the continent.

Some African slaves from Kilwa were transported to the Somali port cities of Merca and Barawa where they were forced to work at plantations near the Indian Ocean and in the Shabelle River Valley.

With the rise of Zanzibar as a trade center in the nineteenth century, Somali entrepreneurs began purchasing East African slaves through the Indian Ocean slave trade in order to develop plantation agriculture in the Shabelle River region. Reluctant to farming for themselves, Somali plantation owners relied on slave labor to produce a surplus of grain and cotton to sell in the burgeoning Indian Ocean trade. Slaves were bought or captured from a wide variety of East African groups, including Yao, Zegua, Nyasa, and Makua, and brought by dhow to Somali ports by Arab traders. Slaves purchased by Somali plantation owners lived and labored on family-owned farms in the Shabelle Valley.

During this period of expanded agricultural production in the Shabelle Valley, the more remote Jubba Valley remained largely uninhabited. Partially utilized by small groups of hunter-gatherers, the forested portion of the valley was largely avoided by Somali pastoralists because of tsetse fly infestation, which is lethal to cattle. Its jungle cover, abundant wild foods, and arable land provided a refuge for slaves escaping from Shabelle plantations. Local lore reports that the first fugitive slaves reached the lower valley and established villages around 1840. They were followed by a constant and increasing stream of runaway and manumitted slaves.

Reports by European travelers suggest the lower valley population of ex-slaves had grown from several thousand by 1865 to between thirty thousand and forty thousand by the turn of the century. Abolition decrees introduced after 1900 prompted a massive flight of slaves from Shabelle plantations, and perhaps twenty thousand to three hundred thousand ex-slaves made their way into the Jubba Valley after the turn of the century.

Ex-slaves arriving in the Jubba Valley initially settled in villages along lines of East African ethnic affiliations: Yao in one village, Nyasa in another, etc. By the late nineteenth century, maroon villages stretched up into the middle valley, and the settlement pattern had begun to change. Somali clan affiliation emerged as an important force in shaping village identity, as ex-slaves entering the valley after about 1890 began settling in communities of people who had been enslaved to the same Somali clan. Many people entering the valley around the turn of the century had been enslaved as children or had been born into slavery and thus held only tenuous connections to their original ethnic groups. For them, Somali clan affiliation provided a degree of social organization and identity.

The role of Somali clan affiliation in shaping settlement patterns was strengthened by the influx of pastoral slaves in the early twentueth century. Pastoral slavery has been overlooked in the literature on southern Somalia but was an integral part of Somali life during the nineteenth and early twentieth centuries. Oromo pastoralists, especially women and children, were captured by Somalis during wars and raids. Captured Oromo women became wives, concubines, and domestic slaves, and captured children were brought up as part of the household, but with a slave or servant status.

In some cases, entire Oromo groups were observed as serfs or clients of Somali clans. Manumitted Oromo who settled into Jubba Valley farming villages often maintained ties with their former masters, strengthening the bonds of clan affiliation between Gosha villages and Somali clans. Oromo settled in large numbers in the midvalley area around Bu'aale, and their immigration has been continual since the earliest decades of the twentieth century. While Oromo are not considered to share physical characteristics with descendants of plantation slaves, much intermarriage in the Jubba Valley between the two has occurred.

The introduction of the modern cash economy at about the same time, and with it the practice of slavery, contributed to the breakdown of traditional intertribal economic and social safety networks. As a result, many indigenous Africans lost the customary coping methods that had formerly protected them in times of severe drought. This was particularly true for tribes that were located near the Indian coast, such as the Zaramo and Wazigua, both of which have descendants represented among the Somali Bantu refugees today.

In the late 1830s, there were several years of consecutive drought in Tanzania that resulted in widespread starvation and death. In the hope of averting their families' starvation, Africans without means to weather this terrible period were reduced to accepting Omani Arab promises of wage labor in a distant land. A few Bantus claim that, once their ancestors landed in Somalia, they were sold as slaves on the Benadir coast and later to nomadic Somalis. The African slaves from northeast Tanzania generally worked in the same southeastern Somali regions as those slaves from Mozambique.

Between 25,000 to 50,000 slaves were absorbed into the riverside areas from 1800 to 1890. During this period of expanded agricultural production in the Shabelle River valley, the more remote and forested Jubba River Valley remained largely uninhabited. In the 1840s, the first fugitive slaves from the Shabelle Valley arrived and settled along the Jubba River. By the early 1900s, an estimated 35,000 ex-slaves were living in communities in the Jubba River Valley, in many cases settling in villages according to their East African tribe. In the mid-nineteenth century, an influential female Wazigua leader, Wanankhucha led many of her people out of slavery in a well-orchestrated escape aimed at returning to Tanzania. Upon arriving in the lower Jubba River Valley, where the fugitive slave were eventually able to farm and protect themselves from hostile Somalis, Wanankhucha determined that an earthquake in the valley was a sign that they should settle rather than continue their journey.

Another factor hindering the ex-slaves return to southeast Africa was the perilous social and physical environments in eastern Kenya and southern Somalia. At the time, the indigenous tribes of east Kenya were more hostile to runaway slaves than Arab slave owners. The physical landscape of the Kenyan frontier with Somalia is one of the more inhospitable areas in East Africa. Non-natives trying to cross this area on foot place themselves at great physical risk.

In 1873, the slave trade was forbidden under the British pressure, the first 45 slaves were freed by the Italian colonial authority under the administration of the chartered Company, *V filonardi*. Massive emancipation of the slavery in Somalia only began after the anti-slavery activist Robecchi Bricchetti informed Italian public about the slave trade in Somalia and the indifferent attitude of the Italian colonial government toward the trade. Slavery in southern Somalia lasted until early into the 20th century when it was abolished by the Italian colonial authority in accordance with the Belgium protocol. Some inland groups remained in slavery until the 1930s.

Fugitive slaves who settled in the lower Jubba River Valley with others from their East African tribes were able to retain their ancestral languages and cultures. Later Bantu arrivals, who had begun to assimilate into Somali society while living in the Shebelle River Valley, found the lower Jubba River Valley densely populated and were therefore forced to settle farther north in the middle Jubba River Valley. While the Bantu of the middle Jubba River Valley generally lost their ancestral languages and culture, they faced discrimination similar to that leveled against the Bantu living in lower Jubba River valley. Many of these Bantu adopted dominant Somali clan attachment and names as a means of social organization and identity.

While slavery in southern Somalia was abolished in the early part of the twentieth century, the same Italian authority that had abolished slavery reintroduced coerced labor laws and the conscription of the freed slaves for economic purposes in the agricultural industry in the mid-1930s. Italy had established over one hundred plantations in the river valleys, and an Italian official suggested to the Italian administration that it establish villages for emancipated slaves who would be organized into labor brigades to work on the Italian plantations.

The emancipated Bantu were expected to work solely as farm laborers on plantations owned by the Italian colonial government. The Italian agricultural schemes would not have succeeded without the collaboration of individuals from non-Bantu ethnic groups who themselves were former slave owners. The Bantu were forced to abandon their own farms in order to dwell in the established villages around the Italian plantations. As a British official in East Africa noted, "The conception of these agricultural enterprises as exploitation concessions engendered under the Italian fascist regime a labor policy of considerable severity in theory and actual brutality in practice. It was in fact indistinguishable from slavery.

During the enslavement of the Bantu, the Italians began to free the slaves who had not escaped in 1895, but some inland groups remained in slavery until the 1930s. The Italians introduced coerced labor laws which forced freed slaves to work on Italian-owned plantations. The Bantu were forced to abandon their own villages around Italian plantations. The British abolished this system when they gained control of Somalia after World War II.

Prior to the civil war in Somalia in the late 1980s, the Zigua (Wazigua), who have maintained their ancestral southeast African culture and language more than any other ex-slave Bantu group, were also referred to as the Mushunguli. Since many Bantu groups in prewar Somalia wished to integrate into the dominant clan structure, identifying oneself as a Mushunguli was undesirable. Once in the refugee camps, however, being a Mushunguli became desirable as resettlement to Tanzania and Mozambique. It was predicted on proving a connection to an East African tribe. In this regard, some Bantu refugees with ex-slave ancestry, whether or not they maintained their ancestral language and culture, adopted Mushunguli identification and Swahili language use to differentiate themselves from the other Somali Bantu groups (Lehman and Eno, 2003).

Somalia gained its independence from the British in 1960, and though the country was relatively peaceful until civil war broke out in 1991, the Somali Bantu faced overt discrimination from the Somali majority. After the death of President Siad Barre in 1991, bitter fighting broke out between clans for power, and the infrastructure of the country collapsed. As the Somali Bantu were farmers and had stockpiles of food in a country they faced attacks from bandits and militias. The bandits and militias did not only take food but robbed, raped, and murdered Somali Bantu farmers.

Somali Bantus are culturally, physically, and ethnically different from the Somalis. Somali Bantus have darker skin (in some cases), are typically shorter and more muscular with broader features and most of them having thicker hair than the Somalis. Somali Bantus usually speak Maay (the official language of Somali Bantus, which all Somali Bantus understand). The Bantu people's predominant Negroid physical features are distinct from that of the Somali nomads and give them a unique identity. They are often excluded from political, economic, and educational advancement.

The Bantu, therefore, have had to settle for the lowest and most undignified occupations. When the civil war began in Somalia, Somali Bantus became very vulnerable and were sent out from their farms by armed people of the Somali clans. After much killing, torturing, and raping, along with severe famine, many Somali Bantus fled from their properties without knowing where they were headed. It took up to four weeks to arrive to the Kenyan border, eating leaves off trees and sometimes drinking muddy water while waiting for the rain to drink fresh water.

Most Somali Bantu families died on their way to the Kenyan border due to lack of water, hunger, and disease such as anemia. Somali Bantus and other Somali clans who fled from the civil war were brought to refugee camps by the United Nations High Commissioner for Refugees (UNHCR) and were divided into three different camps: Ifo, Dagahaley, and Hagadera. The Somali Bantus at first thought it was safe to live in these refugee camps, but after in the camps for three years, they realized they were facing the same problems they had in Somalia, such as torturing. It would happen randomly during day-to-day tasks such as when Somali Bantus would collect firewood from the bush.

When the problem increased in the refugee camps, Somali Bantu leaders asked UNHCR to be resettled to their countries of origin like Mozambique, Tanzania, and Malawi, which later the three countries rejected. In 2000, the United States agreed to resettle 12,000 Somali Bantus in the United States. Some people in the refugee camps couldn't believe the Somali Bantus were going to be resettled into the United States. When everything came closer and the resettlement of the Somali Bantus was actually taking place, the security for the Somali Bantus in the refugee camps became even more dangerous.

The International Organization for Migration (IOM) decided to relocate the Somali Bantus to other refugee camps in Kenya, which was safer than their original refugee camps. Somali Bantus went to the new refugee camp called Kakuma, where they lived for one or two years before the first flight of the Somali Bantus came to the United States. There are now about 12,000 of them in the United States today, experiencing a life they had never dreamed of, and especially lives their ancestors never had.

Although there are today no reliable statistical sources, the Somali population is estimated at about 7.5 million people. Of that figure, the entire Bantu population in southern Somalia is estimated at about six hundred thousand, and those with strong East African identification estimated at a fraction of that number.

Some Bantu populations still maintain the tribal identities of their ancestral country of origin. However, unlike the nomadic Somalis, who consider clan affiliation and tribal identification important and critical to survival, most Bantu people identify themselves by their place of residence, which, for those with strong cultural ties to Tanzania, often corresponds to their ceremonial kin grouping (Lehman and Eno, 2003).

The Bantu who were scheduled for resettlement in the United States, therefore, place much less emphasis on Somali clan and tribal affiliations than do the non-Bantu Somalis who have been resettled in the United States. Other Bantu who lived in the vicinity of nomadic Somali clans (particularly those residing outside of the lower Jubba River valley) integrated into the Somali nomadic clan system, which provided the Bantu with some protection and a sense of identity with the nomads.

Discrimination against the Bantu in Somalia largely prevented them from intermarrying with other Somali groups and thus receiving the protection those clan affiliations normally bring. As the scholar Lee Cassanelli stated,

"In Somali society, married women traditionally have served to link the clans of their fathers and brothers, to whom they always belong, with their husbands, to whom the children always belong. Most of the nomadic clans practiced some form of exogamy—marriage outside the clan—to

help strengthen alliances with "outsiders." Wives were exchanged even between clans and clan sections that were prone to fight over water and pasture. These ties helped mediate disputes between clans, since there were always families with in-laws on the other side who would have an interest in the peaceful resolution of conflicts."

Discrimination against the Bantu was not confined to marriage alone, but engulfed every aspect of their lives. As a marginalized group, the Bantu lacked true representation in politics and access to government services, educational opportunities, and professional positions in the private sector. This exclusion also resulted in economic development policies and resource allocations that didn't take into account Bantu wishes and priorities. The Bantu's lineage to slavery relegated them to second-class status—or worse—in prewar Somalia. This overt discrimination also carried over to the Kenyan refugee camps where the Bantu continued to experience discrimination from the other Somali groups.

Like the Bantu from the lower Jubba River Valley, the Bantu from the middle Jubba River valley also regard their village as an important form of social organization. Although Bantu with strong cultural and linguistic links to southeast Africa have been known to a leveled mockery against those who attempted to integrate into the dominant Somali clan culture and language, there is no real hostility between them. In fact, the war and refugee experience have worked to strengthen relationships between the various Bantu subgroups in most cases.

The Somali Clan System

According to tradition, the Somali nation symbolically consists of a vast genealogical tree. Nearly all Somalis descend from a common founding father, the mythical *Hiil* (father of *Sab* and *Samaale*), to whom the Somalis trace their genealogical origin. At the same time, a widespread Somali belief holds that most of them descend from the Qurayshitic lineage of the Prophet Muhammad. The clan and clan families which have high regard for this claim include Darod, Isaaq, Ajuraan, Shikhaal, Geledi, and others.

The predominance of the Qurayshitic lineage attests to the main role of Islamic ideology in the formation and formulation of the early Somali identity. It is against this background that one could interpret the sprouting of Arab progenitors related to the prophet and siring Somali clans.

Legend has it that Darod was expelled from Arabia. Seeking refuge, he arrived at the Somali coast. He dug a well near a larger tree. Then, one day, he was discovered by Dir's daughter, Doombiro, who was tending her flock somewhere in the vicinity. He watered her animals at "his" well. Noticing that the stock had been watered more than the usual times, Dir one day decided to follow his daughter and discover for himself where the water for the animals was coming from. Seeing that there was a third person in the vicinity, Darod quickly closed the well with a large stone and climbed up a tree. Dir and his followers sought Darod's aid after unsuccessful attempts to reopen the well. Darod refused to come down until "the chieftain promised him his daughter in marriage" and allowed him to descend on his own shoulders. From this marriage the Darod clan family is said to have descended.

This story implies to the scriptural tale of Moses (Prophet Musa) found in the Qur'an. In escaping from Egypt, Moses found two sisters near a well.

The girls wanted to water their flock, but the well was covered by a very heavy stone that could only be lifted by four to six people. Moses removed it by himself and helped the girls to water their flocks. The father of the sisters, Shuaib, gave Moses one of the girls in marriage.

Before the coming of the Islamic and Christian faiths to the Horn of Africa, the Eastern Cushitic-speaking peoples had an ancient common religion, which is still professed by the Borana. Aspects of the old religion are still extant in the new faiths adopted by the other groups. One of the most characteristic elements of that religion is connected with the notion of the sky-god called *Waaq*. This name is still used to mean God by the Oromo, Konso, Burji, Haddiya, Tasmai, Dasenech, and others who speak Eastern Cushitic languages. A number of these groups still consider some kind of trees as sacred. For instance, the sycamore is the Borana's temple. They believe that *Waaq* sometimes descends on that tree.

Thus, the ingenuity of some of the Somali mythic ancestors—or whoever the mythmaker was—to have molded the semblance of smooth transition, one that could bridge the old and the new religions.

Another Somali tradition that shows the merging of African and Islamic cultures is the rite that Somali women in the seventh or ninth month of their pregnancy perform, called *Kur* or Madaxshub. The invited women pour abundant oil on the pregnant woman's head, invoking Eve or Fatima, the daughter of the Prophet, in order to safeguard the woman during delivery. This rite is not a part of Islam; it has its roots in the cult of the goddess of fertility and maternity practiced by the Borana women in the same way and for the same purposes. Here Fatima is a covering name for the ancient goddess Ateta, as the Arabian descendant was for the heavenly origin.

In addition to this, the fact that in a variety of clan genealogies, the appearance of the same *Waaq* (sky-god) coincides with the initial adoption of Islamic names. Theophorous names are very common among all Semitic peoples from antiquity until today. So the Islamic tradition has introduced this form of name to the Horn. For instance, *Bidde Waaq* is a loan transition of the Islamic name Abdullah (the servant of Allah). Here the name Waaq no more represents the traditional meaning of "sky-god," but stands for Allah. According to some scholars, this underlines the legitimacy of our assumptions about the Somali *islamization* period.

No less problematic is the actual lineage systems through which Somalis trace their genealogy. The actually memorized genealogy is not the crucial basis for determining one's clan identity, as is commonly believed among the Somalis.

Scholars argue that this comes to show that the Somali clan structure typically is not based on blood relationship, but rather it is a fruit of nomadic pastoral life. The necessity of defense and the movement to new territory necessitated by a constant search for pasture and water have resulted over time in the formation of new alliances and, later, new clan identities.

Thus, the need to fully examine the mythic nature of the Somali clan system is apparent. This short piece is only meant to provoke discussion and certainly is not an end to the discussion. It is perhaps important to critically sift through received traditions so that there might be able to reinvent new and more viable terms of reference for Somalia.

Clan identity and Islam are central pillars of Somali society, with clan dynamics and interclan rivalries magnified by decades of state collapse. Clan and subclan structures are central to Somali identity. From a young age, children are traditionally taught to memorize and recite their clan-based kinship genealogy, sometimes naming twenty or even thirty generations of their patrilineal ancestors.

When the Siad Barre regime collapsed in 1991 and with it the presence of centralized Mogadishu-based governance, interclan violence and power rivalries spiked as a clan structures and identities filled the governance void. The destructiveness of this process contributed to a paradoxical perception of clans that remains noticeable today. Though many Somalis often self-identify based on clan, they nevertheless blame "clannish" behavior for the fractionalization, violence, and the destruction of Somali stability.

Nevertheless, Somali society continues to be defined by clan identities, and clan rivalries frame the balance of power across Somalia. Somali clans and subclans are geographically incorporated rather than clearly divided between homogenous clan territories, although certain subclans exert significant power in specific regions. For example, the capital of Mogadishu is divided among Hawiye subclans while the Rahanweyn continue to play the key role in central Bay and Bakool regions. The Isaaq dominate Somaliland in the northwest, and various Darod subclans reside mainly in Puntland, the north-central provinces, and the southern Jubba region. These geographic divisions often correspond to battle lines, as clans vie for influence and resources.

This complex and interlocking system establishes the rules by which Somali politicians, warlords, and even terrorists must abide. As al-Shabaab has developed in recent years and sought to balance domestic priorities with international jihadi ideals, the role of clan has continued to plague and shape the organization.

Al-Shabaab's strategy and its inability to avoid clan influence has affected the way the group projects force, recruits fighters, and influences the Somali population. In these ways, al-Shabaab has evolved drastically over the past ten years. Initially a relatively small militia, al-Shabaab gained local support as the only effective fighting force against the Ethiopian intervention in Somalia from late 2006 through early 2009.

Today, al-Shabaab is estimated to field roughly 2,500–3,000 fighters, likely augmented by an additional three thousand or so loosely aligned militia. However, much of this façade began falling apart with the Ethiopian withdrawal in 2009 as clan disputes surfaced immediately affecting al-Shabaab's leadership and conflicts with other Somali actors.

A review of al-Shabaab's battles in recent years reveals clear clan dynamics. Fighting between al-Shabaab, allied Islamist militia around Mogadishu, and Somalia's feeble Transitional Federal Government (TFG) surged in May 2009 and again during al-Shabaab's Ramadan offensive of 2010.

South of Mogadishu, al-Shabaab has engaged in clan-based fighting to control the strategically important port of Kismayo. In fall 2009, al-Shabaab seized full control of Kismayo, consolidating power by ousting its former ally, an Islamist militia known as Hizb al-Islam. The group began as an umbrella organization comprised of various clan/subclan factions with alliances intended to reflect a clan-based balance of power. These included the Alliance for the Re-Liberation of Somalia-Asmara, the Somali Islamic Front, the Ras Kamboni militia, and the Anole militia. Alliances in the fighting broke down along subclan lines, with al-Shabaab fighters affiliated with the Mareehan subclan ultimately defeating the Ras Kamboni militia (Ogadeni subclan power base) and the Harti subclan fighters called the Anole faction. Research suggests that al-Shabaab leadership in the Kismayo area, led by Ibrahim Haji Jama al-Afghani, continues to manage al-Shabaab's interests by manipulating a network of clan allies to maintain local control.

The Somali civil war has multiple and complex causes including political, economic, cultural, and psychological. Various external and internal factors have played different roles during the various stages of the conflict.

The most important factor that has created and sustained the clan-based militias' conflicts is competition for power and resources. Somali clans had often clashed over resources such as water, livestock (camels), and grazing long before Somalia became a sovereign country. Using the widely accepted Somalia traditional legal system *(Heer)*, historically traditional leaders settled these conflicts.

However, after Somalia gained its independence, many Somalis moved to urban areas, so the types of resources that are needed and the means used to obtain them have changed. Political leaders realized that whoever controlled the state would control the nation's resources. Access to government resources, recruitment of civil servants, and control of foreign aid replaced control of water wells and access to grazing issues in the countryside. For instance, Mohamed Jama Urdoh, a Somali journalist, observed Somalia's police forces in 1967. He revealed in an investigative report that more than 70 percent (51 out of 71) of police station chiefs were members of the same clan as the then police chief. Moreover, the police chief was just one example of how government officials were misusing their power.

Besides the political sponsorship appointments that characterized the civil service, corruption affected all levels and departments of the government. With regards to government policy, the frequently cited examples include the use of Somalia's police and army forces for clannish reasons. Within two clans, the Lelkase and the Ayr, there is a widespread belief that the government of the day and the police used excessive force against them.

As corrupt as it was, Somalia's first government was democratic. It had checks and balances and people could talk and address the corruption. The Somali leaders of the time were poorly educated novices with little experience in running a government. Nevertheless, the former prime minister, Abdirizak Haji Hussein, had some success in dealing with security and corruption problems during his reign.

However, when General Mohamed Siad Barre took over power in October 1969 things changed. For the first few years the revolutionary council built new institutions and wrote down the Somali language. However, the general's obsession with controlling and consolidating his power to the benefit of members of his clan became clear to all Somalis. Opposition groups were outlawed and no one could criticize the military leaders.

Since elites from specific clans controlled all levels of state power and the economy, the leadership of the opposition capitalized on this opportunity. After the 1977–1978 war between Somalia and Ethiopia, a number of military officers attempted to take over the government. When this coup failed, the Siad Barre regime started to use excessive force against the Majerteen clan (the clan to which most of the officers belonged). This event was the beginning of Somalia's civil war. Other clans such as the Isaaq, Ogaden, Hawiye, Digil, and Mirifle also started opposition groups in order to seize power.

When the Somali Salvation Democratic Front (SSDF), the Majerteen clan's opposition party and the Somali National Movement (SNM), the Isaaq clan's opposition party started their armed struggle against the military regime, Somalia and Ethiopia had hostile relations, so Ethiopia welcomed and armed all opposition groups fleeing from the repression in Somalia. Other opposition groups, such as the United Somali Congress (USC), the Hawiye clan's opposition party and the Somali Patriotic Movement (SPM), the Ogaden clan's party organized their military activities from Ethiopia. Somalia's military government denied people the opportunity to participate in governing. Denied all other avenues to affect the change of the regime, opposition groups resorted to violence. The state's repression, violence, and excessive force justified the power-hungry opposition leaders when they crossed the border and attacked Somalia from Ethiopia.

Mere differences in clan identities themselves did not cause the conflict. Clan identity is not static, but changes depending on the situation. One can claim to be "Somali" if doing so serves one's interests or wish to emphasis the link between two clans at national level. That same person may claim to be "Irir," "Hawiye," "Hirab," "Habargidir," "Sa'ad," or "Reer Hilowle." These terms involve an example of descending levels of one's clan identity. The same is true of other clans regardless of whether they are in the north or the south. Clan identity is flexible. The emphasis is on one level over another reflects the interests and goals of the elites of that level. For example, when opposition leaders wanted to mobilize forces, they emphasized the most inclusive identities: the SNM leaders emphasized the grievances of the Isaaq clan, whereas the USC leaders mobilized the Hawiye clan. The Somali Democratic Movement (SDM), on the other hand, organized the Digil and Mirifle clans in the south.

General Mohamed Siad Barre depended heavily on his own Mareehan (Marehan) subclan of the Darod clans. Opposition leaders from the Darod clan could not use the Darod banner because General Siad Barre was himself a member of the Darod clan. Therefore, the SSDF leaders depended on the Majerteen (Majertan) subclan of the Darod clans, while the Somali Patriotic Movement (SPM) drew its supporters from the Ogaden subclan of the Darod clans.

After 1992 the emphasis changed from inclusive clan identities (for example Darod or Hawiye) to subclan identities such as Harti, Mareehan, Habargidir, or Mudullood. For instance, when the power struggle broke out in 1991 between Ali Mahdi Mohamed and General Mohamed Farah Aideed (who both belong to the Hiraab subclan), the clan identities that mattered became those of the Mudullood and the Habargidir (their respective subclans). These clan identities fueled the conflicts in Somalia, but did not, by themselves, cause the war. In other words, clan identity became an instrument for mobilization.

The availability of weapons exacerbated the Somali conflict. The Somali people were well armed. There were two major sources of weapons. Because of Somalia's strategic location, the two superpowers of the time (the former Soviet Union and the US) competed to arm the former dictator. The second source was the Ethiopian regime, which was arming opposition groups. The availability of weapons, combined with all the above grievances and disputes, resulted in all-out civil war in 1988.

In addition, most Somalis witness people using violence and benefiting from it. In the countryside, young men used to attack other clans and steal their camels. In the cities, the thousands of armed men benefit from using violence to force people to pay them illegally, and then justify their aggression by arguing that Somali clans have been fighting and robbing each other since time immemorial. Moreover, Somali literature provides many examples of poets defending the use of violence against other clans, or at least attempting to legitimize stealing their camels. Use of force as an acceptable strategy is therefore rooted in Somali culture. In fact, one could argue that some features of Somali culture reward criminals who engage in violent activities.

Both greed and grievances are present in the Somali conflict. Somalia's political elites were driven by greed for power and resources, as Abdi Samatar has rightly observed. However, most of Somalia's people have legitimate grievances. The state failed to provide basic services such as security, education, healthcare, and jobs. Moreover, the military government used force to repress people.

Fourteen peace conferences have been held in different cities at different times. Five of these (Djibouti 1991, Addis Ababa 1993, Cairo 1997, Arta 2000, and Eldoret/ Mpegati 2002–2004) were major conferences to which the international community lent its support. Each produced some sort of peace agreement and a new government. However, all of the agreements failed except for the recently concluded Mpegati conference, which faced serious challenges.

Ethiopia's meddling is the most important and persistent factor in the perpetuation of the Somali conflict. This meddling has given shelter and arms to all spoilers (groups and individuals). It has undermined the two most important peace accords (Cairo Accord 1997 and Arta Agreement 2000) and has manipulated the Somali peace process in Kenya and the transitional government that was formed. Ethiopia has frequently sent weapons over the border and at times has occupied several towns in southern Somali. In other words, Ethiopia, a powerful and well-positioned state, is a hostile neighbor that aims to maintain a weak and divided Somalia.

Throughout history Somalis and Ethiopians (particularly Highlanders) have had unstable and poor relations. The two peoples have ethnic and religious differences. From the Somali people's perspective, Ethiopia is one of the colonial powers that partitioned Somalia into five parts. As Geshekter notes, Ethiopia's King Menelik wrote a circular in 1891 to the European forces that were dividing Africa among themselves and demanded his share. King Menelik wrote, "Ethiopia has been for fourteen centuries a Christian island in a sea of pagans. If the powers at a distance come forward to partition Africa between them, I do not intend to remain an indifferent spectator."

The European powers gave the Somali region of Ogaden to King Menelik to appease him and in 1954 Britain gave Somalia's Hawd and Reserve Area to Ethiopia. As a result, two major wars occurred in 1964 and 1977, and hundreds of skirmishes have taken place along the border between Ethiopia and Somalia. The source of the conflict was the Ogaden region, which is controlled by Ethiopia. Somalia has supported and armed opposition groups trying to overthrow Ethiopia's government, and Ethiopia has supported Somali opposition movements (SSDF, SNM, USC, and SPM). All of the opposition groups have started their wars from Ethiopia in order to fight against the military government of Siad Barre, and Ethiopia has been the major actor in perpetuating Somalia's civil war, particularly over the past fourteen years.

Ethiopia openly and effectively destroyed the Cairo Accord in 1997 and the Arta Peace Agreement in 2000. Twenty-eight Somali warlords and faction leaders agreed on a power-sharing formula in Cairo, Egypt in 1997. They also decided to form a national government. At the time, Somalia's warlords and faction leaders were divided into two camps: the Ethiopia-supported Somali Salvation Alliance (consisting of fifteen factions called the Sodere Group or SSA) and the Somali National Alliance (SNA), which consisted of thirteen factions and received limited support from Libya.

Ali Mahdi Mohamed led the SSA, and Hussein Mohamed Aideed was chairman of the SNA. These two groups controlled most of Somalia, and both participated in the Cairo Conference. In many cities, including Somalia's capital Mogadishu, the Somali people welcomed the Cairo Accord by holding rallies and demonstrations supporting it.

Ethiopia actively recruited two of the twenty-eight warlords that were meeting in Cairo. It encouraged Colonel Abdullahi Yusuf Ahmed (the current Somali president) and General Adan Abdullahi Nur to leave the meeting and reject its outcome. From Cairo they went directly to Addis Ababa. Ethiopia started to openly support these two faction leaders militarily and politically. Ethiopia and these two warlords effectively undermined Egypt's efforts to end Somalia's civil war.

Somalia slipped back into violence and a number of cities changed hands. The UN and Western governments showed no interest in intervening in the conflict, while Ethiopia became more openly involved—its army occupied some of the major cities in southern Somalia. In addition, regardless of Security Council Resolution 733, adopted in January 1992, which imposed a comprehensive arms embargo against Somalia, many factions were receiving ammunition and sometimes direct military assistance from Ethiopia.

Against this background, President Ismail Omar Gheulle of Djibouti developed a peace initiative in 1999. He made a speech at the UN General Assembly in September 1999 in which he outlined his plan for addressing the Somali conflict. Gheulle promised to hold a national reconciliation conference in which civil society and traditional leaders would participate. He asked the international community to support his initiative. If the warlords rejected his plan and stood in the way of peace, Gheulle proposed that the international community should consider them criminals. He did give the warlords an opportunity to participate, provided that they respected the outcome of the conference.

As a result, the Djibouti (named after the city of Arta) Conference became the largest Somali-owned peace conference ever held, with more than three thousand Somalis in attendance. Traditional leaders, civil society organizations, intellectuals, and businessmen came together to forgive one another and to establish a national government. The conference elected over nine hundred delegates, who later appointed a 245 seat Transitional National Assembly (TNA), whose members enacted the Transitional National Charter (TNC). The TNA elected a president, who then appointed a prime minister.

This open and transparent reconciliation conference received far more international and Somali support than the Cairo Conference. The regional organization, the Intergovernmental Authority on Development (IGAD), endorsed it. Arab countries gave some financial assistance. The ARABSAT satellite played a positive role, as it broadcast conference proceedings to Somalia and the region through television and radio.

The UN, the USA, and the European Union (EU) also publicly supported the Djibouti initiative. Furthermore, more than three thousand Somalis, including some warlords, participated, whereas only twenty-eight warlords and faction leaders had been invited to the Cairo Conference. The result of the conference was surprising. Somalis finally created a national caretaker government that was widely accepted and welcomed. Hundreds of thousands of Somalis throughout Somalia welcomed the outcome, with the exception of the self-declared breakaway region of Somaliland, which still had substantive issues with the rest of Somalia.

Even though Ethiopia had initially supported the conference and its prime minister attended the inauguration ceremony, it was reluctant to accept and support the outcome of the conference. After the TNA had elected Abdiiqasim Salad Hassan and even before he had nominated a prime minister, Ethiopia convinced Colonel Hassan Mohamed Nur Shatigudud of the RRA to abandon the TNG (Transitional National Government). Shatigudud and several other warlords had been sent to the Arta Conference by Ethiopia in the first place. He had received military assistance from Ethiopia in order to capture Baidoa from Hussein Aideed's SNA faction. Knowing what happened to the factions that directly opposed Ethiopia, he was not in a position to challenge it. Therefore, Shatigudud abandoned the TNG, going directly from New York as a member of the president's delegation to Addis Ababa. He subsequently became one of the staunchest opposition leaders against the TNG.

Whatever its motives, Ethiopia is an important factor in blocking peace-building efforts in Somalia. Since the beginning of the civil war, Ethiopia has been playing with Somali factions—supporting one, destroying it, and then supporting it again. Hussein Aideed, who lost Baidoa because of Ethiopia, became its friend and spoiler in destroying the Arta Peace Agreement. Even more shocking, the Ethiopian regime has always helped many destabilising forces in Somalia (particularly in the southern part).

When Ali Mahdi was chosen to head an interim government in 1992, Ethiopia supported his main rival, General Aideed. When Aideed became stronger and created his own administration in 1994, Ethiopia supported Ali Mahdi and his groups. When all Somali groups signed the Cairo Accord, Ethiopia recruited Abdullahi Yusuf and Adan Abdullahi Nur. When Somalis formed the TNG, Ethiopia organized all the opposition, helped them create the SRRC (Somali Restoration and Reconciliation Committee) and provided military aid to subvert the TNG.

With respect to the peace conference in Kenya, Ethiopia initiated this peace process and has controlled it for two years with the help of Kenya; together they produced a charter, a parliament and a government of their design. When the heads of the Inter-Governmental Authority on Developmental (IGAD) member states met in Khartoum in 2001, Ethiopia pressured other IGAD countries and insisted that the Arta process was incomplete. Then Ethiopia forced a resolution calling for another peace conference in Kenya. At the beginning of this conference Ethiopia started to manipulate the peace process by controlling the agenda and forum. With the help of the host country, Ethiopia gave absolute power to the warlords it supported. Ethiopia and Kenya have also marginalized traditional, religious, and civil society leaders.

By keeping the Somali people divided and weak, the current regime in Addis Ababa believes it can eliminate any threat from Somalia. Moreover, Ethiopia intends to retain for many years the Somali territories that it has colonized, and tries to gain unlimited access to Somali ports by signing agreements with the clan chiefs on unequal terms.

Warlords who are benefiting from the status quo lead most of Somalia's factions. Some have committed heinous crimes and therefore feel uncertain about their futures. These warlords have used violence and intimidation after peace accords were signed. For instance, General Morgan refused to accept a parliamentary seat and attacked Kismayo in 2001. Muse Sudi, Hussein Aideed, and Osman Atto used violence to undermine the TNG (Muse Sudi in 2001, Hussein Aideed and Osman Atto in 2001). Colonial Shatigudud and Colonel Abdullahi Yusuf also engaged in violence in their respective areas.

The Mogadishu warlords' determination to undermine Ali Gedi's government illustrates better how Somalia's spoilers are committed to keep the status quo. Mohamed Qanyare, Muse Sudi, Omar Mohamud Finish, Botan Alin, and Osman Hassan Ali Atto have done everything they can to undermine the transitional government, even though they remain members of the cabinet. In fact they attempted to create parallel administration in Mogadishu and they started to openly denounce Abdullahi Yusuf and Ali Gedi.

Somalia has had many internal spoilers. General Aideed, for example, challenged and effectively undermined the ill-fated UN efforts to restore peace in Somalia in 1993, despite wide support for the UN presence and activities. He wanted to nominate the agreed-upon Transitional National Council members in the areas he controlled, whereas the United Nations endorsed the local people's wish to elect their own representatives. The presence of internal spoilers who are willing to use violence and intimidation, as well as a hostile neighbor determined to help or sponsor them, makes forging and implementing an agreement almost impossible.

Besides Ethiopia and the warlords, the most important factor that has prolonged the conflict is a lack of resources. Menkhause (1998) wrote, "It is not simply a lack of goodwill on the part of the factions that prevents implementation—it is a lack of capacity." Somalia has never had an effective, self-sufficient government. Most of the state's resources have come from foreign aid, mainly as bilateral or multilateral assistance. The civil war has not only destroyed the internal domestic sources that generated an already insufficient income, but has made the whole country dependent on foreign aid and remittances. The Cairo Conference and the Arta peace process in Djibouti both had significant financial problems.

Winston Tubman, the UN Secretary-General's political representative to the Somali peace conference in Kenya, was quoted as saying, "One of the five permanent members of the UN Security Council—China, Britain, France, the US, and Russia—could make a difference in Somalia."

During the cold war, the United States had strategic interests in Somalia. While ignoring its human rights record, the United States deliberately supported the former military regime that led the country into this protracted civil war. Lyons and Samatar noted that "from 1983 to 1990, the United States committed almost $500 million worth of military resources to Somalia." The United States also led an international intervention into Somalia in early 1992, when the combination of civil war and drought caused tens of thousands of deaths from starvation. However, after General Aideed's faction killed eighteen American troops and wounded another hundred, the United States decided to withdraw from Somalia. Afterward, the United States position on Somalia was not clear, for it has adopted a "wait and see" attitude.

Since the attacks on New York and Washington in 2001, the United States has again shown an interest in Somalia. It has frozen the assets of the largest money transfer and telecommunication company (Al-Barakaat) in Somalia, even though an investigation by the National Commission on Terrorist Attacks upon the United States did not find evidence that linked this company to terrorist organizations.

The United States has also listed about twenty Somali companies and individuals as "terrorists" and repeatedly said that it is interested in Somalia because of the war on terrorism. However, the Bush administration's actions and the statements were contradictory. The United States argued that without a functioning state, Somalia could become a breeding ground for terrorism, yet the United States supports the forces that created and perpetuated the chaos in the first place.

According to some historians, the level of American commitment to helping create a stable regime in Somalia was not sufficient. Somalis widely believe that Ethiopia had a green light from Washington to spoil Somalia's peace efforts. Most Somalis believe that if the United States commits itself to Somalia again, it will have an easier time before two reasons.

First, most Somalis grew tired of the senseless civil war. Warlords and faction leaders have failed to bring peace and development. Second, Ethiopia, which received American assistance, was the most important factor that undermined peace-building efforts in Somalia. US pressure on Ethiopia to stay out of Somalia's internal affairs during the 90s would've solved much of the problem, according to some historians. Overall, Ethiopia's hostile policies, the warlords' unwillingness to accept the popular will, lack of resources, and the absence of major-power interest were major factors that perpetuated the Somali conflict (Schaefer and Black, 2011).

From Independence to Civil War

On July 1, 1960, Somalia gained its independence from European colonialism. The two former colonies, British Somaliland (North) and Italian Somaliland (South), united to form a single country. On a national level, political instability was rampant and progress was slow. There were three major issues facing the country: firstly, the question of whether or not the two Somali nations should be united; secondly, with the country being mostly rural and localized, how could political federalism and nationalism genuinely exist; thirdly, what to do about the absence of any legitimate state institutions and infrastructure. For the first nine years Somalia enjoyed successful democratically elected governments, with no single government lasting more than a few years.

Suddenly, Somalia was about to be pushed into a completely different direction in 1969, as the government was overthrown in a military coup by Siad Barre, who became the country's dictator until he was overthrown during the civil war twenty years later.

On October 15, 1969, President Abdirashid Ali Sharmarke had been touring the northern part of the country to witness the impact of a severe drought. Cities in north Somalia suffered a prolonged drought in 1969, the people suffered from hunger. The president's advisers suggested that he not take such trip as there was a conspiracy against him and against democracy. But he insisted to take the trip by responding, "I want to experience difficulties hit by my people . . . If I don't travel there, then I feel that I have betrayed my people and my country. Therefore, it's my duty to take part of their difficulties to get a correct assessment of the situation."

During a tour in Las Anod, one of the bodyguards of the president, Abdulkadir Abdi Mohamed who was sent to Las Anod with the president assassinated him, which caused shock for the country.

On the day of the assassination, Prime Minister Egal was overseas on an official visit, but on his return Egal ordered a meeting with members of his party to decide who should replace President Sharmarke. After an attentive deliberation, Haji Muse Boqor was chosen to replace Sharmarke. This decision angered certain members of the military.

On October 21, 1969, after the traditional five days mourning, a military coup took over key points in Mogadishu, imprisoned government officials, put an end to the constitution, abolished the National Assembly, and banned political parties, successfully putting an end to democracy in Somalia. The coup was operated by Major General Mohamed Siad Barre, who was at the time the commander of the army.

Barre was a brutal despot with a hunger for power accumulation. Being in control of the country's police force and army, he was ruthless repressing his local enemies.

But there were those enemies whom Barre couldn't simply crush, namely the dozens upon dozens of local clans that were located across the country's vast lands; if those clans united, they could easily have organized an overthrow of the government, for the sheer scale of the balance of forces. In order to prevent this from happening, Barre employed various divide-and-conquer tricks on to the clans, "playing on [their] interests and rivalries," so that they'd fight against each other than against him.

Because the country was so localized, social and political power as a whole laid in the hands of the clan elders and other regional forces. Barre sought to address this situation by both shutting down local institutions and establishing his own state forces. He launched a campaign of suppression against the clans, with the aim of making them weak. The clans were said to be outdated institutions that needed to be get rid of.

By creating a big and powerful government that would distribute resources across the Somali economy as needed, Barre hoped to create a dependence of the population on his regime, people would be required to look to the state for security and welfare, which would totally marginalize the relevancy of the clans, thereby making them inoperative. But despite his antitribal strategy, Somalis regarded the regime as essentially clan-based, support by those clans of Barre's extended family.

Also, Barre had imperial goals. He wanted to have armies invade neighboring countries such as Kenya and Ethiopia, annexing vast amounts of their land, thus enriching Somalia. Ideologically, this imperial ambition was called "Pan-Somali nationalism," a notion that sought to liberate all ethnic Somalis in neighboring states and united them into one state, thereby creating a Greater Somalia.

Geographically speaking, the Horn of Africa is situated in a strategically valuable location—it's a close neighbor to the oil-rich Middle East with easy access to the trade route of the Gulf of Aden (via the Red Sea and the Suez Canal), and it makes shipping into the Indian Ocean easier. However, some oil is situated underneath the country's own territory. It's no surprise, because during the Cold War imperial rivalries would try to seek to control Somalia.

Siad Barre always wanted to be a US ally, but because Ethiopia and Diego Garcia were already militarily-active allies in the region, the United States saw no need to accept the offer. So instead, for opportunistic reasons, Barre became close with the Soviet Union, signing a friendship treaty with Moscow in July 1974.

On 1975, a Soviet naval base was formed in Berbera, a small northern Somalia coastal city; the base had a dry dock, missile handling and storage facilities, a communications station, a large fuel storage facility, and a 15,000-foot runway capable of accommodating large Soviet aircraft.

For now, Barre played along with the Stalinist terminology and governance methods—he called his political party the Somali Socialist Revolutionary with the doctrine of scientific socialism; the country was run through state capitalism, including nationalizations; a political bureaucracy was set up, with Barre as both secretary-general of the party and chairman of its central committee. Via a military junta or a Stalinist bureaucracy, Barre was still the unchallengeable ruler, crushing all enemies and forever accumulating more power into his grasp.

In 1974, the US-friendly monarch of Ethiopia, Haile Selassie, was overthrown by leftist guerillas, forcing the United States to withdraw its force from that country. The Soviet Union tried immediately to monopolize its power over the Horn of Africa by developing good relations with this new government.

This was Barre's moment to prove to the United States that he could be a useful asset to them. He broke off relations with Moscow, invaded Ethiopia, and tried to overthrow the government there. The Americans were indeed impressed—they began immediately sending over aid and arms to Barre, and he became a client of the American Empire. The Americans *"armed Siad Barre for a decade, making Somalia one of the world's largest aid recipients. Somali markets were stock with corn from Kansas; USAID Land Cruiser criss-crossed the plains carrying workers of development schemes, the ruins of which now litter the countryside; and affluent villas funded by diverted aid monies sprang up in south Mogadishu."*

As a client of the Americans, *"Barre was able to build Africa's largest army . . . He was able to secure $100 million a year in development and military aid . . . In June 1988, a few weeks after the outbreak of a war in northern Somalia, the U.S. delivered $1.4 million in military aid to the Barre government."*

The aid had conditions to it—services had to be privatized, state belongings had to be sold off, tariffs on foreign capital had to be liberated, total regulations of labor, environment, and health; in other words, Somalia was only going to get US aid if it applied for the IMF (International Monetary Fund)-style Washington Consensus to its economy.

However, by the 1980s, the United States had a cold war military agenda to conduct in south Asia and Latin America. Throughout the decade, Barre was armed and on standby if needed by Washington, but he wasn't given the call. By 1988, with the Cold War winding up, Washington disinterest led to an eventual ending of all support to Somalia; without US money and guns, the process of the regime's collapse was sped up.

By controlling the government, the treasury, the police, and the military, Siad Barre had immense power, for which he endlessly used to further his power accumulation needs; repressive state powers were used to primarily conserve elite privilege. As is the case with most corrupt governments, Barre's cabinet was a clique of racketeers who directly benefitted from his power accumulation and who complemented his despotism with their own.

As the massive amounts of weapons from Washington began flooding into Somalia, there began the growth and development of a new class, the warlords. These were figures who had no direct connection to commodity production in the society, but could heavily influence the economy thanks to the massive weaponry they had access to.

From the early 1980s, it became clear that Siad Barre was going to continue ruling onward as he had for the previous decade, and no one was going to overthrow him. More and more, during this period, a mass militarization was taking place, encompassing all sectors of Somali society.

Primarily, the clans were purchasing arms, to help protect themselves from further invasions by the Barre government. Clan militarism emerged only with the creation of a police state in the 1980s; the clans were arming themselves in self-defense against Barre's repression.

Various militarized political organizations were formed, including the Somali National Movement (SNM) created by Somaliland, the United Somali Congress (USC) formed by the Hawiye clan which was led by Mohamed Farrah Aidid, and the Somali Patriotic Movement (SPM) formed by the Ogaden people.

Also, there was the origins and growth of regional warlords, who were very vicious; gangs of armed soldiers, either acting as militiamen or bandits, began roaming the countryside to rob innocent people. As the civil war progressed, many of these militias and warlords began directly going after the Barre government, which involved conducting clan-affiliated guerilla-type terrorism.

The Somali national army, which was the key device which Barre used to repress the countryside, began to break apart. There was a series of attempted coups and assassinations, along with various mutinies. The first attempted coup came in 1978, when military officers tried to take power. When this failed, they escaped to the countryside, formed a Maoist guerilla organization, the Somali Salvation Democratic Front (SSDF), and continued to fight Barre that way.

For most of the middle decade, the fighting was limited to just the countryside and major rural centers of the country, which meant that little progress of removing Barre was made and where the regime could ignore the conflict, for it didn't directly concern them. In May 1988, when the Somali National Movement began attacking urban military targets, such as government buildings in the cities of Hargeisa and Burco, the possibility of Barre ignoring the problem had ended. Thus he would have no choice but to fight the guerillas and resist their attempts at removing him. In July 1989, the civil war reached the streets of the capital—following "the assassination of the Bishop of Mogadishu," there was a mass riot; this was ruthlessly repressed by Barre's forces, resulted in 450 people being killed, as well as "mass arrests and executions of civilians."

The 1980s was marked as a sad decade for the future prospects of Somali society, because an entire generation was lost to the fighting against Barre. Countless young people, instead of learning a trade and getting a job and living as a contributing member of the community, would join the local clan's or warlord's militia, and participate in the fighting. Their bravery was fully admired, because they were willing to give up everything—their careers, and possibly lives, just in the hope of getting rid of Barre and freeing their country once again. But even so, without skills and crafts being passed on to the youth and without new workers coming into industries, the possibility of social decay was prevalent.

The biggest problem with the civil war was that the now-militarized clans, only interested in their local, regional, and agricultural affairs, had no understanding of how urban and federal government worked. That was going to change in the next couple of years, once Barre was overthrown and the United Nations came in.

As mentioned earlier, with the cold war being fought on the other side of the world, Washington had little interest in Barre's interests or activities. By 1988, with the cold war winding down, this was becoming possible. It was in 1988 that the civil war had entered into Mogadishu, as guerrillas fought against Barre's police and military security forces. It was a standard practice for America, when it becomes clear that one of its client dictators is about to be overthrown, to cut its ties with them before the final act is played out, so that it still has some political capital leftover. This is exactly what happened with Siad Barre, as the flow of arms and cash was postponed, right at the time when the Barre needed them the most.

Despite nearly dying in a car accident in 1986, and despite his cabinet racketeers now demanding him to step down, Barre continued the civil war, perhaps intensifying it. He authorized his forces to be ruthless against rebels, guerrillas, and innocent people—"bombing civilian targets, planting land mines, poisoning wells, and sometimes deliberately destroying livestock." By the end of the civil war, tens of thousands of people had been killed—the Western media estimated that approximately fifty thousand civilians had been killed, but human rights activists say that the figure is more like 250,000. Over half-a-million Somalis became refugees due to the civil war.

The UNHCR established eight refugee camps in Ethiopia. One major tactic of Barre's security and military forces was the use of antipersonnel mines, which resulted in thousands of people either dying or being disabled, "often children who were not aware of the danger." In the northern Somali city of Hargeisa, which became the capital of Somaliland, "85 percent of the buildings were destroyed by aerial bombardment and direct artillery shelling by Siad Barre's troops."

Warfare among rival factions within Somalia intensified, and in 1991, Barre was ousted from his power center in the capital by nationalist guerrillas. The uprising was a success, with Barre stepping down from the presidency, and thus his reign of dictatorship was over. On January 26, 1991, he and his son-in-law, General Said Hersi Morgan, fled to the "southwest of the country," before then leaving the country, first heading to Kenya. A couple years later, he died in Nigeria, a discredited and dethroned tyrant.

Soon afterward, an insurgent group in Northern Somalia (the former British Somaliland) that had begun its rebellion in the 1980s announced it had seceded from the country and proclaimed itself the Somaliland Republic. In Mogadishu, Mohammed Ali Mahdi was proclaimed president by one group and Mohammed Farah Aidid by another, as fighting between rival factions continued, civil war, and the worst African drought of the century created a devastating famine in 1992, resulting in a loss of some 220,000 lives.

A UN-orchestrated truce was declared and UN peacekeepers and food supplies arrived, but the truce was observed only sporadically. Late in 1992, troops from the United States and other nations attempted to restore political stability and establish free and open food-aid routes by protecting ports, airports, and roads. However, there was widespread looting of food-distribution sites and hostility toward the relief effort by heavily armed militant factions.

Efforts to re-establish a central government was unsuccessful and international troops became enmeshed in the tribal conflicts that had undone the nation. Failed attempts in 1993 by US forces to capture Aideed, in reaction to an ambush by Somalis in which twenty-three Pakistani peacekeepers were killed, produced further casualties. Clan-based fighting increased in 1994 as the United States and other nations withdrew their forces; the last UN peacekeepers left the following year. Aideed died in 1996 from wounds suffered in battle.

The country was devastated by floods in 1997 and in the late 1990s was still without any organized government. Mogadishu and most of the south were ruled by violence. The independent Somaliland Republic, although not recognized internationally, continued to maintain a relatively stable country, with Mohammed Ibrahim Egal (1993–2002), Dahir Riyale Kahin (2002–10), and Ahmed Mohamud Silanyo (2010—) as presidents; extensions of Riyale's term beginning in 2007 led to confrontations between the government and opposition. Somaliland had a growing economy, and in the late 1990s began receiving aid from the European Union.

The northeast (Puntland) section of the country also stabilized, with local clan leadership providing some basic services and foreign trade being carried on through its port on the Gulf of Aden. Both Puntland and Jubbaland (in Southern Somalia) declared their independence in 1998. Although Jubbaland was subsequently the scene of clan and sectarian fighting and ceased to have a separate existence, Puntland both retained its own government and participated in attempts to establish a Somali federal government.

In 2000, a five-month conference of mainly southern Somalis that had convened in Djibouti under the sponsorship of that nation's president established a national charter (interim constitution) and elected a national assembly and a president, Abdikassim Salad Hassan, who had been an official in Barre's regime. The new president flew to Mogadishu in August of that year. A number of militias refused to recognize the new government, and officials and forces of the government were attacked several times by militia forces, and the government exercised minimal authority in the capital and little influence outside it. The establishment (March 2001) of the Somali Reconciliation and Restoration Council by opposition warlords supported by Ethiopia, an overwhelming vote (June 2001) in the Somaliland region in favor of remaining independent, and a declaration of independence (April 2002) by southwestern Somaliland, the fourth such regional state to be proclaimed, were further obstacles to the new government's acceptance.

In October 2002, a ceasefire accord that also aimed at establishing a federal constitution was signed in Kenya by all the important factions except the Somaliland region. Fighting, however, continued in parts of the country. The sometimes stormy talks that followed the ceasefire were slow to produce concrete results, but a transitional charter was signed in January 2004.

Meanwhile, the mandate of the essentially symbolic interim government expired in August 2003, but the president withdrew from talks, refused to resign, and had the prime minister (who remained involved in the talks) removed from office. In September 2004, after many delays, a 275-member parliament was convened (in Kenya) under the new charter, and a new president, Abdullahi Yusuf Ahmed, a former general who had served as president of Puntland, was elected that October. Somaliland remained a nonparticipant in the transitional government (and held elections for its own parliament later, in October 2005). Coastal areas of Somalia, particularly in Puntland, suffered damage and the loss of several hundred lives as a result of the December 2004 Indian Ocean tsunami.

The new government was slow to move to Somalia, delayed by disputes over who would be in the cabinet, whether nations neighboring Somalia would contribute troops to African Union peacekeeping forces, and whether the government would be initially established in the capital or outside it. The disputes in Kenya boiled over into fighting in Somalia in March and May 2005, whether the forces of two warlords battled for control of Baidoa, one of the proposed temporary capitals. Some government members, allied with the speaker of the parliament, who relocated to Mogadishu.

In June the president returned to his home region of Puntland, and in July he announced plans to move south to Jowhar, the other proposed temporary capital. A coalition of Mogadishu warlords announced that they would attack Jowhar if the president attempted to establish a temporary capital there, but the president nonetheless did so. The year also saw a dramatic increase in piracy and ship hijackings off the Somalia coast, including the hijacking of a UN aid ship and attack on a cruise ship, and in subsequent years pirate attacks for ransom off the coast were a significant problem.

By 2010 Somali pirates were raging across much of the northwestern part of the Indian Ocean. The pirates were mainly based in South Puntland, around the port of Eyl; the government of Puntland was accused of colluding with them. By 2012, however, antipiracy measures in the shipping lanes had led to a large drop in ship seizures.

In January 2006, the disputing Somali factions agreed to convene the parliament at Baidoa. There were outbreaks of fighting in Mogadishu in February and March of 2006, between militia forces aligned with unofficial Islamic courts and militias loyal to several warlords.

In April, Baidoa was officially established as Somalia's temporary capital. Fighting re-erupted in Mogadishu in April, and by July the Islamist militias had won control of Mogadishu and, through alliances, much of South Somalia, except for the Baidoa region. A truce in June between the government and the Islamist was not generally honored. In August 2006, Galmudug was established as an autonomous region just south of Puntland.

The Islamists, who were split between moderates and hardliners, established the Union of Islamic Courts (UIC) and imposed Islamic law on the area under their control. In some areas their rule recalled that of the Taliban in Afghanistan. They were accused of having ties to Al Qaeda, which they denied, but there was apparent evidence of non-Somali fighters in the militia. Sheikh Hassan Dahir Aweys, a hardliner who became leader of the UIC *shura* (council), led an Islamist group ousted from Puntland by President Yusuf, and was regarded as a threat by Ethiopia for having accused that nation of "occupying" the Ogaden.

As the UIC solidified its hold over south Somalia, taking control of the port of Kismayo in September, hundreds of Somalis fled to northeast Kenya. Also in September there was an attempt to assassinate President Yusuf. There were increased tensions between the UIC and Ethiopia over the presence of Ethiopian troops in Somalia in support of the interim government, a situation that Ethiopia denied until October, when it said they were to train government forces. Eritrea was accused of supplying arms to the UIC, raising the specter of a wider war involving Ethiopia and Eritrea.

In October 2006, government and UIC forces clashed several times over Bur Hakaba, a town outside Baidoa on the road to Mogadishu. A number of attempts over the summer to restart talks between the government and the UIC stalled over various issues. The interim government was split between those who favored negotiations with UIC and the prime minister, who strongly objected to any negotiations. In addition, the government objected to the Islamist seizure of additional territory since the June truce and the UIC to the presence of Ethiopian forces in Somalia.

After increasing tension and clashes between the two sides in November, the UIC demanded that Ethiopian troops leave or face attack. Major fighting erupted late in December and Somali government forces supported by Ethiopian forces soon routed the Islamists, who abandoned Mogadishu and then Kismayo, their last stronghold by January 1, 2007.

Fighting continued into early 2007 in extreme South Somalia. The United States launched air strikes (using carrier aircraft offshore) against suspected Al Qaeda allies of the UIC, and US Special Forces also conducted some operations in South Somalia. The government assumed control over the capital, declared a state of emergency, and called for the surrender of private weapons. Several warlords surrendered arms and merged their militias into the army, but concern over the warlords' forces remained.

Ethiopian and government forces soon found themselves fighting militias opposed to disarmament and motivated also by interclan distrust and anti-Ethiopian sentiment and Islamist guerrillas. Fierce battles in March and April in the capital caused hundreds of thousands to flee and hundreds died. The presence of African Union peacekeepers, who began arriving in March and were stationed in Mogadishu, did little initially to alter the situation, but the situation winded down after the government largely established control in late April. Sporadic antigovernment attacks continued, however, occasionally erupting into more intense fighting.

Also in April, some prominent members and former members of the government formed an anti- Ethiopian alliance with members of the UIC; the alliances subsequently included Ethiopian rebel groups as well.

A national reconciliation conference in July and August, 2007, was boycotted by Islamists and some clans. Divisions in the government between the president and Prime Minister Ali Mohamed Gedi over their respective powers led to Gedi's resignation in October. That same month, tension and clashes between Somaliland and Puntland over the disputed border town Los Anod erupted into significant fighting.

In November, Nur Hussein, the head of the Somali Red Crescent, was named prime minister. By the end of 2007, some six hundred thousand had fled the capital due to the fighting there.

In January, 2008, the government officially returned to Mogadishu, but the ability of the Islamists during the year to seize the towns in South and Central Somalia, including the ports of Kismayo in August and Merka (fifty-five miles/ninety kilometers south of Mogadishu) in November, and the continuing fight in the capital belied the government's gesture toward establishing its authority.

A peace agreement was negotiated between the government and more moderate Islamist insurgents in June 2008; in August both sides agreed to a joint police force and a phased Ethiopia pullback, and in November a power-sharing agreement was signed. More militant Islamists, however, rejected the agreements, which did not diminish violence in Somalia. Radical Islamists continued to make gains, and there was fighting between the radicals and more moderate Islamists; government control was restricted mainly to Mogadishu and Baidoa.

President Yusuf attempted to dismiss Prime Minister Nur in December and replace him, but Nur retained the support of the parliament. Yusuf, who was seen by many as an obstacle to the power-sharing agreement with the moderate Islamists, subsequently resigned.

In January 2009, Ethiopian forces withdrew from Somalia, although occasional incursions occurred in subsequent months and years; moderate Islamists joined the government the same month. Sheikh Sharif Sheikh Ahmed, a moderate Islamist, was elected president; Omar Abdirashid Ali Sharmarke, son of the country's second president, became prime minister the following month.

Hardline Islamists continued their attacks, however, capturing Baidoa in January and other towns in the following months, gaining control of most of South and Central Somalia. Fighting also occurred in the Mogadishu, becoming heavy beginning in May when hardliners seized large areas in the capital (though the government, defended primarily by AU peacekeepers, retained control of key buildings and infrastructure); fighting, at times heavy, has continued off and on in Mogadishu since then. In May, 2009, the interim government officially adopted Islamic law.

By July 2009, an estimated 1.2 million Somalis had been displaced within Somalia by the fighting; some three hundred thousand were in border areas in Kenya. Tensions between hardline allies turned violent in September and October of that year, when two groups briefly fought for control of Kismayo, and fighting between some hardline factions has continued sporadically in South Somalia.

Divisions within the hardliners have been outweighed, however, by the weakness and corruption of the interim government, which in 2010 experienced a power struggle between the president and the prime minister. Tensions between the prime minister and parliament led the president to dismiss Sharmarke in May 2010, however, amid worsening power struggles in the government, the prime minister resigned; Mohamed Abdullahi Mohamed, a former diplomat succeeded him in October.

In July 2010, meanwhile, Somali hardline Islamists mounted suicide bomb attacks in Kampala, Uganda, in retaliation for Uganda's participation in the peacekeeping forces in Somalia. A failed militant offensive in August to seize control of Mogadishu and divisions within the dominant militant group, Al Shabaab, led to some territorial gains in the capital by African Union forces that continued into 2011. In December 2010, the two main hardline Islamist groups, Al Shabaab and Hizbul Islam, announced that they had merged.

In February 2011, the transitional parliament voted to extend its term, which was due to expire in August 2011, by three years; in March, the mandate of the government, due to expire at the same time, was extended for a year. In June 2011, however, an agreement negotiated by Uganda between the president and the parliament speaker called for extending presidential and legislative terms until August 2012, when new leaders would be chosen. Additionally, the agreement called for the resignation of the prime minister and the formation of a new government, and in June, Abdiweli Mohamed Ali, a Somali-American economist, became prime minister.

By mid-2011, food shortages due to drought had become a problem in parts of Somalia, which was hit by its worst drought in sixty years. The drought was especially dire in areas controlled by hardline Islamists, who had banned international aid groups in 2010. Some 260,000 people died and 1.5 million people migrated to the capital as a result of the famine, which ended early in 2012.

In August 2011 hardline forces withdrew from most areas of Mogadishu, but their control over much of south and central Somalia was unaffected by the move and fighting recurred in sections of the capital at times. In October, Kenyan forces invaded southern Somalia to attack hardline Islamists, whom Kenya held responsible for a series of attacks in Kenya.

Kenya agreed in December to incorporate its troops into the African Union forces operating in Somalia, and an offensive by government-aligned Somali forces in conjunction with AU, Kenyan, and Ethiopian troops continued into 2012. At the same time, however, the government remained divided and largely ineffective, and outside the capital a number of self-proclaimed autonomous regions and warlords sought to exercise power in areas no longer under hardline Islamist control.

In February 2012, the hardline Islamist al-Shabaab publicly proclaimed that it had joined its movement to Al Qaeda; the group suffered a series of setbacks in the first half of 2012, losing control in Mogadishu and other towns. By July, many of its fighters had retreated north or toward Kismayo in the south; Kismayo was the most important urban area still under al-Shabaab control.

In August, a national constituent assembly approved and adopted a provisional constitution to replace the Transitional Federal Charter and a parliament was chosen by clan elders; the following month, Hassan Sheikh Mohamud, a moderate Islamist and academic, was elected president. In October, Abdi Farrah Shirdon Said, a businessman, was named prime minister.

Also in October, a Somali-Kenyan offensive took control of Kismayo as al-Shabaab withdrew. Al-Shabaab remained in control of many rural areas in southern Somalia, and at times returned to areas from which they had been expelled after government-aligned forces withdrew. In the first half of 2013 several clan militia leaders claimed to head a new government for Jubbaland in south Somalia.

The formation of Jubbaland, seen as a potential buffer region between Central Somalia and Kenya, was supported by Kenyan forces but opposed by the Somali government. Subsequently, control of the region was contested by the rival militias. A leader allied with Kenyan forces but opposed by the Somali government gained power in Kismayo after fighting broke out in mid-2013, and then was recognized as the region's interim leader. In June 2013, there was a split in Al-Shabaab that subsequently led to fighting between hardline Islamists. The president survived an apparent assassination attempt unharmed in September 2013. Disputes between the president and prime minister led to his removal in December by a no-confidence vote; Abdiweli Sheikh Ahmed Mohamed, a development economist, was then appointed prime minister (Prunier, 1995).

In order to modernize Somali society, Siad Barre introduced in 1975 a new family law that, on the whole, was based on *sharia* (Islamic tradition), but with regard to property and inheritance introduced fundamental changes to the benefit of women. The new law provided for equal property rights. Girls inherited an equal share with their brothers, and in case of divorce property had to be shared equally between man and wife.

The divorce procedure itself became somewhat more woman-friendly, with specific cases outlined in the law under which a wife could apply for divorce. In theory the law restricted the practice of polygamy. Marriage to a second wife was only allowed under specific conditions that had to be authorized by a family court. The new family law was also provided for the punishment of men for domestic violence.

In connection with the introduction of the new law, a whole range of social problems with regard to women's rights, which had not been acknowledged or openly discussed before, were brought to the surface, mostly by urban, educated women. However, as all civil rights were increasingly curtailed, women's options for voice remained also very restricted. Progressive opinions were suppressed and conservative critique was brutally silenced.

Ten Islamic sheikhs were sentenced to death for opposing the new laws as non-Islamic and heretical. In practice, the law was not applied in all strata of Somali society, and educated urban women profited more than their sisters in the countryside. The traditional legal system continued to be practiced in most parts of the country and only a few educated urban women succeeded in profiting from the new freedom and equality that was provided by the law. Women in the rural areas were often not even aware of all the aspects of the new family law and even those in urban areas could often be convinced by the male judges to follow the Islamic tradition.

The Somali Women Democratic Organization (SWDO) was founded in 1977 and became the women branch of the one year earlier established Somali Revolutionary Socialist Party. Its mandate was "to propose, promote, and initiate progressive policies and programs for the advancement of the Somali women." In 1985, SWDO numbered sixty thousand members. Emphasizing the productive role of women as well as their reproductive role, the SWDO contributed to the increased participation of the girls and women in education, businesses, and public administration.

The SWDO was an integral part of the socialist one-party system. In all government ministries it had a representative whose responsibility was to safeguard women's rights and see that no discrimination was practiced. SWDO had branches from the national to the local level; weekly meetings were held to build awareness of women's rights.

SWDO representatives were involved as voluntary lawyers or advocates in courts on issues such as domestic violence or divorce. The organization campaigned for an increase of the number of girls in education, pressed for an increase in the number of women judges and high political functionaries, and recommended a change in the land law with regard to women's ownership, arguing for joint titles for husband and wife in order to ensure rural women's effective access to land for cultivation.

Examining the political developments in those regions where political opposition movements grew stronger in the second half of the 1980s from a gender perspective reveals some specific problems that arose for women and that affected their position. In focusing on women, differentiation is of course necessary—their age and clan, their rural or urban background, all defined the ways in which women perceived and suffered from the effects of latent and then open civil war. The impact of political instability on women was mixed, on the one hand making life for women generally more insecure, on the other hand empowering women at the household level.

Through the clan antagonism that spread through Somali polity and society from the mid-1980s, women were torn between their own clan and that of their husband and children. Women living in mixed-clan marriages suffered from suspicion from both sides of the family. Women belonging to the clans that staged antigovernment guerrilla actions were the least protected.

Marriage patterns in the pastoral areas had been dominated by exogamy—marriages across the boundaries of clan families. Linking different clans, subclans, or lineages by marital bonds had been part of the economic and political survival strategy of pastoral people (*hidid*). The more clan antagonism came to determine state policies and, in response, the formation of opposition after the mid-1980s, the more people turned to their closer clan relatives. This was reflected in a change in marriage patterns as endogamy now provided more security than exogamy.

One of the government strategies for discouraging support for the opposition was intimidation, violent attacks on and rape of women. Women in the nomadic areas were used to moving freely in order to collect water and firewood. Rape or other bodily harm had been rare in the past. The government now suspected them of supplying food and acting as informants for the Somali National Movement (SNM), a Somali rebel group fighting for the separation of Somalia, and they were punished accordingly. The policy of punishing the civilian population seriously increased the insecurity of younger women, in particular, and restricted them from exercising their responsibilities within the larger family.

During the time of antigovernment insurgency, women's role within the family became stronger due to the fact that women took over tasks that were previously the domain of men. In rural-urban exchange it had usually been the men who were responsible for trading journeys, the *safars.*

However, this became too dangerous, as men belonging to the Isaaq clan were suspected of being members or sympathizers of the SNM opposition and were detained by state officials. Pastoral women increasingly took over the trading in town. They did this not only because of the aspect of physical safety (women being less likely to be arrested by the police), but also because women were able to secure trade by using both their marital and their maternal family ties, making them more suitable for the task. The position of women in socioeconomic life was strengthened by this experience, giving them more decision-making power and access to environments that had previously been male-dominated.

As militia fighting in southern Somalia stabilized in the mid-1990s, the Bantu who remained in Somalia were once again able to resume farming. Since this time, however, armed dominant-clan bandits have taken control of the valuable agricultural regions of southern Somalia. These bandits extort protection money from the Bantu in return for not harming them or allowing other bandits to harm them.

Today, the Bantu in Somalia again exist in a state someplace between sharecropping and slavery. Here is how the situation is described:

The war is now concentrated in key resource areas of the south, which are largely, although not exclusively, inhabited by minorities. While planting and harvesting have resumed in many districts of the south, the larger economy is one based on extortion of surpluses from the unarmed to the armed. Because no social contract based on clan affiliation exists between the occupying forces and the villagers, there is no assurance that benefits in the form of relief aid will reach the villagers themselves.

The United Nations, in cooperation with the Organization of African Unity (OAU) and other organizations, looked into resolving the conflict. The secretary-general in 1991 dispatched an envoy to which all faction leaders expressed support for a United Nations peace role. The United Nations also became engaged in providing humanitarian aid, in cooperation with relief organizations. The war had resulted in nearly one million refugees and almost five million people threatened by hunger and disease.

The Security Council in January 1992 imposed an arms embargo against Somalia. The secretary-general organized talks between the parties, who agreed on a ceasefire, to be monitored by United Nations observers, and on the protection of humanitarian convoys by United Nations security personnel. In April, the Council established the United Nations Operation in Somalia (UNOSOM I).

The relief effort was impeded by continued fighting and insecurity. The Security Council in August decided to deploy some three thousand additional troops to protect humanitarian aid. But the situation continued to worsen, with aid workers under attack as famine threatened 1.5 million people.

The United States in November 1992 offered to organize and lead an operation to ensure the delivery of humanitarian assistance. The Security Council accepted the offer and authorized the use of "all necessary means" to establish a secure environment for the relief effort. The Unified Task Force (UNITAF), made up of contingents from twenty-four countries led by the United States, quickly secured all major relief centers, and by year's end humanitarian aid was again flowing. UNOSOM remained responsible for protecting the delivery of assistance and for political efforts to end the war.

At a meeting convened by the secretary-general in early 1993, fourteen Somali political movements agreed on a ceasefire and pledged to hand over all weapons to UNITAF and UNOSOM. In March, the United Nations organized an aid conference at which donors pledged over $130 million. At a reconciliation conference organized by the secretary-general and his special representative for Somalia, the leaders of fifteen political movements endorsed an accord on disarmament, reconstruction, and the formation of a transitional government.

The security council in March decided on a transition from UNITAF to a new United Nations peacekeeping operation—*UNOSOM II*, authorizing it to use force if necessary to ensure its mandate—securing a stable environment for the delivery of humanitarian assistance. UNOSOM was also mandated to assist in the reconstruction of economic, social, and political life. But while UNITAF had patrolled less than half of the country with 37,000 well-equipped troops, the 22,000 United Nations peacekeepers were given the mandate to cover all of Somalia.

The factions, however, did not observe the ceasefires. In June 1993, twenty-four UNOSOM II soldiers from Pakistan were killed in an attack in Mogadishu. Subsequently, clashes between UNOSOM and Somali militiamen in Mogadishu resulted in casualties among civilians and UNOSOM.

In October, eighteen United States soldiers of the Quick Reaction Force—deployed in support but not part of UNOSOM—lost their lives in an operation in Mogadishu. The United States immediately reinforced its military presence, but later announced that it would withdraw by early 1994. Belgium, France, and Sweden also decided to withdraw.

The secretary-general in October held talks in Somalia, while UNOSOM and United Nations agencies continued their reconciliation and relief efforts. Somali elders held reconciliation meetings in various parts of the country, while over one hundred thousand refugees returned to relatively peaceful parts of Somalia.

The Security Council in early 1994 revised UNOSOM II's mandate, stressing assistance for reconciliation and reconstruction, and setting a March 1995 deadline for the mission.

At talks brokered by a secretary-general's envoy, the fifteen major political movements in March 1994 signed a declaration on reconciliation—it provided for a ceasefire, the disarmament of militias, and a conference to appoint a new government. But preparations for the conference were repeatedly postponed.

The secretary-general told the Security Council in September that UNOSOM II's ability to provide security had been reduced by troop withdrawals, budget restrictions, and military actions by the Somali factions. Wider problems included the lack of commitment to peace by the factions and insufficient political will by member states. The council approved reductions in the force.

With faction leaders still not complying with the 1993 and 1994 agreements, the Security Council extended UNOSOM for a final period. It urged factions to enact a ceasefire and form a government of national unity. As no further progress was made, UNOSOM withdrew in March 1995.

During the three-year effort (UNOSOM I and UNOSOM II), 157 United Nations peacekeeping personnel had died. But the United Nations had brought relief to millions facing starvation, helped to stop the large-scale killings, assisted in the return of refugees and provided massive humanitarian aid. Under difficult conditions, United Nations agencies have continued their humanitarian work (United Nations, 2004).

Refugee Crisis

Due to the desperate humanitarian situation, two strategies were created. First, the urban population turned to their rural relatives, to whom they fled. Clan and family networks were the most urgent source of security. During the years of oppression by the Mogadishu government, clan affiliation had become increasingly crucial, as there seemed to be nobody else to trust. The SNM guerilla units were also structured according to Isaaq subclan affiliation, and the SNM relied on civilian clan-networks for material support, safety, and logistics, especially after 1988.

Faced with increasing food insecurity and continuous fighting in all northern areas, during 1989–90 the second strategy was to seek refuge in neighboring Ethiopia. The total number of UNHCR-registered Somali refugees toward the end of 1990 was 381,369. Figures for 1991 put the number of Somali refugees at about 473,170.

As people fled to their respective clan areas across the border, the UNHCR refugee camps reflected specific clan affiliations. This proved an effective way of ensuring the safety of all involved parties—the refugees, the people of the receiving areas, and the aid workers. The vast majority of refugees were Isaaq (367,300) mainly from urban areas. They were located at the Harshin and Hartisheik refugee camps, about seventy-five kilometers southeast of Jijiga. Refugees of other clan origin were mainly Gadabuursi (105, 170) who were settled in the refugee camps Arabi, Darwonaji, and Taferi Ber about fifty kilometers east of Jijiga.

Physical, legal, food, and health security was delivered by international agencies. The status of refugee gave legal security and defined the rights of the camp inhabitants during their stay in Ethiopia. Physical security was provided by the camp administration, policing the area at night and preventing attacks on the refugees from Somali government units from across the border. Basic food and health facilities ensured the survival of the refugees.

The distribution of food and water were a great challenge to the Ethiopian Administration of Refugee / Returnee Affairs (ARRA) and the UNHCR and meant a heavy burden on the receiving areas, especially in Jijiga town. To give an impression of the quantities involved, eight hundred thousand liters of water per day were needed for Hartisheik refugee camp alone. Although logistic problems occurred in the process, the Northern Somali refugees nevertheless found a safe haven in Ethiopia, a meager but steady food and water supply and basic medical care. Social security in the sense of supporting each other with the management of rations and assisting female-headed households of widows or wives of fighters and old people with the problems caused by camp life derived mainly from existing family and/or clan relations. In the camps, women were relatively safe from rape and other forms of violence.

A survey of Hartisheik refugee camp in 1991 revealed that most of the refugees (92.9 percent of questioned refugees) came from Hargeisa, the regional capital of Northern Somalia. The background of the refugees was therefore urban, many of them having been traders, employees in transport, or teachers. In Hartisheik they soon took initiatives to improve on their plight. Teachers among the refugees organized primary schooling for refugee children; some 12,000 pupils were involved, representing about 22.5 percent of the school-age children in the camp. Economic security, basically provided by UNHCR, was complemented by self-help activities to the extent that between 15 percent and 25 percent of the refugee population was, at the time of the survey, involved in some sort of income-generating activities. These were not initiated by aid agencies but by the people themselves.

Refugees were highly differentiated; some managed to salvage their property, cash, and a few belongings, while others have lost everything. Therefore, it was natural that some form of division of labor developed and after about four years of relatively stable settlement, some refugees became petty traders and vendors of food, beverages, firewood, and charcoal. There are also shoemakers, tailors, shops, and small drugstore keepers and mechanics. Others are porters, man- and animal-powered cart owners, or sell their labor to those who are more fortunate.

A vast marketplace developed in Hartisheik where goods and fresh produce, including vegetables of Ethiopian and Somali origin, were traded. By mid-1991, economic security was coming from both substate and trans-state networks. The private banking sector thrived in Hartisheik. One could buy and sell not only by Somali shilling and Ethiopian birr, but also American dollars, Saudi dinars, and other currencies.

Transactions were conducted within the camp, but also via family networks with relatives located in Addis Ababa and, after the first wave of temporary returnees to Hargeisa in the summer of 1991, with relatives who had begun reconstruction at home. Through relatives in the Ethiopian capital, connections for remittances were also established to Somali family members who, as refugees, were spread all over the world. There were regular connections to Jijiga, the town closest to the camp and the location of the aid agency's offices, shops, and markets, among them the daily *qaat* market.

After the overthrow of the Mogadishu government and the end of the fighting, refugees began to return to their home areas, in the case of Hartisheik to Hargeisa. Often, the women and children stayed behind in the camps, while the men determined the security situation at home and began with reconstruction. Regular bus connections existed from Hartisheik refugee camp to Hargeisa city. For a long time, this was the only functioning transport link to the Northern Somali region, after the collapse of Somali airlines and the destruction of the airports. The strong linkages, contact, and exchange with the home area, strengthened through trade and transport, compensated for the fact of living in a refugee camp, of residing temporarily in a foreign country.

With regard to political stability, the Somali refugees in Hartisheik were active and innovative. A basic administrative structure was created which allowed the representatives of the refugees say in matters of camp policy. Refugee committees were formed at meetings held by elders, religious leaders and clan and subclan heads in the presence of local government officials, ARRA, UNHCR, and NGO (Nongovernmental Organization) representatives.

Refugees from Somalia, especially those who originated from west of the Indian Ocean coastal cities, sought refuge by crossing into Kenya at the border town of Liboi (roughly located on the equator ten miles west of the Kenya-Somalia frontier). The Somali Bantus did not have allegiances with other Somali clans and thus did not have any means of protection. Warring factions, looted farms, and rape killed many Somali Bantus, especially those in the lower and middle Jubba regions. They recount these atrocities and explain how they fled on foot, often for five to fifteen days, across Kenya's bandit-ridden northeastern provinces to the sprawling Kakuma refugee camp close to Kenya's far northern border with Sudan, where there are few other rival Somali groups. Overall, the 1,500-kilometer trip takes about thirty hours. It is a huge logistical exercise costing somewhere between $500,000 and $800,000.

Each convoy carries between 250 and 300 passengers. The International Organization for Migration (IOM) has provided nurses, wayside watering points and places for overnight stays and—in collaboration with the Kenyan authorities—taken a number of security precautions. About thirty police in their own vehicles travel with the convoy as it moves through some of the most dangerous zones.

The Somali Bantus' presence in Somalia, where they have always been treated as second-class citizens and deprived of basic rights, can be traced back to the slave trade of Zanzibar's Arab Sultans during the eighteenth and nineteenth centuries. Because of their roots, UNHCR initially approached Mozambique and Tanzania, but both countries lacked the means to take them and eventually the United States said it would accept them.

As a group, they have no desire to return to Somalia and they would be persecuted—if not killed—if they did so. Their homes were long ago seized by Somali clans. The system of discrimination was even perpetrated in Dadaab refugee camp, a settlement of some 120,000 mainly Somali refugees, further emphasizing their special status for Washington.

Highlighting the sensitivity of the issue, the reception and interview center is ringed by barbed wire. Immigration officials feared non-Bantu Somalis would pose as Bantus, and even threaten some Bantu families to say they were fellow members.

The Bantus are also given a two-week crash course in cultural orientation and basic survival skills on how to manage in the West. As Mohammed Abdikadir, IOM operations manager in Kakuma noted, "There are people who have never seen an airplane, so everything needs to be explained, from a boarding procedure to how the social security system works over there."

Acts of genocide were normally committed by state agents, for example by soldiers in the employ of the national military or by militias who have the support of those who hold state power. Somalia is a rare case in which genocidal acts were carried out by militias in the utter absence of a governing state structure. While Somalia's dictator, Siad Barre, orchestrated massacres of his political opponents during his final years in power, local "warlords" in charge of private militias continued the strategy following Barre's fall from power and the collapse of a governing structure.

Somalia's collapse was defined by clan-aligned militias battling each other for power in local and regional arenas, with the unarmed population of the Jubba Valley becoming a particular target of violence and abuse by opposed militias. During the peak of the violence, an Oxfam official called the valley "one big graveyard." While Somalis throughout the country suffered grievously during the peak years of civil war, residents in the Jubba Valley received particularly harsh treatment by militias because of several factors: (1) in the early years of the war, militias of competing warlords battled back and forth across the valley for territorial control. Each year of the war, militias of competing warlords battled back and forth across the valley for territorial control, each side attacking civilians; (2) identified as racial minorities of slave ancestry within Somalia, most Jubba Valley residents held weak ties to Somali clans that were easily broken in the midst of war, which meant that armed clans did not come to their defense; (3) as sedentary peasant farmers tied to the land for their subsistence, valley residents were easily targeted by mobile militias; (4) as an unarmed population, valley residents were defenseless.

Genocidal acts in the valley took the form of mass killings, abduction, and involuntary marriage of local women by militia members, and the deliberate starvation of entire communities by the seizure of food supplies.

Most refugees in Dadaab (located another thirty miles west of Liboi) today settled at Liboi, which also served as the original United Nations High Commission for Refugees(UNHCR) camp in the area. As Liboi grew to over forty thousand refugees, the UNHCR established additional camps: Ifo, Dagahaley, and lastly, Hagadera. Gunfire and banditry in Dadaab force aid workers to live in secure compounds located in the Dadaab Division of Garissa District in Northeastern Province.

The three camps are situated within ten miles of the Dadaab Division town center. At their height, the four refugee camps in Kenya held over 160,000 refugees. With the closing of Liboi, the UNHCR estimated in 2002 that approximately 135,000 refugees remain in the three Dadaab camps.

The Dadaab camps are administered by the UNHCR with the main implementing partners, CARE International and Doctors Without Borders, providing general camp support and medical care respectively. A number of other nongovernmental agencies such as Caritas, UNICEF, and local Kenyan groups have also provided support. The Government of Kenya (GOK) established police posts in each camp and occasionally provides security backup through the Kenyan Army.

Since Dadaab is located in Kenya's inhospitable north, the area's flat, semi-arid and sandy terrain supports mostly scrub brush and is home to an array of wildlife including giraffe, small antelope known as dik, various cats such as the East African Serval and hyenas, which are often seen walking through town at night. Caution must be used while walking out at night. The Somali wild donkey is also prevalent in and around the refugee camps. Both flora and fauna in the Dadaab refugee area have suffered due to habitat destruction, mainly from the cutting and collection of firewood.

Dadaab is a small frontier town with sandy streets, some concrete buildings, and erratic water and electrical service. Along with refugees and the local Kenyan Somali inhabitants, nomads and bandits use Dadaab as a rest and resupply destination.

In the refugee camps, the Bantu settled in the most distant locations (blocks or sections housing approximately six hundred people each) where they, along with other refugees on the periphery of the camp, are more vulnerable to bandit attacks than refugees living near the center of the camps. Settlement of the Bantu in these camp locations was partly a result of their date of arrival in the camps.

Each refugee family in the Dadaab camps is issued a large canvas tent, basic cooking utensils, and a jerry can for collecting potable water from spigots located throughout the camps. Cooking of UNHCR-supplied wheat, beans, salt, sugar, and oil (which are distributed once every two weeks), along with various produce and canned food available in the refugee camp markets, is usually done over an open fire. Refugees dig their own latrines with UNHCR-supplied building materials and supervision. Doctors Without Borders established the hospitals and many health posts that are located in each refugee camp. They, along with CARE International social workers, provide various forms of outreach to the refugees.

In order to protect themselves against nighttime bandit attacks, the Bantu have constructed fortified compounds guarded by armed sentries. Since security for all people living in the refugee camps is inadequate, other refugees have also built protective fencing around their sections. In the first years of the camp, the Bantu suffered violent attacks at a rate that was disproportionate to their population in the wider refugee camp community.

Before a US sponsored firewood collection program was established, refugee women were particularly vulnerable to rape while collecting firewoods in the surrounding bush. Rape was often committed by men from one clan against women from a different clan. In some cases, refugees who were raped claimed that their attackers first asked them what clan they belonged to. Bantu women were especially vulnerable. Rapists could be virtually assured that they were not attacking a fellow clan member or even someone who belonged to a clan that had a security agreement with their clan.

In the ensuing anger and confusion of these rapes, the Bantu accused the dominant clans of this crime. When women from the dominant clans were raped, they sometimes accused Bantu men as the attackers. With accusations being hurled against each community, hostilities occasionally broke out.

Despite this difficult environment, the Bantu have managed to carve out a niche for themselves in small-scale agriculture, operating a tree nursery at one camp and growing produce for local markets in and outside of the refugee camps. The Bantu have also been employed by nongovernmental organizations in the building trades and as laborers (Lehman and Eno, 2003).

In 2002, over 12,000 Somali Bantu were moved to the Kakuma refugee camp in northwest Kenya to be interviewed by the US Immigration and Naturalization Service.

There were originally three refugee camps established in the wake of the Somali civil war, which were originally occupied only by Somalis and Somali Bantus who fled Somalia. They are Ifo, Dagahaley, and Hagadera. These camps were located in Dadaab, Kenya. The town had six refugee camps. As of October 2015, there are only five refugee camps. These include Ifo, Dagahaley, and Hagadera which are the oldest and largest of the camps.

Dadaab is approximately over fifty square kilometers. The three camps are within a radius of eight kilometers. Dadaab camp was originally established in 1991, in response to the influx of Somalis fleeing their country due to the civil war. It was primarily designed to host ninety thousand people. Currently, it holds about half a million refugees according to the UNHCR.

Dadaab is located about one hundred kilometers to the northeast of the town of Garissa and seventy kilometers from the Somali border, five hundred kilometers from Kenya's capital city, Nairobi, six hundred kilometers from the port of Mombasa. Dadaab Camps are home to many people and communities who fled their home countries seeking mainly security and basic necessities such as food and shelter. The camps is occupied by people from Somalia, Ethiopia, Rwanda, Sudan, Eritrea, and Uganda, however, most people in the camp are Somalis. Each camp is divided into sections that are further divided into blocks. A section has a minimum of a block to a maximum of about thirty blocks. Each block is headed by a male and a female block leader. The male and female block leaders elect a male and a female section leader who will be in charge of the section.

All the section leaders will in return elect the overall chairman and the chairlady of the camp. These leaders are very important in the refugee leadership structure since they connect the refugee community with the United Nations High Commissioner for Refugees (UNHCR) agencies. They are also involved in the conflict resolution and management at block level. They closely work with UNHCR in ensuring that refugee concerns are addressed.

Ifo 1 and 2

Ifo Camp was established in 1991. It is the oldest of all the three camps in Dadaab. Currently, refugees from various East African countries are settled in the camp. The camp has a total population of roughly about 84,181 people. Because of the overwhelming abundance of people and arrivals of refugees coming in, Ifo 2 camp was founded in July 2011 to decrease the population increase in Ifo. Ifo 2 is divided into two subcamps, Ifo 2 East and Ifo 2 West, and separated into eighteen sections consisting of four to nine blocks each. In Ifo, vulnerable refugee children are sheltered with other families through a foster home program in the refugee community.

Children are able to play in two children-friendly spaces without fear of being harmed. A safe haven provides a safe environment for women and children facing life-threatening circumstances. These families stay at Safe Haven until they are identified. Obtaining education in the safe haven is difficult. A protection area provides short-term shelter for families experiencing imminent threats. Many security incidents were recorded in Ifo, some were politically motivated. These attacks include the use of improvised explosive devices (IEDs), grenade attacks and assassinations as well as banditry and robbery.

Meanwhile, Ifo 2 has three Children Education and Welfare Centers (CEWC) which provides early learning for children and various foster homes. In order to increase security, the UNHCR increased the presence of police through Peace Winds Japan. Thirteen administration police officers are currently stationed and based at the new patrol base in Ifo 2 West and twenty Kenyan police officers in Ifo 2 East.

Several security incidents have occurred in Ifo 2. In October 2011, two Medecins Sans Frontieres (MSF) staff members were kidnapped and released in 2013. In June 2012, an NPR staff member was killed and two others were injured in a shooting. They were rescued by the authorities three days later in Somalia.

With the Tripartite Agreement between the UNHCR, the Government of Kenya and the Government of Somalia, some refugees in Ifo 2 have expressed their willingness to return to their country of origin and have participated in the voluntary return program which started on December 8, 2014.

In terms of education, Ifo has eight primary schools and two secondary schools including an adult literacy center. The biggest challenge in the camp is the high dropout rates due to a shortage of teaching and learning materials, school uniforms, and stationery as well as the lack of qualified teachers. There's limited services for children with specific needs.

Ifo 2 has ten primary schools (three in Ifo 2 East and seven in Ifo 2 West), and one secondary school. A total of 28,410 children are enrolled in early child development education and primary schools (60 percent boys and 40 percent girls). Mwangaza Primary School and Nasib Secondary School are Instant Network Schools (INS). The secondary school enrollment stands at 3 percent (81 percent boys and 19 percent girls). In order to improve school attendance of children enrolled, the World Food Programme (WFP) is providing food in all ten primary schools. A typical primary education is also linked to Duksis (Qur'an/Islamic classes).

Ifo has six health posts. One of them is a level four hospital called Islamic Relief, which provides surgical needs. Typically, health clinics are overcrowded which results to shortage of time for each patient. One hundred percent of pregnant women receiving prenatal care services are voluntarily tested for HIV. Only a small amount of individuals HIV positive receive care treatment and support services.

Ifo 2 has one level five hospital, which was first opened in June 2013, a maternal hospital and three health posts that are providing medical services to the refugees and members of the host communities. Kenya Red Cross Society (KRCS) has seventy-three qualified national staff that provide health in the facilities. Currently, 86 percent of all deliveries in the camp are done in the hospital, while the remaining 14 percent are home deliveries.

Ifo has seven running boreholes. The average water coverage is about 22.0 liters per person per day. There are about 12,930 latrines, resulting in an average of seven persons per latrine (the global standard is a maximum of twenty).

Ifo is divided into nine sections, which are overcrowded. Half of the camp is considered a flood-prone area. In 2012, canalization was done to drain floodwater away. The shelters in this part of the camp are very poor and some haven't been replaced since the establishment of the camp in 1991. Temporary shelters are constantly being constructed to resolve the problem. Temporary shelters have a timber structure covered by canvas. The Kenyan government does not allow agencies to construct more permanent shelters.

Ifo is supervised by elected male and female chairpersons at the camp section and block level. In total, there are two camp chairpersons, eighteen section leaders, and 212 block leaders. Approximately twenty-seven registered youth groups are currently active in the camp. Their activities include promoting human rights, girl's and women's empowerment, prevention of Sexual and Gender Based Violence (SGBV), counseling and conflict resolution, leadership and social justice, fighting illiteracy, news circulation, multimedia training, promoting sports, and assisting vulnerable groups (UNHCR, 2015).

Dagahaley

Dagahaley Camp was first established in March 1992. For fourteen years, the camp had a population of about thirty thousand. Between 2006 and 2011 new arrivals settled in the outskirts of the camp. In 2011, most of the population in the Dagahaley outskirts moved to the new Ifo 2 Camp. Dagahaley has a transit center for protection cases which is also used when refugees are transferred to other locations.

Dagahaley has seven primary schools, two secondary schools, and one adult literacy center. The primary school enrollment is 33.9 percent. For primary education, the teacher-pupil ratio is 1:53. Of the students in secondary school, 79 percent are boys and 21 percent are girls. The Government of Kenya's ministry of education has installed solar power in five of Dagahaley's primary schools as part of a broad program to ensure power is available to all primary schools in Kenya.

MSF provides health services in Dagahaley Camp using its own funds. Two of MSF's four health posts in Dagahaley Camp were closed. Prenatal care in the MSF hospital has been suspended. UNHCR is working with MSF to assess and cover those gaps.

Supplementary and therapeutic feeding programs are implemented for children. Those with severe malnutrition are admitted to the stabilization center in the camp hospital.

There are seven boreholes in Dagahaley and two outside the camp serving the community. However, the borehole equipment is aging, with low yields from old boreholes. Six elevated steel tanks are connected to 7.63 km of pipes.

Dagahaley is made up of ten sections with an average of ten blocks per section. Lack of land is a challenge. The crowding leads to boundary conflicts and encroachment into public areas—often roads—making traffic access more difficult.

A tree nursery is producing seedlings for both the host and refugee communities. New arrivals have been cutting down trees in the settlements in the outskirts of the camp, leading to conflicts with the host community. Devalued areas around the camp have been fenced into green belts to allow regeneration of vegetation cover. Energy-saving stoves are being distributed.

Community-based leadership structures manage the camp in terms of decision making and sharing information. They are comprised of the overall chair persons, section leaders, and block leaders. Some parts of the committees are engaged in the coordination of daily activities within the camp and closely work with the agencies. The camp management agency is in control of the coordination and management of the leadership structure.

Dagahaley is home to ninety-six youth groups. Their activities also include promotion of sports, female empowerment, Sexual and Gender Based Violence (SGBV) prevention, conflict resolution, assisting vulnerable groups and information sharing.

Hagadera

Hagadera was established in 1992 and is the largest and third oldest camp in Dadaab. The population of Hagadera has decreased by over 45,000 in the last verification period. However, the camp remains highly crowded. Most refugees and asylum seekers who arrived to Hagadera in the last few years are staying with relatives but some twenty thousand have settled outside the designated camp area in the Hagadera outskirts. In order to decrease the large amount of people Hagadera, relocation exercises in 2011, 2012 and 2014 have moved around two thousand families of about ten thousand individuals to Kambioos Camp. Furthermore refugees will soon be relocated to Kambioos Camp.

Protection work in Hagadera include: registration, child protection, physical security, individual case management and SGBV intervention. The Department of Refugee Affairs (DRA) is responsible for registering new arrivals and opens doors for registration. Regular registration of births and deaths continue to take place throughout the year. Quarterly, the civil registrar from Garissa visits the camp to issue birth certificate to refugee children who were born in Kenya.

The camp's security situation has become increasingly calm in recent months but remains uncertain. Insecurity first started in Hagadera in September 2011 with the kidnapping of humanitarian workers and with IEDs installed underground killing and injuring police officers and badly damaging their vehicles that were escorting UN agencies and nongovernmental organizations. In April 2014 it was reported that a UN vehicle was attacked in which the suspects attempted to kidnap a UNHCR staff member. Crimes including banditry have increased in and around the camp. Hagadera Camp has three police posts with a total of seventy-five police officers who are responsible for the camp security.

Hagadera has seven primary schools and two secondary schools and one adult literacy center. Each classroom in Hagadera holds one hundred to 120 students, while the standard is forty students in a classroom. The primary school enrollment rate is 37 percent, while the secondary schools enrollment rate is 14.8 percent.

Four clinics and one hospital are serving an average of 454 patients per day. The hospital has recently begun to provide specialized eye care services.

A huge number of women give birth at home in Hagadera, which leads to health complications. There has been several death reported arising from home deliveries complications and efforts are undertaken to improve the problem. Currently, life birth expectancy is at 88 percent.

The World Food Programme through World Vision distributes food twice a month. At the food distribution stand, refugees obtain food and other resources. The Norwegian Refugee Council (NRC) is the agency for the distribution of nonfood items. These foods consist of 2,100 kilocalories per person per day, which is the global standard.

Hagadera Camp has seven working boreholes. The water supply is twenty-three liters per person per day, which is also above the global standard of twenty liters. There are 201 water taps in the camp and 807 taps, which means that an average of 132 individuals share one tap. The accepted standard is eighty persons to share one tap.

Approximately, 363 temporary shelters will be constructed in Hagadera by the end of 2015. Severe environmental degradation is caused by the overpopulation of the camp. Most of the green belts in Hagadera are currently ruined. There has been numerous fire outbreaks in the camp since 2010. Precautions have been taken to prevent such incidents.

The camp is also divided into sections and blocks with two elected leaders (male and female) representing each block and each section. There are twenty-eight section leaders and 260 block leaders. The last refugee leaders' election was done in August 2013.

A New Era and the Rise of Terror

In September 2012, from the Transitional Federal Government of Sheikh Sharif Sheikh Ahmed to the Somali Federal Government (SFG) led by Hassan Sheikh Mohamud was recognized as the end of Somalia's horrible past.

On January 17, 2013, after diplomatic talks with President Mohamud, US Secretary of State Hillary Clinton announced that Somalia now had "a representative government with a new president, a new parliament, a new prime minister, and a new constitution," and uttered that, for the first time in decades, the United States would recognize the Somali government. Meanwhile, several weeks later, President Mohamud and EU High Representative for Foreign Affairs and Security Policy Catherine Ashton declared, "Somalia is no longer a failed state." Since then, many foreign governments and international organizations have restored diplomatic relations and opened embassies in Mogadishu.

The establishment of a new government has given Somalia hope in changing its past and rebuilding a better future for the inhabitants of the country.

The new government focused on policy positions, including the Six Pillar strategy, a manifesto that outlines the country's top priority issues to palliate suffering from citizens. The newly constituted parliament also represents a step forward.

Within days of his inauguration, the new Somali president articulated a strategy for his government, the Six Pillars, which was perhaps best articulated in an address to the governing Council of the International Organization on Migration:

My administration's goal over the next four years is to put in place the necessary mechanisms to: 1) create stability in the country; 2) speed up economic recovery; 3) build peace and remove the main drivers of conflicts; 4) vastly improve the Government's capacity to respond to the needs of its people by improving service delivery; 5) increase our international partnerships and create closer ties with our neighbors and friends of Somalia; 6) last but not least, Mr. Chairman, I believe that unity at home is what will propel Somalia forward.

Meanwhile, security development is difficult in modern Somalia, and many previous efforts to build police and military forces have contributed to chaos and violence. This occurred because the central challenges of stabilization in Somalia are political rather than militarily.

Past efforts to rebuild Somalia's security forces have been disappointing and unsuccessful. Between 1993 and 1995, the United Nations Mission in Somalia undertook a massive effort to rebuild the Somali police force and judicial system. In addition to training and salaries, the United Nations provided thousands of weapons and hundreds of pickup trucks and high-frequency radios. But when the mission was withdrawn in 1995, the entire establishment collapsed, with most of the equipment ending up in the hands of local militias.

The next serious effort to rebuild Somali security forces followed the establishment of the TFG in 2004. Once again the United Nations took the lead in reviving the Somali police force, but the program was soon mired in controversy as police units trained and paid by the United Nations obtained a paramilitary character, engaging in counterinsurgency operations and—like the armed forces—perpetrating abuses against civilians. The situation was further complicated by the fact that most uniformed forces, whether police or military, were simply clan militias, loyal to individual commanders, only nominally under government control and in many cases hostile to one another. They engaged in shootouts with one another over the revenue from checkpoints, killing civilians, and committing acts of sexual violence.

Ethiopia, the TFG's closest ally, quietly took the lead in trying to train and integrate the TFG's army. But with the government unable to pay soldiers' salaries—chiefly because of rampant and pervasive corruption in the TFG ranks—such efforts was going to fail. Between 2004 and 2008, more than 14,000 soldiers trained by Ethiopia reportedly defected or deserted with their weapons and uniforms.

Following Ethiopia's withdrawal from Somalia in 2009, the job of organizing and training the TFG forces fell to AMISOM. Recognizing the absence of any meaningful chain of command, AMISOM took action to directly enlist the support of various militias to assist in securing Mogadishu. For these fighters, access to AMISOM's supply chain, especially ammunition was often a higher priority than defeating al Shabaab. Staged battles, in which streets and city blocks changed hands by mutual agreement and minimum loss of life, were a common occurrence, planned via mobile phone by clan relatives across the front lines.

A 2011 United Nations report found that most of the ammunition available in Mogadishu markets or recovered from al-Shabaab fighters was from AMISOM stocks. Such revelations did nothing to diminish the TFG's high demands for more military assistance and the lifting of the UN arms embargo on Somalia.

The arms embargo on Somalia was first imposed by United Nations Security Council in 1992 at the height of the civil war in the south. In subsequent years the embargo was broadened into a complex sanctions regime, prohibiting a broad range of threats to peace and security, financing of armed groups, piracy, and obstruction of humanitarian assistance, and violations of international humanitarian law.

The SFG has argued that the arms embargo has prevented it from arming and equipping its armed forces in order to defeat al-Shabaab. But this argument is based on a misinterpretation of the sanctions regime: in 2007, the embargo was modified to permit foreign governments to provide arms, ammunition, military equipment, training, and financing for Somali security forces.

Moreover, immediately after its formation in late 2012, the SFG renewed efforts to have the arms embargo lifted, and when the matter was brought in to the UN Security Council in March 2013, it received a compassionate hearing. The United States was particularly eager for the SFG to be accepted as a sovereign government. But not all council members were convinced that the authority in Mogadishu could be entrusted with unrestricted access to arms, fearing that weapons would continue to end up in the hands of al-Shabaab. Somali government officials tried to address such concerns, unsuccessfully.

A compromise eventually emerged in the form of Security Council resolution 2093, which eased the embargo for a period of one year. But heavy weapons and certain types of sophisticated equipment (e.g., wire-guided anti-tank missiles, night-vision devices) remain prohibited, and the council has imposed new and diligent reporting requirements—the Committee must be notified in advance of all deliveries of weapons and military equipment, and the SFG must report every six months on the structure of the security forces, as well as the measures in place to ensure the safe storage, registration, maintenance, and distribution of military equipment. The council has also mandated its own monitoring team to provide independent reports on these same issues.

Just a week after the Security Council's decision, Somali media reported stocks of arms and ammunition were being periodically stolen from inside the presidential compound, Villa Somalia. And in mid-2013, SFG-affiliated leaders in Lower Jubba and Bakool regions had announced alliances with al-Shabaab, raising the possibility that the jihadists would receive indirect military support from the federal government.

By April 2013, Djibouti, Turkey, and Egypt had pledged military support to the SFG, and the US government had also paved the way for the future military assistance. Not surprisingly, sources close to the Somaliland and Puntland administrations revealed that they were both actively seeking to obtain arms and ammunition to counter the threat from Mogadishu.

Ethiopia's withdrawal in 2009 subdued al-Shabaab's appeal to Somali nationalists and foreign jihadists, but it left the movement in control of the southern Somali economy. Between 2009 and 2012, al-Shabaab raised hundreds of millions of dollars in revenues at ports, airports, markets, and checkpoints.

With the new TFG headed by Sheikh Sharif, communities across southern Somalia had little choice but to accept al-Shabaab's standard of jihad.

Since 2012, the combined efforts of AMISOM, Ethiopian, and Kenyan forces, together with their Somali allies, have changed the map of southern Somalia dramatically. Al-Shabaab has been pushed out of all major towns, and the loss of Kismayo in September 2012 deprived the jihadists of their single most important source of income, ensuring that the movement never regains its former strength. But al-Shabaab continues to control significant parts across south central Somalia, especially in rural areas, targeting people, IED attacks, and even other operations.

On October 29, 2014, UN Secretary-General Ban Ki-moon visited Mogadishu, along with World Bank President Dr. Jim Kim and senior representatives of the African Development, AU, EU, and Islamic Development Bank. The delegation met with President Hassan Sheikh Mohamud, Prime Minister Abdiweli Sheikh Ahmed, and Parliament Speaker Mohamed Osman Jawari. In his public speech, Ban emphasized links between security and development, particularly the importance of public service delivery and strengthening government institutions.

The security situation continues to be unstable in Somalia and in adjoining border regions of Kenya as al-Shabaab carries out further terrorist attacks. On November 22, 2014, al-Shabaab killed twenty-eight non-Muslims (nineteen men and nine women) in an attack on a bus in north eastern Kenya. On December 2, the group killed thirty-six workers at a quarry in the same border region. Al-Shabaab claimed the attacks were in retaliation for raids on mosques by Kenyan authorities. The Kenyan military has responded with airstrikes on the group in Somalia.

On December 3, al-Shabaab attacked a UN convoy in Mogadishu, which resulted in several deaths among people nearby. On December 5, more than fifteen civilians were killed in another attack by the group in Baidoa. The council issued press statements strongly condemning the terrorist attacks in Kenya on November 22 and in Mogadishu on December 3.

There were signs of state building progress in Somalia on November 17, 2014 when Hassan Sheikh Adan was elected as the president of the newly formed Interim South West Administration (ISWA) comprising Bay, Bakol, and Lower Shabelle regions. The formation of the ISWA was welcomed in a joint statement on November 20 by the UN, the Intergovernmental Authority on Development, the EU, and the AU Mission in Somalia (AMISOM). On December 17, the president of an overlapping, rival six-region state, Madobe Nunow Mohamed, reportedly reached a power sharing agreement with the ISWA.

The humanitarian situation has continued to deteriorate in Somalia, risking another famine. After drought conditions earlier in the year, southern Somalia has had severe floods, further exacerbating food insecurity. More than one million people are in urgent need of humanitarian assistance, which represents a 20 percent increase within the last six months, and another two million people face threats to their food security.

According to the Office for the Coordination of Humanitarian Affairs (OCHA), Somalia currently has the largest humanitarian funding gap (measured in terms of contributions as a percentage of the consolidated appeal) within the last six years. As of November 21, contributions were 39 percent ($365 million out of $933 million) of the request for 2014.

The warring parties in Somalia's long-running armed conflict continue to displace, kill, and wound civilians. Restrictions on humanitarian access exacerbate the human rights and humanitarian crises.

Al-Shabaab abandoned several towns after a joint military offensive by the AMISOM and the Somali National Armed Forces in 2014. However, Al-Shabaab maintains control of large areas of south-central Somalia, where it administers public executions and beatings and restricts basic rights. Al-Shabaab carried out deadly attacks in government-controlled areas such as Mogadishu, targeting civilians, including lawmakers and other officials.

Somali government security forces, African Union (AU) troops, and allied militias were responsible for indiscriminate attacks, sexual violence, and arbitrary arrests and detention.

The Somali government largely failed to provide security and protect rights in areas under its control. Ongoing insecurity in government-controlled areas, including Mogadishu, and political infighting and reshuffles detracted from progress on justice and security reform. Political efforts to establish federal states influenced interclan fighting in some areas.

On December 13, 2013, government soldiers shot dead Duduble clan elder Suldan Abdinasir Hussein Hassan at a checkpoint in Lower Shabelle; the country's military court issued warrants for the soldiers, but they were never apprehended, reportedly due to their commanders' protection.

Somalia's National Intelligence Agencies, NISA, routinely carried out mass security sweeps, despite having no legal mandate to arrest and detain suspects. NISA has occasionally held detainees for prolonged periods without judicial review and mistreated suspects during interrogations.

Government forces and clan militia regularly clashed, causing civilian deaths, injuries, and destruction of property. In December 2013, government forces attacked KM-50 village, where they fought a local militia, beat residents, and looted and burned homes and shops. Several civilians were reportedly killed and many civilians fled the area.

The Somali government continued to rely on its military court to conduct justice for a broad range of crimes not within its jurisdiction in proceedings that fall short of international fair trial standards. The court in 2014 sentenced to death and executed fifteen people, thirteen of whom were not members of the Somali armed forces.

Reports indicate that al-Shabaab continues to carry out targeted killings, including beheadings and civilian executions. On June 2, the group publicly executed three men accused of spying for the federal government and foreign governments in the port-town of Barawe. Al-Shabaab also administers arbitrary justice and severely restricts basic rights.

Al-Shabaab regularly targeted for attack civilians objects, particularly in Mogadishu with a significant increase during the Ramadan holiday. On February 13, a suicide car bomb attack on a United Nations convoy near Mogadishu International Airport killed at least six civilian bystanders. Al-Shabaab claimed responsibility for the killings of three lawmakers in July and August.

Sexual violence in Somalia also remains unknown due to absence of data and failure of reports. Internally displaced women and girls are particularly vulnerable to rape by armed men, including Somali government soldiers and militia members. Government forces and allied militia have also taken advantage of insecurity in newly recovered towns to rape local women and girls. The government endorsed an action plan to address sexual violence, but implementation was slow.

Some soldiers from Uganda and Burundi deployed as part of the African Union Mission in Somalia sexually exploited and assaulted women and girls on their bases in Mogadishu. In some cases women and girls were offered humanitarian assistance, medicine, and food in exchange for sex. Few women filed complaints due to a fear of reprisals and an absence of effective and safe complaints mechanisms. At time of writing, the AU and troop-contributing countries were investigating allegations of sexual abuse and exploitation by AMISOM forces. Thus far, accountability for these abuses has been limited despite AMISOM commitments.

Al-Shabaab in particular targets children for recruitment and forced marriage and so attacks schools. The UN documented recruitment and use of children by government forces and allied militia.

In August, the UN expert on children in armed conflict raised concerns about the unlawful detention of fifty-five children, reportedly formerly associated with armed groups, in the Serendi rehabilitation camp in Mogadishu.

Government authorities committed to implement action plans signed in 2012 to end the use of child soldiers, as well as the killing and maiming of children, but progress has been slow.

According to the UN, over one million people, many of them displaced persons, face food insecurity, and 120,000 Somalis have been newly displaced since the beginning of 2014, as a result of ongoing military operations.

Tens of thousands of displaced people remain in dreadful conditions in Mogadishu and are subjected to evictions, sexual violence, and clan-based discrimination at the hands of government forces, allied militia, and private individuals including camp managers. Government plans to relocate displaced communities to the outskirts of Mogadishu, but forced evictions by private individuals and the authorities increased in July and August.

Ongoing attacks on humanitarian workers, insecurity, local power struggles, and restrictions imposed by the warring parties posed challenges for humanitarian agencies trying to address basic needs. For example, on December 18, 2013, unidentified gunmen killed three Syrian doctors and one Somali doctor while traveling to a health post outside Mogadishu.

Somalia also remains one of the most dangerous countries in the world to be a journalist; three media professionals, including two journalists, were killed in 2014. On June 21, Yusuf Ahmed Abukar—a reporter working with Mustaqbal, a privately owned radio station, and Ergo radio, which covers humanitarian affairs, was killed when a bomb exploded in his car. Impunity for these types of killings prevails.

Government harassment and intimidation of journalists in Mogadishu, particularly by NISA, and threats against media outlets increased. On February 11, NISA detained Mohamed Haji Bare from Radio Danan and Ibrahim Mohamed from Radio Haatuf, for three days, beating them severely and threatening them, reportedly for taking photos of a deputy governor previously injured in a car bomb.

Despite the war on terror in Somalia, the country is slowly improving. In early May 2015, US Secretary of the State John Kerry made a historic visit to Somalia, a country no other US secretary of state had ever visited. His trip symbolized both how far Somalia has come—from the darkest days of the civil war, clan fighting, and famine in the 1990s; to the brutal rule of the terror group al-Shabaab in the mid-2000s; to somewhat getting closer to normal—and how very far it still has to go.

According to the Council on Foreign Affairs, the fact that a high US official could enter the country at all speaks of real security improvements. During his visit, moreover, Kerry announced the reopening of a US embassy in Somalia, which had been closed since 1991 when the government of long-term dictator, Siad Barre collapsed. But the fact that Kerry's visit was a brief few hours—during which he did not even leave the heavily-guarded Mogadishu airport—also points to deep and persistent security challenges.

Moreover, his meeting with Somali President Hassan Sheikh Mohamud and Prime Minister Omar Sharmarke comes at a time when the relationship between international donors and the Somali government has soured and the Somali people have grown increasingly wary of their government. The early optimism that the 2012 election of Mohamud by appointed members of the Somali parliament would usher in badly needed changes in Somali politics, toward inclusiveness, effectiveness, and accountability, dissipated long ago.

Compared to the early 1990s or 2011, when al-Shabaab controlled most of Mogadishu and most of central and southern Somalia, with only the semiautonomous regions of Puntland and Somaliland escaping its grasp, Somalia is in much better shape. Security is tenuous, with al-Shabaab and the African Union Mission in Somalia (AMISOM) forces stuck in a draw, and politics has been regressing to many of the same old discouraging patterns.

The rest of 2015 and 2016 are important times for Somalia. They could either resurrect optimism about the country's progress or reinforce disappointment. The current AMISOM mandate expires in November 2015. By 2016, as a compact between the international donors and Somalia government specifies, presidential elections are supposed to take place, a constitutional redrafting is to be finished, and the transformation of a centralized state into a federal one with states formed is to be completed. From the perspective of the middle of 2015, this agenda looks daunting.

After struggling against al-Shabaab for several years and hunkering down in a few blocks of Mogadishu, AMISOM forces, with the assistance of international private security companies and international funding, finally began to reverse the al-Shabaab tide in 2011. As clan militias defected from al-Shabaab, AMISOM succeeded in pushing the terrorist group out of Somalia's major cities. US air and Special Forces attacks against al-Shabaab leadership eliminated some key figures, such as the group's Amir Ahmed Godane, in September 2014 and its previous leader, Aden Ayro, in May 2008.

That said, al-Shabaab is hardly defected—even if its membership is thought to be down to around six thousand with the most potent and hardcore *Amniyat* branch down to perhaps 1,500. (Such estimates, given by the Somali government officials and international military advisors, need to be taken with a grain of salt, since the capacity of insurgent groups to replenish their ranks often outpaces the capacity of counterinsurgent forces to kill or arrest the group's members.)

The group's spectacular terrorist attacks in Kenya and Uganda, such as the one on Nairobi's Westgate Mall in September 2013 and on a teaching college in the city of Garissa in April 2015, don't necessarily mean that al-Shabaab has lost the capacity to operate in Somalia. In fact, if anything, al-Shabaab's operations have become more targeted and more effective, and generate more casualties with the militant group losing fewer fighters. The fact that the group has deeply infiltrated Somali military and police forces helps it in that regard.

During his trip to Kenya on July 25, 2015, President Obama committed the United States to an intensified fight against terrorists in East Africa, announcing that his administration would expand support for counterterrorism operations in Kenya and Somalia, including increased training and funding for Kenya's security forces.

"We have to keep that pressure going even as we're strengthening the Somali government," he said at a joint news conference with Kenyan president Uhuru Kenyatta.

Obama acknowledged that al-Shabaab terrorists retain the capacity to attack "soft targets" in both countries, even after years of American drone strikes and efforts from a regional, US-backed counter terrorism force based in Somalia. But he said al-Shabaab's territory had been "systematically reduced."

Obama came to office vowing to move the United States off a perpetual war footing and promising to wage a smarter, swifter war on international terrorism. But his East African sojourn serves as a stark reminder that even years into his presidency the long, difficult fight against terrorism remains a central and vexing component of his foreign policy (CNN, 2015).

On August 3, 2015 Somalia's president gave a defiant warning to al-Shabaab insurgents a day after they killed at least thirteen people in a bomb attack on a hotel that houses several diplomatic missions. The suicide vehicle attack, the latest in a string of bomb blasts and killings in the war-torn Horn of Africa nation, came as US president Barack Obama left neighboring Kenya and headed to Ethiopia, both key nations contributing troops to the African Union force battling the al-Qaida-affiliated al-Shabaab.

The White House strongly condemned the "abhorrent" attack. "The devastation was huge, and so far thirteen people, all of them innocent civilians, have been confirmed dead," Somali government security officer Ahmed Ali said.

"Some of the wounded died the next day, while other bodies were recovered under the wreckage of nearby buildings." Initial reports had put the death toll at six. The Jazeera Palace hotel is home to the missions of China, Qatar, and the United Arab Emirates, and is popular among Somali government officials and foreign visitors.

Beijing said on August 3 that one of its embassy staff was killed and three others slightly wounded. "African Union troops helped rescue survivors, including Kenya's ambassador to Somalia," spokesperson Paddy Ankunda said.

The hotel has also been the target of al-Shabaab attacks in the past, including in 2012 when suicide bombers stormed the hotel while President Hassan Sheikh Mohamud was inside.

Despite the challenges of being struck by al-Shabaab, Somalia is improving both physically and diplomatically. For many years, Somalia has had terrible human rights record with always in the list of the world's worst countries for human rights violations.

Somalia's minister of Human Rights and Women's Affairs, Sahra Mohammed Ali met with senior officials from the United Nations offices in Mogadishu to discuss on ways of developing the human rights situations in a country recovering from two decades of civil wars and lawlessness.

She said the government is determined to work on the eliminations of human rights abuses and deal with those who violate. The current government has failed to tackle rights violations despite making pledges in public several times. Its human rights record has been mixed with the security forces being involved in sexual violence against women.

Somalia: Facts, Culture, Belief, and Heritage

Country Name: The Federal Republic of Somalia
Capital City: Mogadishu
Other Major Cities: Berbera, Hargeisa, and Kismayo
Major Rivers: Shabelle and Jubba
Official Language: Somali
Currency: Somali shilling (1 shilling=100 cents)

The Somali Flag

Blue is said to represent the bright sky. The star stands for freedom. The five points of the star stand for the five historical areas of Somali people: Italian Somaliland, British Somaliland, French Somaliland (Djibouti), the Ogaden region of Ethiopia, and northeastern Kenya.

Somaliland is the north-western territory that declared independence from the rest of Somalia in 1991. Somaliland has its own elected president and parliament, but has not been internationally recognized as an independent nation.

Religion

The religion of Somalia is Islam and almost all Somalis are Muslim, adhering to the moderate "Sunni orthodox" version of Islam. They are reputed to be practicing Muslims, meaning they believe in Allah alone (one

God) as the unique creator and sustainer of the universe. They also adhere to Islamic values and morality, which require purity of body and soul, and observe food and drink prohibitions, such as abstaining from pork and alcohol. Muslims follow the five pillars of Islam:

Shahadah- to make a statement of belief: "There is no God but Allah and Muhammad is the prophet of Allah."

Salah- to pray five times a day while kneeling in the direction of the Qiblah (Kabah) located in the Holy City of Makkah in Saudi Arabia

Zakah- to give money to charity for the poor

Sawm- too fast for thirty days during the month of Ramadan

Hajj- to travel to the Holy City of Makkah

Hijab

This is the Islamic traditional dress worn by women. Religious beliefs require women to wear long dresses which cover their bodies and hair. Hijab or head scarves are very common for Muslim women.

Holidays

Two major holidays (Eid) Muslims celebrate: Eid-ul-Fitr and Eid-ul-Adha. These holidays are based on the Islamic calendar that is based on the lunar year, and is ten or eleven days shorter than the solar year. This means Islamic holidays don't fall at the same time each year according to the Gregorian calendar. For both holidays, Somalis gather to eat, buy new clothes, and kids receive presents, mostly money, known as *Xaqul-eid*, from family and friends.

Eid-ul-Fitr

Eid-ul-Fitr is a celebration held at the end of Ramadan, the month in which Muslims fast. When Muslims fast, they abstain from eating and drinking from sunrise until sunset. Eid-ul-Fitr is celebrated for three days in Somalia.

Eid-ul-Adha

Eid-ul-Adha is also celebrated for three days in Somalia. It is celebrated on the tenth month (*Dul-xijja*), which is during the hajj season (the season for making pilgrimage to Makkah). A week before this holiday, Somali families clean their homes thoroughly. Somali women typically bake cookies known as *Macmacaan*, a kind of spice cookie. The word *Macmacaan* itself means "sweetness.") People get together for the Eid prayer at the mosque early morning and families and friends get together for a big feast after. For Eid-ul-Adha, Muslims slaughter goats or even cows and offer the majority of the meat to the needy, and also make their annual charity donations.

Henna

Henna comes from North Africa, Egypt, India, and parts of the Middle East. Henna has been around for thousands of years. It comes from a plant in which the ground-up leaves produce a strong dye. It's used to paint designs on women for special occasions such as weddings, Eid, parties, and holidays. There are many different designs and patterns. It is usually worn on the hands up to the elbows, but it can be done on your feet, neck or back. Henna artists earn money by designing and applying henna.

It can stain clothes. However, these stains are not removable so you have to be careful.

Marriage

In Somalia, marriages can be arranged or by choice. However, Islam encourages marriage to be a choice by the individual seeking to marry. Either way, the bride and groom are allowed to talk to each other before the marriage is official.

The common marrying age in Somalia is around fifteen or sixteen. Traditionally, the establishment of the family unit follows an intricate traditional ceremony where gifts and affluence takes place. For example, when a prospective couple agrees on marriage, the man usually informs his parents to seek the hand of the bride. Parents have influence on the choice because marriage is not only an individual contract, but also a union between two kinship groups. Several elder kinsmen make the formal request.

If the proposal is accepted, an initial gift (*gabati*) is paid and the proper bride price is negotiated. In some areas, it involves several hundred heads of camels. In return, what the bride's family pay is known as *dhibad*, consisting of all the elements and furnishings of the house, in addition to a flock of sheep and goats. The bride's family is responsible for the ceremony also, which lasts for a week or three days. Then, an Islamic priest (*wadaad*) makes a proper contract and the groom pledges a personal price (*meher*) to the bride. This is payable to her if the marriage breaks up. Usually, a bride does not change her name and is considered a life- member of her birth family.

Weddings

Traditional Somali weddings have various ceremonies. On a Somali wedding day, there is a dinner of traditional food of rice and meat for the men of the two families and their friends. This is when the formal Islamic wedding agreement takes place.

The women have a wedding party in the evening. The groom and his family are expected to pay for these celebrations. It is a tradition in Somali culture that a new bride remains in her home for a week after her wedding. On the seventh day there is a women's party for the bride, which is optional. On this occasion the bride will wear traditional costume, *guntiino* with beads. The guests circle the bride singing and each lays a scarf (*shaash*) on her head. This event is known as *shaash saar*, which basically means putting the scarf on the bride's head. This is a form of respect due to her for being married and is a symbol of her becoming a married woman. The *shaash* is of silky material and can have many patterns and colors, but is different to the scarves worn by unmarried women.

Another event that takes place after seven days is that the bride's family provides food and gifts for the groom's family. Traditionally, the food and sweets are placed inside special decorated containers called *xeedho*. These are wrapped in cloth and tied tightly. They have to be unwrapped by the groom or a man in his family.

Naming Convention

Somali names have three parts. The first part is the given name and specific to an individual. The second part is the name of the child's father, and the third part is the name of the child's paternal grandfather. Thus siblings, both male and female, will share the same second and third parts of their names. Women, when they marry, do not change their names. By keeping the name of their father and grandfather, they are, in effect, maintaining their affiliation with their clan of birth. Somalis also identify themselves or use what is known as *abtrisiimo*, which loosely means "family lineage traced back to the clan/tribe."

Reproduction

Childbearing usually commences shortly after marriage. A woman's status is enhanced the more children she bears. Therefore, it is not unusual for a Somali family to have seven or eight children. The concept of planning when to have or not have children has little cultural relevance for Somalis. Expectant and mothers who newly delivered benefit from a strong network of women within Somali culture. Before a birth, the community women hold a party (similar to a baby shower) known as *Xaawo iyo Faaduma* or *Sagaaleyesi* for the expectant mother as a sign of support. Births most frequently occur at home and are attended by a birth attendant.

Breast-feeding

Breast-feeding is the primary form of infant nutrition. It is common to breastfeed a child until two years of age. Supplementing with animal milk (camel, cow, and goat) early in the neonatal period is common and is especially true during the first few days of life, as colostrum is considered unhealthy. Camel milk is considered the most nutritious of animal milks. Few Somalis use bottles; infants are commonly offered liquids in a cup. A mixture of rice and cow milk is introduced at about six months of age, and solid foods follow soon after.

Circumcision

Male circumcision is performed at various times between birth and five years of age. It is performed either by a traditional doctor or nurse or doctor in a hospital and considered a rite of passage to manhood. The uncircumcised are considered unclean. Both boys and girls are circumcised during a ceremony and celebration. Boys and girls are kept separated. Somali girls go through the process of female circumcision after they are born. This custom originally came from Egypt and is one of the unpleasant sides of Somali custom.

After 1980, the old government tried to outlaw this practice but people were still practicing it. In short, this practice means to remove the clitoris and surrounding part of a girl's private part. This practice doesn't relate to the Islamic tradition whatsoever. In many places, many Somali families fight against this practice. This practice has an impact on the life of a Somali girl especially during her menstrual cycle. Not only do they miss classes, but also become sick for about three to seven days in a month.

Fashion and Clothes in Somalia

For everyday use, Somali women wear a *baati*—a long loose cotton dress made in many patterns and colors. It is usual for women to cover their hair with a scarf. These often match the material of the dress.

For special occasions such as weddings, parties, or Eid, Somali women will wear a *dirac*. This is a silky, shiny and highly decorated top dress. It is often transparent, which is why it's best to wear a dress underneath it.

Sometimes Somali women wear an outer dress called a *jilbaab* that covers from head to toe and *niqab* that covers the face. Somali women like to wear gold jewelry including necklaces, bracelets, earrings, and rings. Women often receive jewelry as a wedding gift.

Men wear *khamiis*—a long loose overshirt that is suitable for a hot climate. Men usually wear small hats. For relaxing at home a man will often wear a *macawiis*—a long cloth wrapped around the body and tied at the waist. The traditional costume of Somali women is a long cloth that is draped around the waist and over the shoulders. This is called *guntiino*.

Birthdays

Birthdays are not celebrated in Somali culture. Rather, forty days after the birth of the baby, there is a gathering known as *afartanbax*. It is not a birthday celebration but just eating together to support the mother and to welcome the newborn.

Death

In Islam, life is considered sacred and belongs to Allah. It is believed that all creatures die at a time determined by Allah, and no one knows when that time is except Allah. For this reason, when a patient is determined to be terminally ill, a time frame for when death might likely occur is not offered.

In Somali culture, community support is an integral part of the bereavement process. Community members cook, babysit, and pitch in financially to cover funeral costs and help family members of the deceased. Death follows burial as soon as possible, and everyone is involved. Qur'an plays an important role in sickness and death, and Somalis pray for the ill and bereaved sincerely.

Food

Somali culture has its own concept and attitudes regarding food, such as what is proper food and what is not. There are rules and customs concerning food that have to be observed. For example, certain portions of meats are reserved for guests only. In Somalia, people eat when they are hungry.

Children will be out playing and will only come home when they are hungry. Guests arrive and the hosts will cook for them, even at night, without asking them if they need food. Asking implies one is not hospitable. When people are eating, they will invite you to join.

It is improper to refuse food. Somalis believe that eating alone is not good for one's health. When a Somali invites you out for a meal, you know that he/she will pay the bill. You do not need to have money, you just go. Somali people use the Somali term, *Soo dhawoow* which means welcome.

In Somalia, no matter how poor they are, guests are welcomed. They don't worry whether they have food in the house, the idea being that even water, or just conversation, is enough.

Use of Right Hand

The right hand is considered the clean and polite hand to use for daily tasks, such as eating, writing, and greeting people. If a child begins to show left-hand preference, the parents will actively try to train him/her to use the right hand. Left-handedness is very uncommon in Somali culture.

Visitation

One of the aspects of the Somali culture is expecting visits from relatives, friends, neighbors, and other community members without prior notice. These visits can take place any time during the day. Somalis do not ask their visitors what they like to eat or drink, because their visitors will decline—it is shameful for guests to ask for anything. The host will offer what is available (often the best the family has), especially Somali tea.

It is important in Somali culture to visit those who are sick, families with newborn babies, bereaved families, and wedding events. While approaching the house one is visiting, the visitor will call or announce his/her presence by calling out the Somali phrase *Hoodi-Hoodi*, which means "I'm here!" The host will respond with *Soo dhawoow*, which means "welcome." Once inside the house, the visitor stays in a certain area. The rest of the house is out of bounds.

Family Values

Somalis deeply value the family. The strength of family ties provides a safety net in times of need. The protection of the family honor is very important. So it is a loyalty, which extends beyond the family and extended family. Living with extended families is the norm. Young adults who move to the city to go school usually live with relatives rather than live alone. Similarly, unmarried people tend to live with their parents or extended families.

The family system is very strong and the decision-making process in Somalia is beyond the parents' decision. Other relatives and close friends have influence in the decision-making process as well. Respect is paid to the elders of the community who are addressed as "aunt" or "uncle," even though they are not relatives.

Elders help encourage considerate behavior in clan/family disputes, conflict resolutions, payments of blood indemnity, setting up for grazing and water rules in the nomadic lifestyle, and are effective in mediating and setting these issues.

Somali children are raised with much love but are also disciplined and taught to work from age five or six, with little time for play. In spite of numerous hardships, Somali children are known for their sense of joy and abundant laughter. Children are taught independence and self-reliance and to carefully observe the world around them.

Education

Education for Somali children in all but the wealthiest urban families was practically nonexistent, except for training in reading the Qur'an, before the early 1970s. Boys in rural areas attended outdoor schools where they learned Arabic using wooden slats. Before independence some attended Roman Catholic schools, where they learned Arabic or Italian.

Under Siad Barre, a Latin-based alphabet was created for the Somali language, which previously had no written form. The leader undertook a massive literacy campaign in Somalia and achieved some success, although many nomadic children still do not attend school, and many others, especially girls, dropped out after four years of primary school.

Students learned reading, writing, and arithmetic as well as Arabic, animal husbandry, and agriculture. When the civil war broke out, most secular education stopped, as schools were bombed and the government, which hired teachers, collapsed.

However, some determined teachers struggled on during the 1990s, especially without pay. Students continued to come, eager to learn even when there were no chairs or desks and no roof on the school. With the absence of a government, parents contributed what they could toward school supplies so their children could continue to get an education.

PART 2

SURVIVING SOMALIA: OUR JOURNEY TO AMERICA

My memories of Africa consist of the many times I played the part of the African version of *Dora the Explorer*—except in my case, I nearly die in all my adventures. My father was working in Nairobi. His job was to help merchants sell their goods. He didn't get paid much from it. He was paid only a couple of cents. Though he worked in order to provide us with food and clothing, the money he made was only enough to supply him with food and shelter for a week. Because of that reason we only got to see him every three months. On the other hand, my mother made a living piercing people's ears. Every morning she would leave to the market with her bags containing materials used to pierce ears, with my sister Malyun on her back. Malyun was a baby during those days. When my mom left to do business, she would leave me with our neighbors.

However, I didn't like staying at my neighbor's house because she had sons. I couldn't stand boys and couldn't help but be as far away from them. My neighbor's sons freaked me a lot. I'm not sure why. Maybe it was because they were so tall. So as soon as I saw that my mother had left, I would sneak out of my neighbor's house and walk back to my house, which was only a block away. I would sit behind my house where there was shade and sit there until my mom came back. I don't know if the neighbor ever tried to look for me because I did that quite often and got away with it.

When my mother came back home she would find me sleeping on the dusty ground with bugs crawling and flying all over me and the sun shining right at me. My mom told me that she couldn't help but cry seeing me in such position. Sometimes, she would stress out about what to do with me. Life was very difficult for her. Her mother and siblings were not there to help her raise me and my sister, and my father was miles away trying to earn as many coins possible to make sure we lived.

Meanwhile, my mom then decided to leave me at my aunt's (my father's half sister) house. After a while I started to hate going to my aunt's house. Every time we ate, my male cousins would finish the food from me before I even started eating. In Somali culture everyone ate from the same plate together. I disliked my male cousins too. They had no etiquettes when it came to eating, which is why I chose not to eat sometimes. But my older cousins were really fun. Even though I wasn't the youngest in the house, they treated me like a baby. My older male cousin, Abdikadir would give me piggy back rides and lift me up and down as if I was on an airplane. I would also play hide-and-seek with my older female cousins, which I enjoyed a lot especially at night when it was hard to find each other. Since I was going to my aunt's house on a daily basis every year, I got bored doing the same thing every day. When Malyun grew older, at least to be able to walk and run, she had to stay at my aunt's house with me. But one day, we decided to sneak out and go to my great cousin, Rahma's house. Cousin Rahma was my favorite person in the whole world after my mom. My mom told me that both of them practically raised me and that I would always try to find a way to get to her.

Sadly, my aunt would always catch me and Mal leave and demand us to come back instantly. I loved her, but I was sick of coming to her house. I started to realize why my mom trusted my aunt so much. She was too protective of us which was really annoying to me. But my adventures did not stop there. They began at home when my father came back.

One evening while playing *dhaka dhaka* (tag) with friends, I was bitten by a scorpion and almost got killed in a stampede of donkeys later that night. I didn't understand why I was the only one bitten. Then again I was always barefoot; it started making sense to me after a while. Dadaab was very sandy, and with the temperature being so hot, my feet were always burned. I don't think my parents had money to buy me sandals, because I know if they knew my feet were burning so much they would've done something about it. I was told to play outside only when there was shade out, but I didn't listen to my parents. I was always ready for an adventure and would leave the house anyway.

Meanwhile, the poison of the scorpion caused me to hallucinate. My legs were numb. I couldn't lift them up. Even though I saw a herd of donkeys coming toward me, I was incapable of running. I kept calling out to my neighbor named Mat Hassan. He was probably about forty years or older. For some reason he would always be out at night, while everyone was sleeping, doing God knows what. He was the only one who could save me that night. So I called him three times, *"Aw Mat Hassan!" Aw* means mister in my language. Prior to me being outside late that night, I was experiencing strong hallucinations and thought my family left me abandoned at home. They placed me on a bed made of mud, which was very uncomfortable. The bed was only for my parents to sleep on or when my sisters and I became ill.

In my vision the house was very dark. I failed to see my parents and my two siblings sleeping on the floor. I thought they left me, and I somehow managed to get out of the house without them realizing I had left. There were no locks on the doors in the refugee camps, only a few heavy objects to block the door just in case armed men invaded the camps. Although, to this day my parents and I still question how in the world I escaped.

As soon as I got out of the house it was very dark, similar to how the sky looks during midnight. Seeing the herd of donkeys made me regret leaving the house. My parents heard me calling out to Aw Mat Hassan, and that's when they realized I had left and came out to get me. I don't think I've ever been that scared in my entire life. I'm sure my parents made sure they had many heavier objects blocking the door since then. But my troubles didn't end there.

Then, there was a time when me and my sister, Malyun, tried to sneak from my aunt's house again and leave off to my cousin Asha's house. We've never been to her house before and so we thought we should visit that day. It was all my idea, poor Malyun was always there in my schemes and got in trouble with me.

We successfully sneaked our way to Asha's house. For the first time ever, I felt free. Since that incident, I don't think my dad trusted my aunt with us. Later that day on a dark scary night, we got lost on our way home from Asha's house. I didn't understand why my cousins didn't walk us home. I was only five years old and Malyun was three.

After walking for several minutes, Malyun and I found ourselves in the middle of the woods. I remember looking up in the sky and not being able to see stars or the moon. It was that dark! We could barely tell if the ground was actually the ground, because it seemed like we were standing in the middle of a humongous pit sixty acres wide. The next thing we knew, we were in the center of a huge pit. I still have no clue how we ended up in a pit. An hour later, we saw flashes of beaming lights shining down on us. It was of course, my distant cousin Amina's father along with my mother and a few of our neighbors.

Apparently, everyone in town was searching for us. I don't recall what happened after that, but I'm pretty sure my parents didn't let us out of their sight ever since. My mom had already lost a child before, my older brother who was only a few months old in a previous marriage. He died naturally when my mom was fifteen years old. She was not going to lose any more kids.

While Malyun and I were off on our expeditions during our childhood, we failed to see what was really taking place in our country. We weren't thinking about why my mother would just suddenly leave every morning and send us off to my aunt's house. We didn't know why we weren't able to see our father as often as we should have. We didn't understand why every once in a while some Caucasians would suddenly show up in our town or why the other kids felt the need to be so excited about the Caucasians' sudden visits. I didn't understand where they were coming from or what they were doing in the refugee camps.

It was about the age of eight when my mother started to tell me all the things that were taking place both in Somalia and Kenya. However, at the age of six, I knew my country was facing hunger and lack of necessities as it was shown in the UNICEF commercials I've seen on television when we first came into the United States. From my mother's stories arose how she and my father met. Originally, my parents were born in Somalia. My mother, as well as her father, were born in a small town called Bardheryerey, but my grandmother was born in Mogadishu, the capital of Somalia. My grandmother's maternal grandfather was from the Hawiye clan. Together they were living in Bardheryerey along with my mother's nine siblings and other relatives. It wasn't an easy life for my mother's family in the town.

Often times, a group of Somali men armed with weapons would suddenly invade the town. My mom recalls seeing about seventy or more armed men every day and night. The men would come in different groups due to clan differences. They would come from all angles surrounding the town to make sure no Somali Bantus escaped. They threatened to kill any Bantus that they laid their eyes upon. Many times they were there to rob the Somali Bantu families of any possessions they had.

The Bantus were farmers who grew many crops including corn and bananas. The cities of Somalia at the time were going through conflicts and food shortages. So the armed Somali men came to rob food crops from Somali Bantus like my mother's family. But robbing food was the lesser of the problems Bantus faced. My mom recalls seeing the armed men rape women and girls. They would kill the men and boys of the families they captured. If a woman was pregnant with a baby boy, the baby was often killed by the armed men, but if it was a baby girl the baby would be left alone, but in some cases killed. Unfortunately, boys only had death as an option, whether young or old.

The armed men in most cases forced male family members to rape their female family members. If Bantu men refused to do such thing, they were killed. Predominantly, the armed men were the ones who would rape the Bantu women and girls. After raping the women, they would insert a bayonet in their vaginas and tear it apart, which resulted in death.

One day while my grandmother and her mother were sitting and talking, a small group of the armed Somali men invaded their house. The men commanded my grandfather to rape my mother. My grandfather refused after being told to rape his daughter several times, knowing that he would be killed if he didn't. My mother was always his favorite, and he would never do anything to hurt her. So he refused and, at that moment, my grandfather was shot and killed.

After killing him, they went after my grandmother and her mother and commanded them to give them every possession that belonged to my grandfather. During that interrogation, my mother's older brother, Abdi, came in a hurry to the scene. He told my mother to leave, because the men would come back to rape and kill her. My mother refused to leave her father's dead body saying, "They killed my father and they're going to have to kill me as well. I will not leave my father here." My uncle grabbed my mother despite her response and told her to run as far as she could. That was the last time my mother saw her mother, grandmother, and her older brother. She didn't know if they survived until someone told her they were still alive in Somalia when she settled in America fourteen years later.

My mother also had two younger siblings named Jafar and Johara. They were about five and six when she last saw them. Luckily, they were taken to Tanzania during the *Habat Kanta* period, which is referred to as the years before the Somali war and conflict began. This was the period in which many rich Somalis fled the country and settled in parts of Europe and North America. My mother's uncle who was in Tanzania sent money to my great grandma so she could bring my aunt and uncle to Tanzania in order for them to receive education and escape the violence. My mother was told to leave, but since she was so close to her parents she didn't want to leave them.

Uncle Jafar and Aunt Johara don't remember anything about the time they fled to Tanzania since they were so young. *Habat Sugo* is referred to as the period in which the Somali conflict was taking place. The people who were living in Somalia at the time were poor and couldn't afford to leave the country. This was the situation the rest of the family faced.

My mother remembers her and my uncle Abdi running in different directions, not knowing where they were headed or if they were ever going to see each other. My mother saw a group of Somali Bantus, who faced similar situations fleeing and made a decision to follow them to Dadaab, Kenya where they would live in its refugee camps.

On their way to Dadaab, many people including children died from starvation and harsh weather conditions. The walk from Somalia to the Kenyan border (*hadood*) was prolonged and arduous. It took about fifteen days for my mother and others to reach the border. They survived by eating leaves of a tree called *garass* until they reached the Kenyan border. Unfortunately, many women and children died on their way to Kenya. If a person died all you could do was grab a piece of cloth and some leaves and cover them. You couldn't do a proper burial. If your child died, you had no choice but to leave your child lying in the hot sun and continue with your journey. After reaching the border, my mother and others couldn't enter the country. One reason being it was fenced with barbed wires. Second, the Kenyan government was authorized to allow people to enter the country. My mother and the rest of the people found luck when the Kenyan government and *Medecins Sans Frontieres* (MSF), an international medical humanitarian-aid and nongovernmental organization now known as Doctors Without Borders, came to the border and authorized them to enter the country.

The Kenyan government, as well as MSF and the United Nations, knew about the deadly conflict taking place in Somalia, which is why they allowed Bantus like my mother and others to enter the country. However, there was an exception in entering Kenya. You had to be given a card, which had holes punched in, representing how many individuals were with you. You were to use the cards every fifteen days to get in line for a meal, which was provided by the United Nations. MSF was in charge of providing medical needs.

Settling in Kenya did not stop the armed men from coming in and continuing to terrorize my people. My mom recalls hearing gunshots every night at the first camp she was living in. Oftentimes they would wait in the woods for their victims in order to rape and kill the Bantu women who were in search of finding tree branches so that they could make fire for food.

One day, around the age of seventeen, my mother and nine other girls went out in the woods to get tree branches to make fire for food. Suddenly, they came face to face with armed Somali men. She remembers being so terrified that she didn't think she would live. Three of the girls were raped and killed. The youngest girl—who was about twelve and unmarried—was violently raped and killed by having a bayonet inserted in her vagina and ripped up. Luckily, my mother was able to flee.

Originally, there were ten girls, but by the time they came back to the camp there were seven of them left. Because of that terrifying experience, my mother sees scenes such as that in her nightmares till this day. My mother told me that almost all Somali Bantu women and girls who were born and raised in Somalia experienced rape by armed Somali men. The only ones who hadn't encountered rape were those who were luckily born in the refugee camps like me.

My mother stated that the day she and her friends were attacked in the woods was during her engagement to my dad. At the time my mother was living with one of her uncles since neither her mother nor her grandmother made it to Kenya. My great uncle and my father urged her not to go to the woods constantly, knowing the dangers she would face. But my mother was sure that she would come quickly before the bandits came into the woods. She wanted to be helpful to her aunt and bring tree branches for her. So she went anyway. After a few minutes in the woods the bandits came in. They started violently raping my mother's friends.

Luckily, my mother didn't get raped or *koofsi*, because of her quick action. She smeared her feces all over herself so that they wouldn't rape her, which worked. But because they were so upset she did that, they beat her severely to the point that she was taken to the hospital and remained there for weeks. My father constantly visited her in the hospital to make sure she was okay.

My parents first met at my paternal great uncle's house. My great uncle was married to my mother's great aunt. My father felt in love with her after seeing her beauty, because she was very bright and saw how hardworking she was. My father had been married three times before. He told me that his previous wives were very lazy and disorganized. He had been looking for a woman who was hardworking and helpful. My mother was the perfect woman for him. They married a few months later in July 1997.

Meanwhile, my parents, as well as many Somali Bantu families, experienced even more hate and discrimination at the refugee camps. Once some minority Somalis started fleeing from Somalia and settled into the camps, some of them were very disrespectful when they heard that the Somali Bantus would be resettled to the United States.

The majority of them came to the camps for a better life and did not want to be involved in another conflict. Some of the rude Somalis, especially women, would say things like, "Who would take these monkeys or donkeys anywhere?" The women kept saying, "They think they're free just because they're going to America. It doesn't matter how much education they will receive in America, they will always be dumb. Look at how happy those donkeys are." It was very shocking to me when my mother was telling me about what was being said to the Bantus.

I couldn't believe that we called each other Muslims, but we couldn't even respect each other as human beings. I didn't understand why the appearance of a person influenced assumptions about them. Everyone was a refugee, I didn't see how some of the Somalis found humor in such situation.

In order for the Somali Bantus to be able to go to America without any altercations with the Somalis, they were displaced from Dagahaley to Kakuma. Kakuma was the last camp the Bantus settled in before migrating to America. They were placed in Kakuma from Dagahaley by means of bus, which was either provided by the government of Kenya or one of the refugee organizations.

In order to successfully be able to live in America, the Bantus had to go through examinations held by US agencies. The first agency dealt with providing application for US resettlement, the second was in charge of updating people about their applications. The third agency dealt with approving and disapproving people from US entry. My mother remembers the third agency's name as INS or Immigration and Naturalization Service. After all the applications were processed it took about a month or two to hear the result of our application. We were notified that we were approved on migrating to America on September 2003. Our family received the flight schedule to leave on October 10, 2004 for the United States on September 2004. We were expected to land in the United States the next day, October 11, 2004. Until it was time for us to leave, we were moved to Goal Accommodation Center in Nairobi. We rode a plane from Kakuma camp to Nairobi, which was about four hours long if not more. We stayed in Goal for about a month. Goal was essentially for any refugees who were bounded for the United States. You could not go to America without staying in Goal for a while. Unfortunately, when the time for our departure came, my mother collapsed and had a miscarriage. At that moment our flight had to be rescheduled. She was experiencing a hemorrhage and was hospitalized. She had a miscarriage at the airport on our way to board our flight. The miscarriage happened when my mother was startled and in shock after my sister Malyun was vomiting violently in which her eyeballs suddenly became completely white. At that moment my mother fainted out of fear, which caused the baby to die in her belly. I remember crying so much and people rushing to her as she laid on the ground. I thought my mother died that moment. I was six years old and had no idea what was happening. I remember crying myself to sleep after a while. My sister Sahara was only a year old and was held by my father when my mother collapsed. My mother was hospitalized for about a week and received treatment and medication until our next flight. We stayed in Goal Accommodation Center in Kenya for another month until our next flight which was scheduled for November 22, 2004. Some of my dad's friends were also scheduled to leave that day, except they were to live in Texas while we were set to live in Louisville, Kentucky. My parents greeted them with good-byes and hugs and we all boarded our planes.

A few hours later we arrived in Louisville on November 23. Once we were brought to our home in Deena Drive my mother stated she felt a sigh of relief and nourishment. She said she felt that she could raise her kids in America and was confident that we would attain the best education that we could ever receive in America.

Appalling Reminiscence

Being able to live in America was a relief for my parents; it was an escape from all the nightmares and tragedies they faced back in Africa. However, living in America was going to be a great challenge for us. When we first settled in Louisville, Kentucky, we were given an apartment home in Dena Drive. Every Somali Bantu in Louisville including my parents pronounce it as "Dena Dareva." Generally, most parents from Africa aren't able to pronounce certain words in English correctly. The neighborhood was comprised of many town buildings that were constructed beautifully. Some of the residents had balconies. We unfortunately didn't because our house was downstairs. I wanted to know what it felt like to live upstairs with a balcony. There were people living above us. They had balconies. The neighborhood was really quiet. You could barely see people coming outside. The refugee agency in Louisville had already provided everything we needed for our house, from kitchen utensils to furniture. It was the first time we had ever seen any of those things. We had a stove, toaster, and television with no knowledge of how to use it. There were about two occasions where my parents had to take us to a local restaurant, Rally's.

I remember sitting outside on the benches with a plastic red umbrella hung above us. We all ordered chicken sandwich with fries and drinks. The food was very new to us, but delicious, as well. Since then, I have developed a love for fries. My mom later learned to use the stove and we no longer needed to go to Rally's. I kind of enjoyed being able to eat such delicious restaurant foods, but we obviously couldn't continue to depend on restaurant foods. It was very clear that that required a lot of money. The first dish my mom cooked was spaghetti. She would put spaghetti in each of our blue plastic bowls. It was very strange, because in Africa we always ate together as a family in one big plate. Apparently, eating was different in America too. Of course, I wasn't complaining. Back in Kenya whenever I visited my aunt, her kids would always finish the food before me. We couldn't even get seconds since the family was big and there wasn't enough food to go around. So having our own plate or bowl of food was a good thing for me in America. The best part of living in America was being able to have our own rooms, including a bathroom, kitchen, and a living room. Back in the refugee camps, everything was located inside the house.

The bedroom was both the living room and where you slept. The front door was where you made fire and cooked food. You had to walk outside in order to use the bathroom, which was really scary at night because there were concerns of safety. You never knew when bandits were going to attack. In our apartment, Malyun and I shared the same room. Sahara shared a room with my parents since she was only one year old. Our room already had a bed placed in it along with cool, small pillows and a small television. I don't remember how my parents' room looked because I already thought ours was cooler. Since we arrived in the United States at the end of the year, we couldn't attend school. So we spent our time exploring our surroundings and observing how things worked. Figuring out how the television worked was one of our discoveries. Some of the early shows we watched were *Dora the Explorer* and *Seinfeld*. The shows were very strange to us. We couldn't understand anything the characters were saying.

We didn't even realize Dora was speaking Spanish until a few years later. I didn't know English, but I assumed that's what Dora was speaking. The most bewildering thought Malyun and I had was how on earth Dora was talking. I actually thought there was a world of cartoons somewhere in America where you could see Dora and her friends as they appeared on television. If there was such a thing, I was going to go. I remember being so fascinated by everything on the show. Until we could start school, watching television was all we did. Our social workers brought us boxes of toys on one occasion so that we could amuse ourselves with them, along with a few coloring books and art supplies. I remember getting a large flat box of crayons and markers. We had a Sesame Street coloring book as well as a Barney and Friends coloring book. We didn't know how to color. Looking through our coloring books, we scribbled colors all over the pages. The faces of the characters on the page were unknown because we scribbled them off with our markers and crayons.

My dad was obsessed with watching army movies. Every time he changed the channel of the television in the living room, we already knew it was going to be something graphic and violent. Whenever he put on such movies, I would be so frightened that I wouldn't even eat dinner. Going to sleep was also a struggle. I didn't like watching people get shot and killed. The most annoying thing was how loud the machine guns were—or it could be the fact that my father had the volume up so high.

I really loved living in Dena Drive. It was very clean and peaceful. In front of my house was a building that appeared to look like a hotel. Until this day I'm still not sure if it was a hotel. I loved watching the sun rise and set above the building. Right next to the building was the freeway. I always thought it was a way back to Kenya. Sometimes I wished to drive on the freeway because I was feeling homesick for Dagahaley Camp and my friends. When I was younger, I never saw my country Kenya as a poor country. I saw Kenya as a place where I belonged, because I had my friends and family and that's all I needed at the time. Oftentimes, I questioned myself about how we got to America and why we left our home. Living in Kenya, I didn't experience any horrific experience except when I was bitten by a scorpion and nor did I think we were facing any hardship. So, suddenly being moved into the United States was very perplexing for me.

After living in our apartment home in Dena Drive for about two months with less to do, it was finally time for me to start school. I was enrolled in Wilkerson Traditional Elementary School in January of 2005. The school is part of the Jefferson County Public Schools system. I didn't realize it was a public school until I was sixteen. In some states, uniform schools were private schools, which is why I had the assumption that Wilkerson was a private school the whole time I was a student there. I loved attending Wilkerson very much. The school was big. The building's exterior was brown with blue and white windows because of the window blinders. Wilkerson was shaped like half of a circle with an opening. It's one of the reasons why I loved the school. It was different from how other school buildings were constructed. Wilkerson had a huge playground area with monkey bars, a track field, three connected large slides with frog-shaped entrance, swings, a basketball field, and a baseball field. I fell deeply in love with the school after seeing the playground area for the first time. Every morning we had homemade breakfast, which included pancakes and breakfast patties. Sometimes we had wrapped breakfast like pop tarts and hot pockets. I obviously didn't know what I was eating. Luckily, Mr.

Muhammad, the Somali interpreter, was always there to tell the kitchen staff what we could and couldn't eat, because as a Muslim I couldn't eat anything that contained pork. Mr. Muhammad also spoke Swahili and helped other African students who spoke Swahili. At Wilkerson we wore school uniforms: navy or white shirts and navy or khaki pants or skirts.

As an immigrant, attending school was a bit of a challenge for me—not so much academically, but socially. I was placed in K5 with a teacher named Ms. Lynch. She looked somewhere in her late forties or early fifties. Ms. Lynch had blond-grayish hair and wore glasses on her forehead half of the time. She was very nice and friendly, but it was of course nerve-wracking for me to be in a place with lots of strangers without my parents' presence. I later learned to suck it up and try to interact with my classmates. I couldn't really play with the other students because I was too nervous and shy, but there was a huge pink doll house that always made my day in the classroom. It was as big as a television set. You could get into the house through its doors and peek out the windows, and it even came with baby dolls that resembled the American Girl dolls. The dolls came in different races, black and Caucasian, and had their own cribs, clothing, and supplies. That was how I spent my playtime. I didn't really understand why I was going to school at the time. All I remember was being able to play with dolls, puzzles, and blocks all day and having really long naps. I'm sure my teacher read books to us at times, but I don't remember that. I enjoyed kindergarten very much. Once I got used to it, I didn't worry so much about being in a place with a couple of strangers. However, there were times when I felt I had to start interacting with the students in my class. They seemed nice and interested in knowing who I was. I actually wanted to make friends with my classmates. I just didn't know how that would be possible, because I couldn't speak any English. Unfortunately, there was one kid who I disliked, because of the way he always treated me. He seemed to hate me before he even got to know me; I was confused.

Was it because my face looked funny to him or the hijab I was wearing? I believe his name was Christopher. He looked mixed, chubby with big cheeks, and seemed to look angry at me almost every day. Was it because I was wearing a hijab or was I just simply awkward to him? I wasn't sure why he always made mean faces at me. I thought maybe he was going through personal problems, but that didn't make any sense because he was always happy around the other students, who were Caucasians and at least one black student. There were probably more black students, but all I remember is seeing a lot of Caucasian students. After a while I realized he didn't like me. Fortunately, I didn't care what he thought of me because I knew I didn't do anything to make him feel that way about me. One day I was put in timeout because he got me in trouble. It was the day I thought I was doing better in interacting with the rest of the students.

Four other kids and I, including Christopher, were seated at the same table. I guess they thought my accent was funny because I remember they use to laugh at everything I said. I didn't care. I was laughing along with everyone. I was so happy to see that the students found me cool and some were even teaching me to say some words in English. I remember one of the girls taught me how to say "cup" and "cookie." All of a sudden, Christopher joined and tried to teach me a new word as well. At first I kind of felt suspicious about him being so nice to me. As the forgiving person I was, I fell for his trick. He taught me to say "shut up." He had me repeat the phrase several times until everyone heard it. While he was teaching me the word, he would burst out laughing and that's when I thought something was wrong. I didn't know how to speak English, but I attempted to talk to one of my classmates, hoping she would explain to me what the phrase meant. I kept repeating the phrase "shut up" to her in order to get her to tell me the meaning of the word, but she yelled out, "Oh, Zeynab said shut up!" I remember Ms. Lynch coming up to me very frustrated. She said some things that I didn't understand at the time, but I knew she was telling me that I was in trouble. I was confused. I didn't understand why I was in trouble for repeating what someone else said. What was even more upsetting was that some students saw Christopher telling me to repeat the phrase, but no one had the courage to back me up and tell the teacher it was all Christopher's fault. It was almost like some of the students feared him. That was the first time I had gotten in trouble at school.

Unfortunately, that wasn't the only scary situation I faced in kindergarten. Wilkerson had a tradition every spring where students were able to get on balloon rides with professionals. Meanwhile, I was scared to death at such activity. When it was my turn to board the hot air balloon, I started crying. My teachers didn't know why I was crying but they later understood I was afraid of riding the balloon. In my understanding, I thought the teachers were sick of us as students and used the balloons to get rid of us. I thought the balloons were going to be used to send us somewhere far away to keep us away from them. I ran out of the school backyard and into the school, all the way to the office. Administrators asked me what was wrong. I couldn't explain it to them and continued to sob. They assured me I could stay in the office until everyone was done with their balloon rides. I felt better with their words of comfort, but continued to have fears of my teachers. It was hard to live in a new society where you had no knowledge of everything around you.

Life was not only hard for me but also for my parents. They suffered and continue to suffer the most, even today. I remember one summer night fireworks were being cracked and my mom mistook them for gunshots. So she hid me and my two sisters, Malyun and Sahara, under the bed with her. My father was out working. My mom didn't know what to do, so she thought hiding us under the bed would be best. We were under the bed in our room for about fifteen minutes until the entire firework sounds suddenly stopped. It was of course Independence Day, but we didn't know what it was at the time. No one had told us anything about the activities Americans do during certain holidays. My mother thought the event was the Somali war all over again. Even after Independence Day, she recalls hearing occasional gunshots. I wasn't aware of any of that. However, I do remember the many times my parents risked walking to the Catholic Church near our house every winter in order for me to get tutoring on certain homework assignments. We didn't have the right winter gear on during the harsh winter of 2005. There were times I didn't have homework but my parents would still take me to the Catholic Church to be a part of educational programs the church offered. We were often walking more than ten blocks and even passed railroad tracks to get to the Catholic Church. Neither of my parents had a car so we always walked. Sometimes, friends of my parents would drop us off.

My parents didn't think they were wasting their time and energy at all. They knew they wanted me and my sisters to be successful and educated. They knew exactly how they were going to make sure that we achieved those goals. Their response was always, "You only achieve success through harsh circumstances and obstacles." Just like in Kenya, where kids suffered hunger and miles and miles of walking in order to attain a quality education. Not only did my parents go to the church for my educational purposes (I was the only one going to school at the time), but also to get certain papers and documents translated. It was a daily routine because none of us knew how to read or write. Sometimes there were Somali translators at the church. When my parents couldn't get a hold of one, they would call a friend of theirs who lived on the other side of Louisville to translate for them. Often times my parents struggle was finding a translator.

When I was younger, I always cried out of sadness in seeing them suffer so much. It hurt my heart to see them look exhausted, frustrated, or even hopeless at times. I would often cry in the bathroom without them knowing. Then I would wash my face and dry myself so that they didn't know I cried. I was always afraid that if they saw me crying they would too. I always promised myself to try to do my best in school so that I can make them happy and guaranteed them that I would create a brighter future for them and my relatives in Africa, because that was our purpose in coming to the United States. I made sure I did my best in school for their sake. My parents were my motivation.

Almost on a weekly basis they lectured me and my siblings about the importance of obtaining education. They would tell us how lucky we were to get the opportunity to receive education in America and that we must really take an advantage of such opportunity. As soon as I became a third grader a few years later, my father started to really challenge us.

My dad began to help us improve our reading and writing skills. On weekdays we were only allowed to do homework and read books. During breaks, we were only able to watch the news. We could only watch PBS Kids and Nick Jr. shows on the weekends. When summer came, my dad would keep us in the house and make us read all sorts of books. We would read novels, certain elementary books, newspaper articles, teacher's edition books, and make us write two page summaries of what we read. He had us copy down excerpts from books in order to improve our penmanship. Then we were supposed to come up with our own stories three pages long and translate them in our native language to him. On top of improving our reading and writing skills, which we did from morning to afternoon, my parents wanted us to keep our language and heritage. They always told us to not lose our language. This way, Africa was still a part of us. My dad also had me translate what was reported on the news including when President Bush made remarks or when there was an election. I also had to translate what presidential candidates said. It was truly challenging, but my father pushed me to challenge myself at all times. During break time in the summer, rather than watching television, we were allowed to play with our friends outside. We were allowed to play outside from about 3 to 6 PM every summer. The rest of the evening we spent the time watching one to two shows from Disney Channel and Cartoon Network. However, we also had a curfew time which was around 8 PM. Every aspect of our lives was timed. My parents were very dedicated in showing us that if we wanted to be successful, this was the way to do it.

While still living in Dena Drive, sometimes Isha and Nurto, along with their parents, would visit us. They were our neighbors back in Kenya in the refugee camp. My mom and their mom were very close, so my mother named my sister Sahara after her, which technically in my culture makes them my nieces. The first time they stayed at our house was fun. We had pillow fights in the dark, but Nurto was having too much fun and hit me hard with the thickest pillow on my face. It nearly knocked me unconscious. After that I was always afraid to play with her. That incident was when I developed my fear of the dark until I reached third grade.

During the spring of 2005 my family moved into the neighborhood of Arcadia. Our house in Dena Drive was flooded. We had to move. There was no flood in the city at the time, but there was something wrong with the pipes in the house that caused the flood. We weren't at home when it happened. My dad was working; my mother along with me and my siblings were at the Catholic Church for homework help. The landlord couldn't do anything about the flood and said we had to move. The carpet in our living room was soaked up. The apartment was closed down for rent for a while. It's probably fixed up today for potential renters. A family most likely lives in it today. It was a very nice house in a peaceful area.

I was very upset about moving. I loved living in Dena Drive. I knew wherever we ended up next wasn't going to be as peaceful as our neighborhood in Dena Drive. I was really going to miss the sounds of the cars going up on the freeway at night. The view of the freeway and the hotel-looking building during sunset was what I was truly going to miss even more.

Arcadia homes were also town buildings as well, but they were smaller, older, and rusty. In Arcadia we had two bedrooms just like in Dena Drive. The kitchen was dirty. Things often fell apart, such as the cabinets. The cabinets were also very dusty. The bathroom was even worse. I didn't like our new home. I would often ask my mom when we would move back to Dena Drive. She would tell me that this was now our home. There were times when I saw mice running around. That was the worst experience I had in the house. I'm not a fan of little critters, especially when it was mice and rats. They're just little scary creatures to me that steal your food every once and awhile. I think the reason why they were so scary to me is because I've never seen such creatures in Kenya.

A few months later, on September 10, 2005, my brother Abubakar was born. I didn't know my mom was pregnant. She was really skinny. I never thought she was pregnant. The news of having another sibling was amazing to me. I've always loved kids, especially babies. Babies were so cute to me. They had this power to bring joy and happiness into your life. Abubakar was born in Norton Hospital. We spent the night at Isha and Nurto's house, which was the building next to us, when my mom was giving birth. It was the first time we slept over someone else's home; something my mom would never agree to in other situations. It wasn't because she didn't trust anyone; it was because she couldn't distance us from her. Since my dad was in the hospital with her we had to sleep over their house. The night my mom went into labor, we had to take our uniforms to Isha and Nurto's house so that we could change in the morning and head to school. I regretted doing that. I lost my uniform skirt, which I really loved because of its ruffles. Isha and Nurto's room was huge and you could easily lose things in it because all of their belongings were splattered on the floor. So I had to wear one of Isha's uniform skirts until they could find mine, which never happened. I spent the rest of my elementary school year wearing her skirt. I didn't like borrowing people's things, but I got used to wearing Isha's skirt since I couldn't spend the rest of my life being upset about one little skirt.

During our stay at their house, Nurto managed to give Malyun a haircut on her head and her eyebrows. Malyun was very timid and couldn't fight back for herself. However, I didn't understand what she was thinking when Nurto told her she wanted to cut her hair. It reminded me of the time when my cousin Hawa burned Malyun on the breast and her knee in Africa, because Hawa was playing with fire and couldn't control herself. People always did things to Malyun and yet she wouldn't do anything about it. It was always when I wasn't around. Isha and I were playing "shap" which was a game we played with rocks when Nurto gave Malyun a haircut. I was so mad because Malyun's hair doesn't grow fast like everyone else in the family. Plus, I wasn't a big fan of short hair when I was younger.

Meanwhile, my parents decided to name the baby Abubakar. My dad constantly claims that he always wanted to name a son Abubakar. I, on the other hand, insisted that the name came to me in a dream. In my dream, a man came to me and suggested he was my Uncle Abubakar. The dream was kind of odd. The place where the man approached me was an oasis surrounded by palm trees in the middle of a desert. According to my dream the location was supposed to be Kenya. It was a bit strange because Kenya didn't look like that. My focus was on the name Abubakar; I thought it was unique. So I told one of my parents to name the baby Abubakar. However, to this day my father still believes that it was him who decided on my brother's name. I could also be wrong, but I did however have such dream.

Abubakar was born during my first grade year. My teacher was now Ms. Butler. She had long blonde hair. She was very slim and fashionable. All the teachers wore uniform shirts with any bottom wear. Ms. Butler was always rocking her outfits. She was very cool, but talked a bit fast for me. You didn't want to get in trouble in her class, because she would confront you like she was your parent. Sometimes I would see her talking to students who got themselves in trouble. She wasn't mean and nor did she yell at students; the way she looked at you if you did something bad would scare you. My favorite part of Ms. Butler's class was when she read books to us. She had a set of books near the blackboard that she would read to us within each week. I loved when she read the jumbo books to us. They were big. We were able to see the images on the book clearly. I remember Ms. Butler read a jumbo book to us about animals that were obsessed with pizza and were in search of it. That book made me hungry. I was thinking about the pizzas rather than focusing on the story. My absolute favorite book that Ms. Butler read to us was *Wayside School Is Falling Down*. All of the characters were so unique. There was something funny about all of them. The book was truly amusing to me. It took us about two to three weeks to finish the entire book because Ms. Butler was only reading about three pages to us a day. She also read *Charlotte's Web* to us. The best part was being able to watch the actual movie. I was a visual person and often daydreamed a lot. Watching the movies from books we read was one of my favorite things to do.

Art was another subject I enjoyed in first grade. I loved to color. Our teacher was a black woman who appeared to look west-African, because of her strong accent. She was very skinny and wore dresses often. I loved the way she wore her lipstick. She had dark red lipstick on the outline of her lips and pink-reddish color in the interior of her lips. I thought it was pretty. I don't remember her name. For many weeks she would tell us about different instruments. Then, she would pass them around for us to look at. All the instruments looked like the ones used in west Africa. Sometimes, she would give us coloring pages of instruments and we would color them.

The art teacher was very calm and understanding. She was always smiling. She loved being around students. Unfortunately, I haven't seen her since first grade.

One of the students in my first grade class named Caitlin was, very skilled at drawing. She always had her long brown hair tied up in a ponytail with a ribbon that came in different colors each day with different print designs. She had pretty brown eyes and wore glasses. She could already draw an actual horse in first grade. Caitlin was very good at art and my coloring technique was actually inspired by her. I remember during the month of April we were coloring bunnies and Easter eggs. Caitlin would first outline the picture on the coloring page with a marker and then get a crayon the same color as the marker she used and colored it in. The result is a cleanly colored page. I was so amazed by how her coloring page looked, that I still use that same coloring technique today. Caitlin, along with her best friend Marie, was very smart. Both of them, and another student name Matthew, often had the highest grades in the class. I always tried to do my best just like them.

Being an immigrant was no excuse for me. At the time, I always believed I could do anything if I set my mind to it. I watched television shows that always encouraged kids to believe in themselves, so I always took those messages seriously. Caitlin was very quiet and hardly talked. Meanwhile, Marie did, but at the right time. There was a time where Marie was caught talking while the teacher was talking. The teacher warned her not to do so again, but Marie thought she got in trouble and started crying. I felt bad for her because she has never been in trouble nor was she in trouble. I guess she was not used to being told not to do something. Meanwhile, the girls were inseparable. They sat next to each other in every class and during lunch. I remember during lunch time Marie would share her lunch with me when she didn't like what her mom packed her. Sadly, her mother always put a bag of unshelled sunflower seeds in her lunch box, which she didn't like. So Marie would give it to me every day because she knew I loved sunflower seeds. There was a time when I also shared my lunch with one other person. It was my classmate Kirsten. She had a curly strawberry blond hair. I brought *samosas* to school one day for lunch. Kirsten had never seen such food before, so she kept begging me to let her taste one. At the time I only brought two and I was starving so much because I didn't have breakfast that day. So I let her try a piece of it, then she liked it and wanted more, so I had to hand her the whole samosa even though I had already bit off it. That was before I knew I had two samosas. I didn't mind her asking to try one. It looked like she was open to learning about other people's culture and I appreciated her for that.

One problem I had in first grade was that I wasn't good at writing, but my father constantly encouraged us to practice. The word *can't* was not in his dictionary. He did not like that word. Even now, he pushes me to learn new things. He always reminded me that having experience in numerous of things was good and that it would look great when I applied for a job in the future. In class we would often write prompts and the teacher would post our prompts on the bulletin board outside our classroom. Sadly, I would sometimes walk up to the bulletin board and felt like my writing was not as good as the other students. But I took that as an opportunity to work on improving it. Sometimes it was very frustrating because I didn't know a lot English words. What was even more frustrating was not being the student of the month. In order to be the student of the month you had to have a good behavior all month. You also had to do really well on your assignments all month. In terms of behavior I was great. I never got in trouble. But since there were many smart students in class, it was almost impossible for me to be student of the month. Every last Friday of the month our school had an assembly in the gym.

We all sat on the floor. The blockage that separated the gym from the cafeteria was taken down every last Friday to make room for all the students and parents who were visiting. We walked into the same song every assembly—the song called "Lean On Me." It was quite catchy. In the assembly the principal spoke to us, announcements were made; sometimes the principal and the vice president did comedy skits for us. There was a red plastic cup shaped like an apple given to students of the month for each grade level that contained treats. One of the reasons why I wanted to be a student of the month was to see what was in the apple. I always thought it was a little apple sculpture until my sister Malyun got one in her first grade year. I was a second grader. I was happy that she was able to get one. She shared all her treats and goodies with me. I also wanted to be a student of the month in order to show others that I might be an immigrant, but I am also very intelligent as well. First grade had a lot of ups and downs for me, but there were some good times too. Every once in a while we watched movies in class before certain holidays or just for fun. My favorite movies we watched as a class were *Scooby Doo*, *The Magic School Bus*, and *Charlotte's Web*. Other times, students would bring in cupcakes and other treats to celebrate their birthdays. I remember when it was Matthew's birthday. His mother brought cupcakes and Papa John's pizza. I didn't know what was going on. I thought we were supposed to choose between pizza and cupcakes. So I chose cupcakes. Turns out we were going to have both. Unknowingly, I chose cupcakes because I didn't think I would taste something so good like that ever again. I loved pizza, but as a child I loved sweets better. Ms. Butler kept asking me if I was sure I just wanted cupcakes. I responded yes even though I wanted pizza, because it tasted so good. I was nervous to change my mind. I thought I would get in trouble if I did. After I ate my cupcake, I still got a slice of pizza. I think Ms. Butler noticed I wanted one even though I said I didn't. The party was fun.

Although everyone was having a great time, Matthew didn't look too happy even on his birthday. He was always quiet and never smiled. He was nice, but I guess he was just very timid. He just acted like how he normally behaved, quiet and independent. He ate by himself on his seat while everyone else were eating together and talking to each other. His mother and Ms. Butler were standing by the front table where the party supplies were, talking about something pertaining to him. It sounded like they were talking about how well he does in school and his achievements. He was very intelligent and well-mannered; it was great to see his mother proud of him. I wasn't used to seeing parents proud of their children, especially in my Somali community. Part of it wasn't their fault. They were often too busy working extra hours to pay their bills that they didn't have time to see how their children were doing at school.

Other fun things I enjoyed doing in the spring during first grade was when we were celebrating Thunder Over Louisville. It was an annual kickoff event for the Kentucky Derby Festival. During Thunder Over Louisville fireworks were displayed over the Ohio River. It was always held on April, two weeks before the first Saturday in May. During the week before the Kentucky Derby we would create art relating to the fireworks display and the Derby Festival. We used glitter and glue to create fireworks and draw the bridge on the Ohio River. Then for Derby week Ms. Butler gave us each a coloring page of a racing horse that year. Mine was Barbara. She was very famous. Her coach was a girl with a pink jacket and I already fell in love with the horse just for that. We colored our horses and placed it on our bulletin board on the hallway. I enjoyed holidays and festivals in Kentucky because we got to color pages relating to the celebrations. I enjoyed art and coloring very much in elementary and even today. It took away my stress of personal problems and made me feel at peace.

Though first grade was fun and challenging at times, I remember the time when I made the worst decision of my life. As Muslims, females are required to wear hijab for modesty. I was only about seven years old in first grade. My parents never told me why we had to wear the hijab. In Kenya and Somalia we Somalis wore the veils even if we weren't fully practicing the religion of Islam. My family, including me, are Muslims who practiced the religion to its fullest. Though my parents made me and my sisters wear hijabs, we didn't understand why we had to put it on and why we had to dress so modestly.

I was often told to wear long skirts, because at the time I only wore pants. When my mother told me to wear certain things, I didn't hesitate, so I wore anything that was handed to me. I didn't really care. But one day I decided not to wear my hijab to school, which was a horrible decision. I put my hijab in my backpack which was in my locker. Then, the class sat down on the carpet for reading time. Every time we sat on the carpet for reading Ms. Butler would say, "Hands on your shoulders and your eyes on me." As a class we had to respond, "My hands are on my shoulders and my eyes are on you." After our response Ms. Butler asked me why I pulled my shirt up to my head. She told me I couldn't keep doing that all day, plus it was uncomfortable for me anyways. I looked weird doing it. My neck was hurting as well.

Then, I had no choice but to pull my shirt down and show my hair. It felt awkward. I was embarrassed. My hair was braided into cornrows. It was on a winter day, so the breeze of the cold air on my hair gave me chills. I felt guilty and vowed to always wear my hijab next time. My parents never found out. I took my hijab out of my book bag at the end of our reading time and put it back on. I knew I had done something my parents would not be happy about. Luckily, they never found out and I never mentioned it to them.

The whole purpose of the hijab was strange to me because when I was outside in the neighborhood I could walk around with my hair showing, but when I was going out to public places I had to wear it. I never questioned my parents about it because it was rude in my opinion. Plus, you couldn't question my parents—you had to do what they commanded you to do. A year later my parents enrolled us into an Arabic and Islamic class to learn about our religion and learn to read the Qur'an as it appeared in Arabic.

Second grade was a blast. I had the coolest teacher anyone could ever have. Ms. Nolan was a blonde, but she was probably originally a brunette before because of the brown strands in her hair. She was very funny and sweet. When it was time for recess, she let me and my friend do her hair on the benches of the playground. Ms. Nolan was too nice; I don't remember her punishing students at all for bad behavior. Students were always good because she really loved kids. She brought us treats at times. One day she baked cupcakes and brought them for us. The cupcakes had pink icing and white and pink sprinkles. I don't think the boys mind that it was pink. Everybody loved cupcakes even if it had girly colors on them.

Second grade was full of fun and laughter. Almost every day at the end of the day, we would play heads up seven up. That was my favorite game. In Ms. Nolan's class, we always got our work done so that we could spend the rest of the day outside at the playground. In my memories of attending Wilkerson, almost every time we went outside it was always sunny. The grass was almost always green. Kentucky weather was nice in the spring. I remember waking up in the morning and feeling cold, but by the end of the day when we were in school it would get really hot to the point that everyone would carry their jackets in their hands. That was normal Kentucky weather during the spring.

During recess, my friend Haway would ask Ms. Nolan if she could play with her hair. I was always shy and couldn't ask to play with her hair too. I thought it was a weird thing to ask. But when Ms. Nolan did let Haway play with her hair, I did too. Haway and I were pretty much best friends; we did everything together. We were also cousins by marriage, but she didn't know that nor did I want to tell her. I thought that would ruin our friendship. Haway and I had great times together in second grade. We experienced many funny situations together.

I remember the time when Ms. Nolan brought her dog Gizmo to class. We had already told Ms. Nolan we were afraid of dogs. She said she would make sure he wouldn't come near us. However, the students sitting near us wanted to pet him, so Gizmo ended up coming near us anyway. Haway and I jumped up on our desks and stood there screaming at the top of our lungs until Gizmo went toward Ms. Nolan at the back of the classroom. Meanwhile, one of the boys who was also Somali and sitting next to Haway was trying to shoo Gizmo away from us. I think he was scared of dogs too, but he was trying to impress me. I wasn't impressed anyway because I didn't have any feelings for boys. I spent my entire life trying to stay away from boys. Plus, my mom always told me to stay away from boys and not make friends with them. I knew she was trying to tell me I should never get a boy as a friend because it would lead to dating, but because of my age she wanted to say it in a way that I could understand. I didn't even know what boyfriend was at that age. Even till now, the only time I talk to boys is when I'm put into a group with boys at school or through my work as a community activist. I consider boys that I work with my colleagues rather than friends because I try to avoid the word *boyfriend.*

Plus, it was always awkward to me when my friends talked about how handsome some boys were. I would often change the subject and they fell for it almost every time. Also, the Somali boy was the half-uncle of my half-sister. His dad is my half-sister's grandfather, but he didn't know that. My point was that he was wasting his time. I wanted nothing to do with boys, even now.

One of the other funny memories with Haway was when the entire second grade class went to a six-day swimming class. Haway and I knew we couldn't swim and that bad things might happen during our lessons. At first, we both had no swimming suits to wear nor did we know where to buy them. But luckily Marie lent us two of her swimming suits and bought herself another one. She let us have it after the sessions. We had no idea what was going to happen in the swimming pool. Everyone was separated into groups. Every student was divided into different section of the swimming pool. My friends Haredo, Makay, and all the other Somali students were put into one group. I was kind of jealous because I wanted to swim with Haredo and Makay. Haredo was also my best friend and neighbor. Unfortunately, Haway and I were put into a group with the other students. I later felt comfortable in my group because there were no boys.

When the lesson started and Haway and I went into the water, we wouldn't let go of the railings in the pool. We were so scared to drown. The instructor kept urging us to let go but we couldn't. We were scared for our lives. When we did let go, we started climbing on top of the instructor's shoulders. In my mind, I kept saying, "It was your fault that we had to let go, I'm not trying to die today, I'm just going to climb on your shoulders." We felt bad, but we were also terrified. We were relieved when she taught us how to swim back to the edge of the pool where we felt safe. After the sessions were over, we kept laughing about our experience for several days.

During the autumn of my third grade year on September 10, 2007, my fourth sister Fatima was born. We called her Fay-yaray for short. She was surprisingly born on the same day as Abubakar. She was a very pink baby. She didn't have brown skin like us. She was born completely pink. She had tiny Asian eyes and nose. When people came to see her they would joke and ask my mom if she was the daughter of Jackie Chan. Jackie Chan was the only Asian Somalis knew because of the movie Rush Hour, which many people watched that year. My mom didn't find the jokes funny. She thought people were thinking she cheated on my dad. My mother was always serious about her family life and hated when people had unpleasant statements to say. I also thought my sister was a little different, but I thought that was cool. I've always wanted sisters of different ethnicities when I was younger. I was definitely happy to have another baby sister. That meant I had more sisters to play with. Plus, I loved the idea of being looked up to and I wanted more sisters so that I could be a role model to them.

During my third grade year in school, I started to experience things that were not new to immigrant students. Some teachers at school failed to realize that language and academics isn't the only troubling circumstances immigrant students face in the classroom. While most students are able to fully communicate with teachers about their problems and struggles, immigrant students don't get that opportunity. For instance, a student faced hardships at home due to family problems which is normal for immigrant families. Because the student sees his parents struggling he will likely be moody and disruptive in class because he can't tell his teachers about his problem. For many students, communicating their problems is often a partial solution to their problems, because they know that people are looking out for them and willing to help them cope with their problems.

I experienced a similar situation when I was in third grade. One day I came to school with a fever. I constantly slept throughout my classes with my head down on the desk. I remember during math class, Mrs. Collins, who was my math teacher at the time, was in the middle of teaching the class. She saw me sleeping throughout the lesson and suggested I "flip the strip" until it was on blue. We had small pieces of strips in the classroom with all the students name labeled on the packs of the strips.

The strips were small laminated papers colored red, yellow, green, and blue. Green meant that you were good, yellow was a warning, red meant that you had to have ten minutes of time out during free time, and blue meant that you couldn't have any free time and had to sit on the bench all day until recess was over. Mrs. Collins wasn't aware that I had fever. She must have thought I was awake all night watching television or something. I couldn't tell her that I had a fever because one, I could barely move a muscle and two, I've always been afraid of talking to my teachers. She suffered from migraines so I never really saw her look happy. That might be why I couldn't talk to her about anything. Her co-teacher Mrs. Armstrong wasn't there that day, but I always felt comfortable talking to Mrs. Armstrong. Mrs. Collins and Mrs. Armstrong switched every day. Mrs. Armstrong taught us Mondays and Wednesdays while Mrs. Collins taught us Tuesdays, Thursdays, and Fridays.

I didn't have the gut to tell Mrs. Collins I had a fever and that's why I kept sleeping in class. Mrs. Armstrong was a very happy teacher. She came to help me with assignments even when I didn't ask her for help. She sometimes knew if we were feeling down or not in a good mood. The day I was sick, when free time came, I spent the whole time sitting on the bench. I didn't really care because I needed to take a nap and that's what I did during that time. No one asked why I was sleeping so much. After recess we had our last class, which was called "The Assessment Lab." I believe it was a class where we learned to write essays, because all we did in that class was write. But by the end of the class when we all got in line to go back to our home room, I started throwing up. So I ran to the bathroom as quick as I could while still throwing up.

I felt a lot better after that. My headache and my fever disappeared at that moment. I remained in the bathroom for about ten minutes, because I thought I would throw up again. Then, I went to the office to change and went back to the classroom. I couldn't go home since it was the end of the day anyways. However, I'm sure me sleeping in class started to make sense to Mrs. Collins when I returned to class. I didn't blame her for not understanding. Third grade wasn't always bad. It was fun during the holidays because we got to watch movies related to the holiday that was going to be celebrated the coming days. Whenever we had movie days, the teachers brought food and drinks. Sometimes some of the students would bring treats in for everyone. My favorite was during the Christmas holiday where we got to watch *How the Grinch Stole Christmas* and *The Polar Express*. We got lots of Christmas candies and cookies among other treats.

School was very important to me. One of my best memories in school was being able to attend ESL classes with Ms. Otley. She was perhaps the best ESL teacher anyone could ever have. People often ask me why my English is so good and why I sound like a native speaker. It was all because of Ms. Otley. Also, because when I learn a new language I always tried to pronounce every word as a native speaker would. With the help of Mr. Muhammad with translation, she taught all the African students at Wilkerson how to read and write successfully.

Every day during third hour, Ms. Otley would grab me and some of my other Somali and Sudanese classmates to her classroom to work on our reading and writing skills. She did this one at a time. While she was helping the previous students who were there before me, she would let me get on the computer and play games on educational websites such as PBS Kids, Game Goo, and Star Fall. My two favorite sites were always PBS Kids and Star Fall.

On Star Fall, I was able to listen to every letter of the alphabet and hear its correct pronunciation. I was also able to listen to books being read to me and hear the pronunciation of each word in a particular story. Meanwhile, PBS Kids had all sorts of fun activities and games. I could watch episodes of my favorite shows which included *Maya & Miguel*, *It's A Big Big World, Arthur, Caillou,* and *Dragon Tales.* My favorite activities were coloring certain characters on the online coloring book and building a nest house for Snook.

When it was my turn to sit down with Ms. Otley, she had me read books to her. Then, she would pull out some words on index cards and tell me to repeat them. After that, I had to trace and write certain words and sometimes even my name. It was a daily task, which I enjoyed very much. I loved the one-on-one attention I got with her. I couldn't get that in my regular classroom. Not only did Ms. Otley help us academically, but she would take all the ESL students out on field trips to theaters and fun zones.

I remember the day she took all fifty or more of us to go see *The Nutcracker.* The play was very scary to me. The giant rats scared the living out of me and the creepy music that played whenever the rats came out. I was overjoyed when she took us all to McDonalds after the play. The McDonalds we went to has a huge playground area, which was so fun. It had slides and tunnels. We even got to sit on the lap of Ronald McDonald. Even though I enjoyed the trip, the play gave me nightmares in the coming days. I couldn't even use the bathroom at night for several days. So, I decided to deliberately wet my bed for a couple of nights, which only made my mother mad.

As I grew older, I started to realize ESL class was keeping me from learning other skills. By the time I was in third grade, I was reading and writing at my grade level. However, my problem and weakness was math—one reason being because I wasn't present in class when math was being taught. Ms. Otley would pull me out of the classroom every day during math class in third grade. I remember knowing I was horrible at subtraction when it came to borrowing. I knew how to do simple subtraction already, but borrowing was a difficult concept for me. The frustrating part was that Ms. Otley only taught us how to read and write; math wasn't one of the lessons we were taught in ESL class. I knew Ms. Otley would've listened if I had told her I wasn't good at a particular subject and would've done everything she could to help me get better at it. But of course, the shy person I was I couldn't tell any of the teachers my problem. During math hour I would sit in class feeling hopeless about never understanding the concept of borrowing. Things then started to change when I found out we were moving. I still didn't understand the whole borrowing concept.

It all happened during the summer of my fourth grade year. I was going to be a fourth grader a month later. I was playing with my friends Nimo, Haredo, and Sawoomu on a July night when my father suddenly called me to come in the house for a second. My father and I were very close. He often told me things before anyone else. I came in the house and into the kitchen where my father was sitting. He then broke the news to me. He told me that we would be moving to Milwaukee soon. As soon as I heard the news, I felt my heart tear into pieces. I asked my dad why we were moving. He responded that we were moving in order to live closer to our family members and attend an Islamic school so that we could learn more about our religion.

At first I didn't understand why we were moving, because all of my dad's friends and some relatives were living in Louisville already. But then, it became clear to me that my dad missed being around his cousins, uncle, and aunts. My dad grew up in Somalia with his aunt and uncle who were around his age. They were all raised by my dad's great-aunt. He missed that close family niche. Also, because my dad enjoyed visits from his cousins from Milwaukee, it made him want to move even more. My dad is very close to his uncle. They are like best friends; they called each other almost every day to talk about different issues or share their solutions to family problems.

I knew it was my great-uncle who encouraged my father to move to Milwaukee because he was always very good at motivating people to do things. My father told me not to tell anyone that we were moving. As soon as I went back outside to play with my friends, they asked me what happened because I obviously had a sad expression on my face. I told them nothing and continued to play tag with them. Since our moving day was unpredictable and unknown to me and my siblings, I tried to make every moment of my time in Louisville count. I knew my parents weren't telling us because they thought we would panic.

When August came around, school was back in session. I was now a fourth grader and had new teachers. In contrast to my third grade year where I had two teachers, I now had four teachers. Ms. Boyd was my math teacher, Ms. Pritchett was the reading teacher, and Mr. Decker was the science teacher. I forgot the name of my history teacher, but he was pretty cool. I no longer had Ms. Otley as my ESL teacher. I guess I advanced out of ESL class. I was now in a program where I read books in my grade level just like all the other fourth graders in school. I forgot the name of my teacher for the program since I didn't really get to know him in such short amount of time, but he was super cool. I mean really cool! From the books he read to us, I learned cool new words like *tarantula*. It was a pretty cool word for such poisonous creature. I remember the day he described the behaviors of tarantulas to me and two other ESL students. It was very amusing. He tried to make us laugh all the time and was great at it.

I remember the day we were moving as if it was a week ago. My sisters, Malyun and Sahara, and I had only been in school for about three weeks. School started Monday, August 11, 2008, and we were moving on Thursday the 28th right after we came from school. Those weeks were Sahara's first time attending school. She often cried a lot. I had to take her to her class every morning and every time I tried going to my class she would cry. I would try to cheer her up and tell her I'll be there to walk her to the bus after school was over. No matter what I said I had to leave her sobbing every morning so that I wasn't marked tardy. I felt horrible about it, but I had to. When I finally came to get her in the afternoon she would run toward me and hug me and wouldn't let go of my hands. I thought it was cute, but I also understood what she was going through.

When I first started kindergarten, I had no one to talk to or hug like Sahara did. I had to let things happen and go with it. I remember coming home on the 28th of August with pretty much everything packed up. Everything was wrapped in boxes. All of our toys and bikes were out to be given to our neighbors who were all my distant cousins. I was so upset. I left almost all of my school supplies in my locker. I didn't even get to say good-bye to my friends at school including Haway, Marie, and

Haredo. I didn't get to say good-bye to Ms. Otley, Mr. Muhammad, and all my previous teachers. I didn't understand why my dad didn't let us know ahead of time that it would be so soon. All those times I thought we were going to move a year later, not a month later. Sadly, I couldn't do anything about it and had no choice but to get ready to settle in a different place with different people for the second time. I was disappointed that I was leaving my friends behind, but I was also looking forward to being able to see my cousins again in Milwaukee.

On the day that we were moving, my uncles came—Abass and Maliko, who were my dad's cousins. In Somali culture, your parent's cousins are considered your aunts or uncles because the word *cousin* is used the same way as brother or sister. They came together to help us load our belongings in the car. When we were all done packing, they drove their red minivan with all our belongings while my parents and my siblings and I rode in our blue Sienna Toyota minivan. It was pitch dark when we left. All of our neighbors came to say good-bye to us three hours before. When we left, all I could think of was the many wonderful memories I had in Louisville, especially at Wilkerson.

One of my all-time favorite memories was going to the school's library every day. When I was in second grade, I read pretty much all of the Junie B. Jones and Arthur book series. My favorite Junie B. Jones books were *Captain Field Day* and *Almost Flower Girl*. I always read all the Junie B. Jones books in one day, from the library to the school bus and sometimes at home later the day I checked it out. I just loved Junie B., the main character. I always read the books to find out what Junie B. did next in her scenarios. *Almost Flower Girl* was my favorite out of the series because I was given an opportunity to be a flower girl for my neighbor's wedding, and I needed to know what to expect as a flower girl. I was eight years old.

At the wedding, while it was fun being a flower girl, my partner left me on the dance floor by myself. She was so nervous that she started crying. It was probably because hundreds of people were looking at us and the camera lights were flashing on our faces. While I wasn't use to all that, I was thinking about being the best flower girl I could be and wowing the crowds with my dance moves that I didn't have. My partner—who I believe was named Layla—and I had a silvery long dress on with our matching ponytails. Her hair was longer. Prior to the wedding, I asked my mom why I couldn't wear weave. She responded that Layla and I had long hair and that we didn't need weave. I wasn't comfortable showing my hair, which is why I asked for weave.

Meanwhile, *Captain Field Day* was also my favorite book because Wilkerson held an annual field day event on the last day of each school year. It was always a fun and exciting day for all the students in school. We received free candies of our choice, and played many amusing games, including relay races. It was a whole day of fun. We didn't have classes on field days. It was always held in our school's backyard, which was humongous. I really enjoyed experiencing such event, and so reading it from Junie B. Jones's book always made me look forward to field day. I always read the book the days leading up to field day. Also, once every spring there was a day in the library when we could get one free book and an accessory with it, whether it was bookmarks, stickers, pens, or mechanical pencils. Though I really needed bookmarks because of all the books I was reading in elementary, I always chose mechanical pencils. They were just so pretty to me with the various colors and patterns on them, especially the neatness it produced in writing. Most of the books I chose had to have some sort of pink coloring on them, which is why I always picked out Hello Kitty books or fairy books. There was always a section that was all pink and that's where I went each spring. Pink was my favorite color at the time. I have never seen such a beautiful color before. As I grew older, I would eventually fall in love with the color purple.

While on the road to Milwaukee, I also recall my time living in the Arcadia neighborhood from the end of 2005 until the summer of 2006. We had so many great memories. Every weekday after school we used to go to the community center to get homework help, get snacks, and play many fun games. We would play soccer and tag in the backyard of the community center after completing homework. Sometimes, Ms. Otley came to the center to help us with reading comprehension. It was so fun having a teacher from school come into our neighborhood to help the students. All of the students at the center really liked her. This gave me a chance to brag about her being my ESL teacher at school. I just loved being able to see her after school in my neighborhood. In the summer, the staff of the community center would take us out on field trips.

One summer, we went swimming at a park miles away from Louisville. There were about thirty ESL students and maybe four or five staffs with us. I almost died in the swimming pool at our trip because Nurto pressed my head against the water for about ten seconds. I became very angry.

She was doing that to other students who were younger than her as well. I didn't understand why she was doing such dangerous act, so I stepped out of the pool and didn't go back in it again to avoid death. We did camping activities like making s'mores, eating wheat crackers, and hiking in the woods. Besides the pool incident, I really did enjoy the trip. However, since I didn't have a swimming suit, I swam with my underwear and a tank top. I'm still surprised my mom let me wear it.

When we left Louisville, though I would miss my friends and family, there were some memories I wanted to leave behind and hoped it didn't haunt me when we settled in Milwaukee. The most horrific event that occurred was when I lost four of my precious cousins. They were murdered by their father. I've only seen the three oldest since we rode the same bus to school. We didn't attend the same school. The bus went to different schools. This is common in Louisville. Sadly, it happened during my third grade year in the summer of 2006.

The two weeks that we rode the bus together were the first and last time I would ever see them. I knew they were my cousin's kids, but they didn't know we were related. They were very young. The oldest was Siad, but we called him Sidi like his father. He was eight years old, a year older than me. The next oldest was Famaay. Shani and Khadija were the youngest. Sadly, I never got to see Khadija, who was only two years old. When I asked to see her pictures after they were buried, I was told their pictures were burned as well. In my culture, when people were deceased their pictures were supposed to be burned because the deceased were no longer living. Their clothing and shoes were given away to other kids.

During the many-month-long funeral, I put on Famay's shoes one night, hoping I could feel her spirit somehow. Thinking about that now, I feel kind of stupid. Their murder was very graphic, according to their mother and grandmother. It all started when my mom's cousin, their grandmother, had suspicion that something was wrong with the house. This she got from the constant howling of the owl on the tree every night. To some Somalis the howling of the owl was a sign of bad news.

One day my cousin Fatuma, the children's mother, decided to go on a trip to Ohio to buy clothes with a male cousin of hers. Her male cousin was the driver. There were other women coming with her as well. In my religion, it's wrong to go somewhere with a male who isn't married or closely related to you as a female. You can't be around a male cousin either or touch him, because he's able to marry you if you wanted. Her husband,

Sidi (Siad), became very jealous that my cousin was going to the trip with her male cousin. He didn't want to see any man near her. He suspected that she was cheating on him with her cousin. He told her not to go, but she did anyway, because the trip was very important to her.

She wanted to buy new Somali clothing for her kids. So she left. The kids were left with their grandmother and their father. When my cousin came back several hours later, she told her mother she could leave now that she was back. The grandmother however, suspected that something bad would happen and kept telling my cousin, Fatuma, that she wanted to stay.

My cousin kept urging her mom to go back to her house to care for her other grandkids who lost their mother in a car accident. She finally left after my cousin stated that everything would be okay. Sidi, my cousin's husband, wanted to make sure the grandmother left so he could finally kill the kids. As soon as she left around midnight, he first came to my cousin in the living room and knocked her unconscious with a machete, so that when he was murdering the kids, she wouldn't be able to contact the police. He also raped her, which led to her pregnancy with a fifth child (who's currently the oldest).

Then, he went to the kids one by one. The oldest, Sidi, was struck with a knife in his head and then beheaded. Investigators stated that according to his injuries, Sidi showed no sign of struggle, which meant that he was either knocked unconscious first or was sleeping when he was killed. Second, he slit the throat of Famaay. Third, Shani the four-year-old was beheaded while she was pleading to her father saying, "Why are you doing this to us, Father?" He cut her fingers off first then beheaded her as well. All the girls showed signs of trying to fight back their father during their murders.

Every time people hear about Shani's last words they get emotional. She was so young and innocent. The last one to be beheaded was Khadija, the two-year-old. She was an easy slaughter because she was so small. While my cousin was knocked unconscious she could hear her kids screaming for help and their blood gushing on the floor. Sidi didn't behead the mother, because he thought she was already dead when he knocked her unconscious. He knew the kids were very important to her so he killed them. It was typical for older men to get jealous when their younger wives were seen with younger men around their age.

When my cousin gained consciousness, she slowly tried to reach the phone and called the police. By that time, Sidi had already left the house. The police came to her house a few minutes later. A citywide search for

Sidi began. The news of the murder was all over the city of Louisville and dominated headlines and local news channels. Sidi was later caught driving a truck after the sun rose hours later by someone who had recognized his face on television. He surrendered and turned himself in at the police station. The news of the murders of my cousins brought a huge wave of sadness to the whole Somali community as well as to the city of Louisville. Everyone was mourning perhaps until the rest of the year. It took my cousin Fatuma and her mom many years of mourning because the kids spent most of their time with the two of them.

My cousin Fatuma was hospitalized so many times and became mentally disabled for a long period of time due to the loss of her children. The kids were very well-mannered and were hardly seen outside. After they were buried, many people started making conspiracies about their death and flashbacked the problems that might have led to the murder. According to my mom, Sidi came to our house a week before the murder to tell my mom that he had been having problems with his marriage to my cousin. He stated that they would argue a lot and that she was so stubborn.

As my mom always told every parent who had problems, she told him to think about their children and what they want for them in the future, as that was more important, and to stop arguing in front of them because it would sadden them. She also told him to forgive his wife and just keep praying for things to get better. When my mom told me that he came to my house once, I was frightened. I had never met or seen him. The one time I heard about him is when he kills his children. I was in shock. I kept thinking about how he would probably come back to kill us one day now that he knew where we lived. The day I was told about the murder, I didn't eat the whole day and slept with the light on. Malyun and Sahara didn't know what was going on so they obviously didn't understand why I was so scared. My mom and I didn't mention it to them since they were too young to understand.

Others in the Somali Bantu community were talking about the fact that the woman who previously lived in the same house of the murders killed her own son as well. It was sort of like a conspiracy everyone had. It was said that an African American woman who lived in the house shot her only child, a toddler fatally. People started claiming that it was a house full of bad spirits that made people kill.

My mom's cousin, the grandmother of the kids stuck to her belief that the owl was telling them that something was wrong with the house.

I remember one day the children's dad came to pick them up from the bus stop and embraced them. He then handed them some candy. Some witnesses say that he asked the kids how the candy tasted. They responded "very sweet." Witnesses say that he then told them "that's how sweet you guys will be" in our native language. That response gave people chills. The grandmother of the children mentioned that when my cousin left for Ohio, she was awake the whole night. She just knew something terrible would happen that night. People were even saying that she was awake the two nights before the murders, as well. She wasn't quite sure what the bad feeling was at the time. She even wanted to take the kids to her house and spend the night there, but the father refused. He suggested that if she was going to babysit them, it would be at their house. According to my cousin, she and her children used to live in Portland, Oregon, but they moved to Louisville to get away from him. She also told the court that he had threatened to kill her and her children once before.

Of course the only thing on everyone's mind at the time was why anyone would kill their own children and who consented that he marry my cousin, a young innocent girl. She was married to him when she was thirteen years old back in Africa. My mom told me my cousin's mother married her to him because he had money at the time.

Some families gave their daughters away for marriage in order to get money from it. Sidi was about twenty years older than my cousin. In Africa, parents married their daughters to older men on purpose, mainly because he had some money that the girl's family could benefit from. Some girls were lucky and were arranged into marriage by men around their age group. I don't understand why many Somali parents married their daughters to men that they knew nothing about.

Many marriages of young girls to old men resulted in domestic abuse or seclusion away from society. I have a great-cousin who was also married to an older man. At the time of the murders he was in his late fifties, while she was still in her twenties. She is never seen outside. Her husband doesn't want her to see other men because he's afraid she might fall in love with a better-looking, younger man. As loyal as she was, she always did what he wished. Despite all that, she lives a miserable life. She has about six kids (or more now) from him and is never seen smiling. Her father was the one who married her to her husband. I didn't understand how he could live with such decision. Most fathers would want their daughters to be happy.

In Islam, Muslims should know that they can't force their children into a marriage they don't want to be in. That was forbidden by the Prophet Muhammad himself. From relationships similar to my cousins', my father told me that if I reached the age of marriage I am free to marry whoever I want, no matter what my future spouse's ethnicity is as long as he was a good practicing Muslim. As good as that may sound, I hated when people talked about boys and marriage to me. I always felt that I was too young to hear or even talk about such things. Any time people brought that topic up, I felt like punching something.

Meanwhile, I was so upset about the fact that I never got to tell my cousins that we were related. They only knew me as one of the kids on the bus who would at times say hi to them. When we went to school every morning after the murder, every Somali Bantu child in Louisville was advised by their parents not to talk about the murder in school. Our parents were afraid that they would somehow be arrested just by being related to the murdered kids. I didn't understand why they were so scared to talk about it.

Since my mother made me promise not to tell, I had to lie to my teachers when they asked if I was related to the children. I believe I admitted it to one of my teachers though because I trusted her. Plus I couldn't keep secrets or promises for long when I was young. I felt guilty. People could easily tell if I was lying. As a child I was also a motor mouth. I was also nosy. I was always in my parents' conversations, and when the adults in my neighbor were talking, I would just suddenly wind up in their conversation. My mom would always tell me, "You can engage in adult conversations when you turn fifteen." But I never listened. Plus my mom's friends and our neighbors loved me for being so nosy because I always gave direct answers and knew the answer they were looking for. They thought I was too mature for my age. It was funny because I always thought the same thing. Because of my maturity, even now my parents don't make any decisions without asking for my input.

In the meantime, my cousins' heads were all buried in one grave. Their bodies were probably placed in that same grave as well. I overheard my mom say that they were all buried in one grave, because they were very young. After their burial, I had many visions where they all got out of the grave and their skeletons came walking to my house in search for me. I was still in complete shock for many months. I couldn't believe that someone you've seen a few hours ago can just suddenly die minutes later.

I didn't think about death so much when I was younger until this incident took place.

My parents would watch the news to see what would happen to Siad Ali Biyad (the murderer's full name). They always prayed that he would stay in jail until his death. He was later sentenced to life in prison on June 7, 2011. The town building they resided in was demolished and rebuilt again a year later.

The second-worst situation I experienced in Kentucky was the night I thought I had lost my mother. It was during a summer evening. I was outside at our front door chatting with friends. The older boys in the neighborhood were playing soccer in a small yard behind our town building. My mom decided to go visit my baby sister Fatuma's *samoy's* house. When she went to visit Fatuma's *samoy* (someone you're named after), they decided to take a walk around the yard the boys were playing soccer in. Then out of nowhere, one of the boys kicked the ball so high that it hit the back of my mother's head. She was knocked unconscious. She was lying on the ground similar to the way victims of murders would lay.

Her hijab fell off and was a few inches away. Her hair was visible for everyone to see. I saw the whole population of Somali neighbors in the Park Hill neighborhood come toward the scene to look at my mom lying on the ground. I asked my friends if we should go see what was going on. I assumed that my cousin Asha was dropped again and broke some more bones. While we were walking to the scene, I saw my aunt Isha crying and running past me. Everyone looked so sad. I then tried to walk through the crowd to take a good look at who the victim was.

There she was—my mother lying on the ground with her hair and arms uncovered. No one could tell if she was breathing. Her eyes were shut completely. As soon as I saw her, I was in shock and broke down into tears. I was crying so much that I didn't even see the paramedics come and place her on the ambulance. My friend Sawumoo then took me to her house, which was the building across my building, along with my siblings. I spent the whole night crying until I got a call from my dad saying that my mom would be okay.

Luckily, I had a really great friend who was constantly trying to calm me down and stating that my mother wasn't going to die. I believed in my heart that she wouldn't. I kept telling myself that God wouldn't take my mother from me, because I was too young to experience such tragedy. I started thinking about life without my mother, which made me cry even more.

A few days after my mother left the hospital, the boy who kicked the ball to her head came to apologize to my mother. Ever since the incident, he hadn't come outside because he felt so bad. His mother urged him to visit my mother, which he was too nervous to do. I, along with my mother and others, saw the incident as an accident. We didn't want him to keep blaming himself for something that was nondeliberate.

Another horrible experience in Kentucky was the many times my parents would argue about things I really didn't understand at the time. According to pretty much all of my aunts on both my mom's and dad's side of the family, my parents argued since I was a baby. They even got divorced a year after I was born. That explained why my sister was two years younger than me, because usually Somali women gave birth every year. When they somehow remarried, my mom became pregnant with my sister Malyun. Sometimes I would think about how life would be if they hadn't remarried. I wouldn't have Malyun by my side and would be controlled by an evil stepfather.

I was also told of a story where my mom knocked my dad unconscious. I didn't blame her for acting that way because she was previously in an abusive marriage. Her previous husband often abused her just because he felt like it. There were no police in Kenya to stop incidents like that. Also, my father was and still is very stubborn. Oftentimes when my parents argued it made sense to me.

In Louisville while my brother Abubakar was only about a few months old, my dad had gotten married to another woman without telling my mom. She didn't find out until she heard the neighbors talking about it and it became a rumor. My mom became upset that people knew what was going on in my dad's life but she didn't.

The following year in 2006, my dad's second wife gave birth to his fourth daughter. Her name was Muna. My dad and her mother had already divorced a few months before she was born. My dad took us to Norton Hospital, the same place my mom gave birth to Abubakar, to see Muna. At first I wasn't sure if I should go because my mother was still upset about the whole situation. I thought me and my sisters would get in trouble if we went to visit our half sister. When we came back home, my sisters told her about our visit to see our baby sister. My mom didn't get mad at all. Instead, she asked us how it went. I was relieved. I should've known my mom was very kind to people even if they hurt her at one point.

Usually my parents argued when we were at school. However, when we were living in the Park Hill neighborhood, my parents would argue nonstop. It was on an almost monthly or sometimes weekly basis. On every occasion of their arguments I would cry. Malyun, Sahara, and Abubakar had no idea what was going on so they always continued playing around while my parents were arguing. I, on the other hand, would cry from the beginning of their argument to the end. My biggest fear was always them ending up divorcing. Even at the age of eight I didn't want to see that happen. I knew I wouldn't be able to succeed in life without them together. I never told them why I was crying when they asked, but they knew I cried every time they argued. I was afraid that if I told them I was afraid that they would divorce, they would proceed to divorce. I thought they would take that as a great idea, so I always kept it to myself.

Park Hill was filled with Somali Bantu families. We were all surrounded by each other. Each building had a unit number and the address on the door. We lived in 1626 B. Moore Court Building 26. My friends Sawumoo and Haredo lived in Building 25 right in front of us. Nimo lived in the same building as me. Our houses were connected. In my room, I could hear her and her sister Muna talk, through the wall. Sometimes I thought about what would happen if I drilled a hole through the wall so that we could talk to each other and have sleepovers without our parents knowing. I had a wild imagination as a child. That all seemed too risky and dangerous, so I never bothered to do it.

Most days, I had the best time living in Park Hill. I never understood why it was called Park Hill because it wasn't the most attractive place to live. There were murders almost every week. I saw RIP written all over the place even on street light poles and the sidewalk. I knew it meant someone died, but I didn't understand what the letters stood for. The neighborhood was only settled by Africans and African Americans. I remember being so scared when we moved in the neighborhood in June of 2006 because some houses looked like there had been a shootout.

It was a very hot day. We were moving from Arcadia. My dad left me in the house by myself while he went to the parking lot to get the rest of the boxes. The parking lot was a block away. The door was unlocked. I stood by the door because I was so scared. In case someone came through the window, I would just run out the door. While I was waiting for my dad to come back, a guy came out of the door next to us. I was so scared. He was big and dark. I assumed that if he had seen me he would try to kill me, so I moved away from the door and went farther into the living room. When I saw my dad coming through the window I walked back to the door again. I've never been so relieved to see him. I also thought the guy would pull out a gun and shoot my dad.

Luckily that didn't happen. As soon as my dad came in, I stood by the door again because I felt brave with my dad's presence. The guy waved at me with a smile and I waved back. I didn't feel scared anymore because he seemed nice after a while. I eventually learned his name, which was Terry. He lived next door to us with his sisters Missy, Joy, Dorothy, Berta, and their mother. After a couple of weeks we had gotten close to them. Missy would braid our hair sometimes. We spent most of our time playing with Dorothy and Berta, the younger siblings. Berta was two years older than me. Dorothy was probably one or two years older than Berta. We spent every summer playing with dolls and their makeup set. It was fun. Missy would do our hair in their house. Our best time together was during Independence Day. Missy and her siblings would buy a lot of firecrackers and teach us how to light them. It was too scary for me, but the African boys in the neighborhood did it. Being able to bond with Missy and her siblings put an end to the stereotypes Africans had about African Americans. Some Africans had assumptions that African American men were violent and dangerous. It also put an end to the stereotypes African Americans had about Africans. We now started to see ourselves as equals. Since our parents as Somali Bantus never went to school, they didn't know about the history of slavery or African Americans. Somali Bantu parents feared African Americans because they were afraid of being shot or killed. This was of course from hearing about the shootings in our neighborhood on television and even witnessing some shootings, which all involved African American teens at the time. Most of the shootings were between young adults fighting over girls.

I didn't understand why our people feared everything in America. They acted as if their lives were put on surveillance, as if the US government was constantly watching their every move. When I went out to ride my bike one summer, my mom told me not to ride my back in certain parts of the neighborhood. But I didn't listen; I rode my bike all over the neighborhood. That day when I went riding behind our building, a man with braided hair came up to me and hit me in the eye. I was the only one outside in that area.

I had the Aquafina bottle label on my eyes. I didn't see who the man was. After that incident, I never went bike riding again. I was afraid I would get kidnapped the next time.

Many horrible things took place in Park Hill. They all usually happened in the summer. I wasn't present at the setting of this incident, but one summer two males were shooting each other right in front of the door of my cousin Makkah's house. They were in a big argument about a girl they both dated. Apparently, the girl was dating both of them simultaneously. They both wanted her to themselves so they each grabbed a gun and kept shooting at each other. Luckily, no one died, but I thought the whole incident was vacuous. If I were one of them I would have just left the girl for the other guy and not waste my time with a woman like that. I would have told myself that there are a lot of other beautiful, trustworthy women out there. Why spend my time with this one? As violent as the men were, I'm surprised they didn't put their anger on her, as well. Maybe they did, but I haven't heard of anyone talk about what they did to her after the incident or if they were arrested for the shooting.

The most tragic event that occurred that summer was when my friend Halima's brother was electrocuted. Halima was the same age as Malyun. I was nine years old. Her brother was around the age of thirteen or fourteen. He and two of his friends were playing around the electricity plant, which was bizarrely located in Park Hill. They were being the ludicrous teenage boys they were and decided to get into the power plant.

Halima's brother declared that he was brave enough to go inside the fence of the power plant and touch the electric wires. As brave as he claimed he was, he went into the fence and touched the wires. Then out of nowhere, his whole body was electrocuted. The T-shirt and pants he was wearing were shredded up to his chest. It was as if his shirt and pants were shredded by a shredder. He had burn wounds all over his body. Smoke was still emanating from his body. His friends were able to bring him to the porch of his house. The house was across the street from the electricity plant.

He was brought home crying. One of his friends knocked at the door and told his mother to come out. As soon as she came out she was shocked at what she saw. She was speechless and almost looked paralyzed when she saw her son. She then burst into tears. It was a beautiful sunny day. Everyone was outside enjoying the sunny weather. When they saw Halima's mother crying, almost the whole neighborhood came to her front porch.

People all over the neighborhood surrounded the porch. Everyone was curious about what had happened. The area was crowded. People tried to get a glimpse of what had occurred. Almost all of the mothers were crying, including my mom. My mom described Halima's brother as having his skin cooked like meat. The ambulance was called as soon as possible. It took a while for them to arrive.

Things started to make sense to me that day. A few minutes before Halima's brother was taken to their porch, the whole neighborhood had a power outage. I was in the middle of a television program when out of nowhere the television turned off. It was a bright sunny day. I thought it was weird that the television would just suddenly turn off on a nice day. There wasn't a thunderstorm. I was a bit confused. But when Halima's brother was electrocuted, it all made sense. As soon as he touched the electrical wires, all the power in the area shut down. Oddly, approximately three minutes after the television turned off it was turned back on again. I wasn't aware of what had happened, nor did anyone else, so I continued to watch my program like nothing ever happened. After the incident, Halima's brother didn't go to school for the rest of the year. He had surgery after surgery all year long. It was truly saddening. His friends mentioned that they tried to get him to not enter the fence, but he claimed he was brave enough and refused to stop.

Milwaukee: A City of Change

Moving to Milwaukee was absolutely bewildering. I could feel a small burst of energy making me feel that moving to this city would be life-changing for me and would open a lot of doors for me. I felt that a lot of accomplishments and excitement awaited me in such small city. I was definitely excited that I would be much closer to my aunts and cousins again just like in Africa. Something told me that I was destined to live in Milwaukee and that I was to fulfill my dreams, even though I didn't really know what my dreams were. I was only nine years old. We moved to Milwaukee on the evening of August 28, 2008. I would turn ten years old a few weeks later on September 12.

My family, which now consisted of my parents, Abubakar, Fatuma, Malyun, Sahara, and I were living in my uncle Maliko's house for a few months until we found a house of our own. My uncle lived in an apartment on Richard Street located on the southside of Milwaukee. He only had one bedroom, which meant that Abubakar, my sisters, and I slept in the room in one big bed. My parents and Fatuma, who was one-year-old, slept with my parents on a bed that was placed in the living room by the entrance door.

Despite the small space we had in the house, we also had bed bug problems. My uncle was living with my teenage uncles until we got our own place. However, neither he nor we knew that the mattresses in the house had bed bugs. We didn't know that was the case until the month we were moving to our new house. My mom suspected there might have been bed bugs in the bed we were sleeping on when she noticed my siblings and me constantly scratching every day. Sometimes we scratched until we bled. That's when we had to start sleeping with my parents in the living room. The search for a new house became urgent. I don't think my uncle knew he had bed bugs. Then again, it was weird because my uncle didn't have any bite marks. It was a mystery to me as to how he survived with bed bugs.

Three days after we settled in Milwaukee, our relatives from my father's side of the family came to visit us. They lived in the downtown area just a couple blocks away from Marquette University. It was very emotional and heartwarming to see them again. I got to see my aunts Ayan, Khadija, Fatuma, Samira, and Anisa including some of my uncles who were either teenagers or around my age group, for the first time since leaving Kenya.

During the last few days of summer on certain weekends, we would visit them since we didn't know anyone in our neighborhood. We would leave in the morning and return home somewhere after magrib prayer. It was very convenient for us to visit all of my cousins, aunts, and uncles, because they all lived in the same neighborhood. I remember every time we visited them I wished I lived in their neighborhood with them, which would happen a few years later. Their neighborhood was very clean, green, and there were a lot of kids to play with. Many Somali Bantu families were settled there.

I wanted to be able to play and talk to kids my age. When it was time to leave, we would be so tired from playing and laughing with our cousins that when we came home we were so exhausted and fell asleep.

By the time it was September, my Uncle Maliko had already packed and moved to Cleveland, Ohio. I thought that was kind of strange since no one had told me he was moving nor was I told why he was moving. Two years later he would be married again. He already had a wife and a son in Africa. They were still in the process of being settled in America. Uncle Maliko had left us his house even though I hated it so much. I was glad that he was moving for his own reasons and didn't think that we were taking up his house.

Fortunately, as nice as he was, he left us his desktop computer, which we used to play online dress-up games on Most Fun Games. Most Fun Games was our favorite website to play dress up and put makeup on the characters in the games.

On September 1, 2008, we started school. Our great-uncle enrolled us in Clara Mohammed, a private Islamic school where my cousins (his kids) also went to school. It was very nerve-racking to me on the first day. One of the office ladies took us to our classes one by one. Malyun was taken to her class first. She was put in the third grade classroom where my cousins Ayan, Anisa, and Samira were in. I waved good-bye as I was being walked to my classroom. They were so happy to see us, especially because they thought I was going to be in their class too. The school only had one classroom for each grade level.

I don't remember Sahara being walked to her classroom; I believe it was because she started school a day after us. Meanwhile, it was finally my turn to go to class. I was placed into the fourth grade. I remember walking in shy and nervous. I didn't have my uniform on and I thought that would be a reason students would probably stare at me, as I walked to my seat.

With me being so nervous, there was one person who made me feel comfortable—my future best friend Khadija. She had a white scarf tied on her head. You could see her enormous ponytail. She had really long puffy hair. She kept turning around and smiling at me for at least three times and even said hi at one point.

That day the students were learning multiplication. The teacher, Brother David had called me up to the front of the board to answer a multiplication problem. Every staff at school was addressed sister or brother. I answered the problem correctly and sat back down to my seat, nervously. At the end of math class Khadija started talking to me, which I was happy about but nervous as well. She introduced herself to me and I introduced myself to her as well. Something told me we were going to be great friends. She seemed bright and spoke her mind quite often. She was very outspoken. Students never picked fights or argued with her because everyone feared her and wanted to be her friend.

She was very friendly as long as you didn't get on her nerves. After math class we had Arabic and Islamic studies. Mondays through Thursdays were dedicated to reading, writing, and learning to speak Arabic. Fridays was dedicated to Islamic Studies only, where we learned about the twenty-five prophets as well as some teachings taught by the Prophet Muhammad. My first Arabic class was fun and easy. The teacher, Brother Abdirahman was impressed with how quick I caught up with the class in one week. We worked on memorizing the Arabic letters and connecting them to form words. Since, I understood the lessons very well that Brother Abdirahman asked me to help the students who were struggling.

I learned the Arabic alphabet at an Arabic class in Kentucky, but since the instructor could barely speak English I never really learned the Arabic alphabet before. With the way Brother Abdirahman taught, I was able to learn the Arabic letters quickly. Mainly because instead of memorizing alphabet songs like my class in Kentucky, I was able to learn the Arabic alphabet and the vowel sounds in Brother Abdirahman's Arabic class.

Our Islamic Studies class on Fridays was sometimes frightening to me. This was the day Brother Abdirahman would tell us stories of the Prophet Muhammad. He also talked about topics like the Day of Judgment, resurrection, and the end of the world. All of which were scary topics to me. I thought it was weird that we were being told stories about a man that was living centuries ago. I didn't know what a prophet was. So, when it was said that Prophet Muhammad was born in Saudi Arabia I would ask myself, "where in the world is Saudi Arabia?" I thought it was a land in heaven (jannah).

But when Brother Abdirahman talked about the return of Isa (Jesus), I would have great excitement. I thought it was cool that someone living centuries ago would one day come and eradicate evil and bring peace in the world for a short period of time.

However, when the topic of death came, I would often sit in class pretending not to listen. Many times I'll watch the clock in the classroom hoping that Brother Abdirahman would leave soon for his next class, instead of talking about such scary topics. I think I was the only one scared, or maybe some of my classmates forgot about the whole thing when class was over. When Brother Abdirahman left I would have a great sigh of relief. Sometimes he would continue speaking even when class was over, and I would sit in my seat with my head down asking myself when he would leave. But after a month or so, I got over my fear of the topics he discussed and even wished he continued speaking sometimes. It became interesting to me after a while.

I soon began to love my new school. I don't think I missed Wilkerson at all. The only thing I was still worried about was the school supplies I left in my locker at Wilkerson and not saying good-bye to my friends. I didn't mind Clara Mohammed being such a small school, considering it was private. I still wore uniforms just like I did in Kentucky. Except in Clara Mohammed we wore white shirts short or long, navy pants or skirts, and since it is an Islamic school the girls were required to wear white or black scarves.

Within the first week I made friends. Khadija, who everyone knew and was very popular; Mariam, who was very funny; Makaya was also my friend, but at times we didn't really get along, and also, Salma and Ariauna were my friends. Makaya and Khadija were good friends. So when Khadija and I were getting very close that was a problem for her. This I was told by my other friends, I didn't realize I was stealing someone's friend. One morning during breakfast, Malyun, I, and others were sitting at one of the tables in the cafeteria. Malyun drew a picture on the table with a pencil eraser, and Makaya came out of nowhere and said "That's ugly." Then I responded to her in defense of my sister, "Who do you think you are telling her that her drawing is ugly." Many of the students were afraid of Makaya, but I was new and didn't really see anything frightening about her. Even though I've never been in a conflict, I wasn't afraid to stand up for my sister. I knew Makaya was being mean in order to make me fear her and stay away from her Khadija, but I didn't care.

Plus, Khadija once told me she and Makaya weren't close. They were just friends. All the students were ready to see a fight between us, but I was mature enough to know that it was wrong and would be childish of me to fight her, considering all the kindergarteners and elementary students that were watching us argue back and forth. It was a little embarrassing. Makaya on the other hand wanted us to fight to show people she could beat me up. I didn't want to get in trouble on my second month of school. Despite our conflicts several times, we got to know each other a little more and became good friends after a conflict in fifth grade, which caused all the girls in our class to turn against her.

Besides those incidents, I didn't face any other problems or conflicts at Clara Mohammed. Henceforth, I still carried one more problem with me from Wilkerson. I was good at everything, but subtraction. I still didn't understand the whole borrowing concept. But that was because I was always overthinking everything when it came to math.

It was in fourth grade when I finally learned to do subtraction in terms of the borrowing concept. Since Brother David had many students in the class and some of them had hard time following directions, he couldn't help me one-on-one. But I got lucky one day and he was able to break it down for me. I was finally relieved when I finally learned it. After that I felt unstoppable and believed I could do anything.

Brother David was a great teacher. Every morning before we began class, he would have us read Al-Fatiha from the Qur'an. Then, he would go to different chapters of the Qur'an and read it to us and explain the meaning. Before we came to America, I had already memorized about fifteen surahs from the Qur'an in Arabic, but I had no idea what any of the surahs were saying. In Africa most teachers only taught to memorize surahs. We weren't taught the meaning of each surahs. In Clara Mohammed I had the benefit of being taught the meaning of chapters of the Qur'an through English translations. During Qur'an recitation time Brother David was really serious. You could not interrupt him, talk, or play around. The word of God was important to him and that's what he tried to teach us. For that reason he was inspirational to me. Brother David was Puerto Rican, but when I first met him I thought he was Mexican because I didn't know what Puerto Rican was. I had never seen a Puerto Rican before. I assumed anyone that was Hispanic was Mexican. I didn't have geographical knowledge.

None of the places I lived in Louisville, Kentucky were diverse enough to have such groups of people. During my fourth grade year, Brother David was the coolest teacher in the school, in my opinion. After lunch, Brother David walked us to a park a few blocks away from the school past the KFC restaurant. Getting there was a great exercise. Once we arrived at the park, he would try to get the whole class to play football, but after a few times he stopped doing that because it wasn't fair to us girls. We couldn't run as fast as the boys and some of us had asthma. So instead we did playground activities such as getting on the slides and swings and playing tag. At the end of the day when we returned to school we had our last class, which was math.

When winter came along, we took two trips to the Urban Ecology Center at Riverside Park. I loved going to the Urban Ecology Center. Those trips were the first time I actually thought about nature and saw its beauty. The Urban Ecology Center had mini buses. One of the bus came to our school and picked us up to go to the center. Once we got there we were escorted to a room where we had discussions of the types of animals we would see in our hiking trip. Then, we were taken outside into the woods and were told to spot the birds and animals we discussed about inside. I loved taking the hikes, especially when it was snowing. Everything looked so beautiful when covered in snow. It was a winter wonderland. Being able to see the plants, trees, and animals were exciting to me, especially in the fall and winter.

On our way back into the center after hiking, we would slide through a narrow slide that led us back into the center where it was warm. My favorite part was going through the slide. Every time Brother David asked us where we wanted to go on a field trip we always suggested the Urban Ecology Center.

Even though fourth grade was one of the best years in school, I ended up in a position I never thought I would be in. Since my best friend Khadija and another student named James were always arguing, I tried to intervene one day. It was almost a daily basis they argued about silly things. Sometimes they almost fought. James tried to be brave, but everyone knew he was afraid of Khadija as almost all the boys were, even though she was pretty and didn't look scary at all.

So one morning during phonics the two started arguing again while Brother David left to get something from another classroom. When their argument became very loud and bothersome, I intervened trying to stop them because they were disrupting the class. I believe someone left to get Brother David, because their argument was getting more personal. When Brother David got back he asked who was involved. Everybody stated it was Khadija and James. Then, I spoke stating, "I tried to stop them." Then Brother David suspended the two including me. I was shocked and scared and a bit confused. I didn't know what to tell my parents. Even though it was a very scary moment for me, I ended up telling my parents what happened anyway. Luckily, my mother believed me. She knew I would never get in trouble. She knew I was the type of student who would try to prevent conflicts from occurring.

The next day I had to stay home and go to daycare with my mom since she worked there. I felt so embarrassed because almost all the parents kept asking me why I wasn't in school. So my mom had to constantly explain my situation several times that day. I felt very ashamed of myself, then again I knew I did nothing wrong. The next day when I returned to school Brother David asked me why I didn't come to school the day before. I asked myself, "Wasn't he the one that gave me the suspension?" He then told me that I was never suspended, which confused me even more. I told him that he said that I was suspended verbally out loud two days before. He then explained to me that if I was suspended, I would've received a paper saying that I was suspended. I was shocked and embarrassed. "I ruined my perfect attendance for no reason," I told myself.

That made me so upset that day. I told myself that I stayed at home and daycare for no reason the day before. I loved daycare when my friends were around when we didn't have school. But I also loved school as well. I was mad about missing several of my favorite classes. Meanwhile, Khadija and James were still suspended. They were suspended for three days.

While fourth grade was filled with fun and games and some turmoil, we learned so much. The best part of attending Clara Mohammed was that I learned more about my religion and that's what my parents wanted us to gain from the school. Every Friday we had Jummah prayer, which is a congregational prayer held on Fridays during Zuhr prayer at masjids (mosques). Clara Mohammed was also a masjid. Staff members would pull out large green carpets to sit on. A combination of all the students, staff members, and visitors came down for the prayer service.

For almost all the students including me, listening to the lectures was the hardest part. We all often fell asleep. Teachers had to keep us awake. The service was about an hour and fifteen minutes long. It was hard not to sleep. It was even harder in the summer because it was very hot, especially when it took place in the cafeteria, where the warmth of the kitchen spread throughout the first floor. The lectures were often given by Brother Imam Shaheed, who was one of the founders of the school. He was older and the way he lectured didn't appeal to the students. However, when Brother Abdirahman lectured almost none of the students fell asleep. This was because he spoke in a loud, attentive voice. I felt bad we slept through Brother Imam's lectures, but it wasn't something we could control. I often told myself not to sleep during service, but I couldn't help but sleep. But most days, I was able to stay awake throughout the whole lectures of Brother Imam.

Brother Imam was very knowledgeable about many things concerning the religion and black history. Sometimes he would even tell me about the history of the Qur'an during the enslavements of Africans in America, during my lunch hour. There were times during lunch when I would visit him in his office and hear his perspective of questions I had regarding politics, our religion, and even black history. Sometimes I would be late to class because I enjoyed listening to him.

I always valued his opinions. He would even allow me to borrow his books, which were predominantly about the history of Islam. My favorite book I borrowed from him was a biography of Prophet Muhammad. The book was very heavy and thick. I borrowed it from him in spring break during my sixth grade year to that summer. I took the book with me to daycare every weekday during the summer. While all the kids were playing together during free time, I would sit on the side of the fence of the daycare's small playground and read the day away. Some of the students would make fun of me for reading so much and call me a nerd. I hated when they called me a nerd, because I see myself as a curious person not someone who only cared about academic related things. Plus, I dislike when people label others.

When reading the biography of Prophet Muhammad, it was difficult to grasp what I was reading sometimes, because some of the kids would come toward me and urge me to play with them. I often refused. But there was a time when I did want to take a break from reading and have a little fun. The kids were getting splashed with water from a water hose at the daycare. It was a really hot day and I thought that was a great way to cool down. So I joined the rest of the kids and had a little fun for a few minutes.

Then, I went back to reading after drying off. I learned so much from the book. I learned a lot about the Prophet that I had never known. Such as how he was a descendant of Ibrahim and how both of Ibrahim's sons were descendants of the Jews and the Arabs. I thought that was very interesting. It made me think that maybe all the prophets were related and maybe we humans were all somehow related. I spent my seventh grade summer trying to comprehend and finish the book. It wasn't an ordinary book that I could just read and return as soon as I was done. I took notes as I read it, which is what I always did and still do to books I find very fascinating.

When school was back in session in the start of fifth grade, I learned Brother David was no longer teaching at Clara Mohammed anymore. I was a bit saddened by the news. I only knew him for at least a year. I thought he was the coolest teacher I ever had. He opened our eyes to things we hadn't known. I was grateful to have him as a teacher because I was learning so much about my religion from him that I wish I had known before. Little did I know I was going to have another awesome teacher in fifth grade.

For the first two quarters of fifth grade, I had a teacher named Brother Terrence. He was very quiet and very relaxed. He talked very low and slow. Most of the time, the class had to be very quiet in order to hear him. Sometimes I thought he was sick because of the way he talked. He blinked very slowly too. It was like when someone was given a lethal injection and slowly dying. I was afraid for him at times. But after a while, I started to realize that's how he's always been. After a few months, he and his family moved to Arizona. I wasn't sure why.

Now I had another teacher named Sister Kalimah. She and her sister, Sister Rasheeda had moved from Chicago. Sister Kalimah was the fifth grade teacher and Sister Rasheeda was the math teacher for the middle school students. She was a great teacher. We always had a great time with her. I remember in the spring she would take us outside across the school to do yoga workouts. We weren't as flexible as she was so we often encountered some difficulties as a class. Sister Kalimah also took all the girls in the class shopping sometimes. I remember one spring we went shopping at Bayshore Mall along with Sister Rasheeda and their younger sister nicknamed Zayzay. It was also my nickname, so I often got confused who was being called. We had so much fun together. During lunch break, I bought Italian spaghetti. I choked on one of the strands and ended up coughing for about five minutes. After that, I took a break from eating spaghetti for a month, afraid that I would choke on it again.

Though Sister Kalimah was very nice and sweet, there was a time in fifth grade when I felt I was treated unfairly. We were playing a game in which the boys and girls had to compete against each other. Since the school was a private school, our class size was small. There were twelve students in the class, six boys and six girls. We were to split up into two equal groups. For some reason even though there was an equal number of boys and girls, I was placed in a group with the boys. At the time I was a girly girl and never liked being near boys and didn't really know how to interact with them. Boys were strange to me. I then refused to be a part of whatever the game was remembering what my mother always told me.

My mother always advised me to stay away from boys and not make friends with them, so that's why I didn't end up falling in love with one I guess. She was trying to prevent me from ever having a boyfriend, which some of my friends had. But at that age I was too young to understand that. My mom's saying was something every Somali mother told their daughters. It wasn't an unusual thing. However, my friend Ariauna got along with the boys very well. I didn't understand why she couldn't be in a group with them instead of me.

Meanwhile, I thought I had the right to not participate, because I knew my mother wouldn't approve of such decision. I ended up getting in trouble that day for my action. I had to stand outside of the classroom for fifteen minutes. Sister Kalimah came to me ten minutes before my time was up to see if I still wanted to play. I still refused because I felt that I had to respect what my mother told me. So I stayed out for a while. I felt bad that I had to do that, but I had to respect my mother. I didn't make a big deal about it because I felt I was honoring my mother. Sister Kalimah was still a great teacher despite all that.

Sister Kalimah was very cool. She would play *nasheeds* (Islamic songs) in rap forms and as normal songs. It was very soothing and helped us work better and quicker. It was my fifth grade year when the girls and I formed a singing group. Every year for black history month we sang songs and even did a few dances. We continued our singing and dancing tradition for black history month until seventh grade.

There was a day in fifth grade when we had a talent show. We were going to sing and dance to Michael Jackson's "They Don't Really Care About Us." After practicing several moves we were finally ready. When the day came after school, I only had a few hours to go shopping for a cute outfit for the performance. My mom had my father take us to Rainbow. I quickly grabbed a long sleeved black shirt with a crop top-looking purple jacket.

When we came back my father took my mother to the hospital. She wasn't feeling well. So I had to cancel an hour before the performance. My father advised me to babysit my siblings while he and my mother were at the hospital. At that time she was pregnant with my sister Aisha, but she was nowhere near her due date. My mother was experiencing hypertension, nausea, and other pregnancy symptoms.

I was sad that I was going to miss the performance, considering the fact that I didn't have a way to get a hold of my friends to tell them I wasn't going to make it. I didn't have any contact with them. My parents believed that I was too young to talk on the phone unless it was a family member. However, I had to stay home and help my mother out when she returned from the hospital. It wasn't the first time that I would cancel an engagement in order to help my mom with her needs. As the oldest child, it was going to be a problem for me in the coming years.

In fact, when my sister Aisha was born a few months later, my mother was taken to the ER the night she returned home from the hospital. I was left home to take care of four kids and a newborn baby even though I was only eleven years old. My parents trusted me and knew I was mature enough to care for infants as I've done for all my siblings. Plus, I was the only person they could depend on. With such trust, I couldn't let my parents down. Luckily, my mother came home around midnight feeling a little better. That night I realized what my responsibilities were as the oldest and promised to be there for my mother. I was going to do such uneasy tasks two more times on the birth of my younger siblings.

Meanwhile, sixth grade year was filled with academic challenges as well as a lot of competition. Sister Rasheeda's math class was very competitive, but we learned a lot as well. Anytime our class took a test or a quiz, Sister Rasheeda would announce the three students with the highest test scores. I remember it was always me, Khadija, and my other friend Samira. Surprisingly, the girls always scored high. I knew the boys were smart enough to score high as well, but they didn't try their best when it came to academic games. I guess they had it in their mind that the girls would always score higher than them. It was good that we girls did better than the boys, but I could also see how it was hurting their self-esteem. Of course, me and my friends were willing to help them but they were always either nervous or too embarrassed to seek our help. I could see that point of view, but I also didn't want them to think they were also not knowledgeable. I believe everyone has a talent in something. The boys were definitely better than us in a lot of things outside of academics; sometimes to the point that we didn't like playing with them because they always won in things like sports and rap battles.

Meanwhile, the students who had the highest test scores were taken out shopping with Sister Rasheeda and Sister Kalimah. I remember the day we went shopping one spring. It was a beautiful sunny day. Brother Rashad, Sister Rasheeda's husband picked us all up using the school van to the mall. Fortunately, they picked each of us up from home. Even though the plan was that the trip would only consist of me, Khadija, and Samira; Makaya and another female classmate were included because Sister Rasheeda was very sweet and knew they were our friends. So they came along with us. We went to Grand Avenue Mall located in downtown. My favorite shop at the time was Rainbow. So we all went there and found the prettiest striped sweaters. Khadija and one of my other friends chose the red striped sweater. Samira and I wanted to get the turquoise one, but she didn't have enough money, so I was left to buy the sweater myself. It was a bummer because I really wanted us to match and have a twin theme going on. After shopping and walking around for a couple of hours, we went to the food court to eat.

That's when things fell apart. As a young girl I loved spaghetti so much and decided to get some from an Italian restaurant in the mall. I ate my spaghetti in a rush. I was that hungry. Ten seconds later I started choking and hacking. I kept coughing the rest of the trip. Since then, I didn't eat spaghetti for about a month. That day I really thought I was going to die choking on a spaghetti strand.

Unfortunately, Sister Rasheeda and Sister Kalimah only did about two more shopping trips. I guess things got very busy in their personal life. We however, did some fun things during the school year with them. I think Clara Mohammed became very fun and exciting when they were teaching there. I always say that they're from Chicago, so they know how to have fun. They were the best and very smart as well. I wouldn't have won "best project" in my school's science fair during sixth grade without Sister Rasheeda. Every year Mr. Murphy, my sixth grade teacher, always picked our project for us. The whole class usually had the same project. I being so stubborn wanted to be different and challenge myself to do something a little more challenging and unprecedented.

Since Mr. Murphy constantly played cassettes and documentaries on astronomy I remember learning so much from Galileo and Isaac Newton. I was an astronomy nerd at the time. I would often study astronomy in my free time, especially during spring break. The one scientist I found very fascinating was Isaac Newton. I studied almost all the discoveries he made. That's when I developed my love for physics and Isaac Newton's three laws. I remember people talking about how hard physics was, and that made me look into physics as a science project topic. I knew our project was going to be challenging, and so I went with it as a science fair project anyway. I enjoyed being challenged. However, I knew I couldn't do a project with all of Isaac Newton's three laws, so I had to choose one. After looking into all of them, I realized I resonated to the second law (the law of acceleration). That's when my project goal was to find out how acceleration affects mass.

At first, I wasn't sure what kind of experiment I could conduct to solve the problem. For some reason I came up with an idea to buy a toy car and somehow create a steep hill. I changed the weight of the car by increasing mass each time and rolling the car down the steep each time. I was to record the time distances each time I increased the weight of the car. Sister Rasheeda helped me write an equation for the time and distance it took the car to go down the steep. Our equation seemed very accurate. My group, which consisted of Khadija and my other friend Qamar went to Sister Rasheeda at least three days to make sure we solved our mathematical equation correctly. At the time, we were doing twelfth grade level work for our project. Mr. Murphy, who was our homeroom teacher and taught science and social studies, seemed a little jealous that we weren't asking him for any help like the other students. So, one day I pretended to ask him a question just to make him feel better and went to see Sister Rasheeda a few minutes later. He seemed happy again. Sometimes he felt that way just to be funny, but not this time.

I didn't want to make him feel bad, but Sister Rasheeda was the one with a math degree and I really needed her for the project. I felt kind of bad that I was doing all the work, but I had to make sure our project did well in the science fair. But I couldn't have done the experiments without my partners. Khadija was the one who bought all the materials. I only bought the display board. And Qamar just settled in America a couple months before. She didn't know much about science to help us out at the time.

So, I explained to her what we were doing during the experiments. I didn't want her to feel left out just because she couldn't speak English. Everyone had a group but her. She was my close friend and I didn't want her to feel left out. So I claimed her. And during our presentation I had Qamar demonstrate our experiment. She had to increase the mass of the car by piling items on the car while I explained what she was doing. Khadija on the other hand timed the results during our demonstration. Then, Khadija and I took turns explaining what was presented on our display board. My voice was obviously sort of shaky, while Khadija talked enthusiastically as she did typically.

I was extremely nervous. Our judge seemed nice and calm. I thought we had a better chance of winning because he constantly told us not to be nervous before we began our presentation. After our presentation, the judge told us we did very well, but I thought that was something every judge said even if your project and presentation was horrible.

I didn't think we would win, because even though the judge was very nice he didn't seem impressed, and that's the face I was trying to avoid. Instead, I put in my mind that this was another failed science project. Our first impression was the feel of relief that we didn't get Mr. Sales to judge us. Mr. Sales was the husband of our school's vice principal. He sold snacks in the cafeteria. He was very harsh at grading. We had him as a judge several times the years before and we lost every time. It seemed as if he cared a lot more about how attractive the display boards were than the research information that was provided. I saw a lot of senior high school students who had wonderful projects and researches, but somehow ended up losing. I thought some of their presentations were better than ours.

We would find out the results of our project a couple months later in the spring. Unfortunately, I was diagnosed with strep throat which was very devastating. I never experienced such pain before. I couldn't eat or drink for a week prior to my diagnosis. Then, I developed fever which lasted for about three days. The first night of my fever, I thought I would feel better and went to school anyway the next day. That of course was a big mistake. My fever only got worse that day. I couldn't keep my head up or keep my eyes open.

Luckily that day, we weren't switching classes and spent the whole day watching astronomy-related documentaries. I took that time to take a nap hoping it would reduce the fever and headache I had. Sadly, that didn't help either. My head was hurting so bad that I couldn't stay asleep. Later in the afternoon, sometime around lunch, I threw up. I still had a fever even though my headache was reduced. The next day, I didn't show up at school. I received a shot for my strep throat on the part of my body I never imagined would ever be shot. My butt. My sisters Malyun and Sahara also received the shot on that area. All three of us had strep throat. We couldn't sit straight for a week. We had to tilt on one side when we sat or simply lay down. At first my mother thought it was probably from the powder lemonade drink we had a week before our diagnosis, because we developed strep throat the day after we bought the powder drink. I also thought the drink caused it because I kept hearing about many foods and drinks containing some form of bacteria in news reports.

Meanwhile, my doctor stated that we got the shots on our butts because we didn't have enough muscles on the upper part of our body since we were so skinny. The day of the science fair announcement, I was laying on the floor in my living room. I was glad I wasn't in school because I didn't want to hear that someone beat me in all winning places, even if it was second or third place. Suddenly, out of nowhere Qamar called me while I was watching the news with my father as we always did. She called me with full excitement. I thought something was wrong with her. Almost as if someone drugged her. I never heard her so happy before on the phone. She usually called me for homework help or to talk about school problems. It was quite a surprise for me.

She kept yelling, "We won, we won!" I asked her what we won because I had no clue what she was talking about and the teachers never announced when winners of the science fair project would be revealed. Qamar then yelled, "We won the science fair!" I kept telling her to stop lying to me.

But then she swore by Allah (God) and I knew when Qamar swore, she was telling the truth. Plus, she never lied to me. It was just too good to be true. Then, I started to believe it. After all these years of several failing projects, I actually created a winning project. We won the $100 award and a trophy. We won a category that I myself never heard of, Best Project, which was beyond first place. Someone else won first place. I was so proud of myself and my team because we beat high school students and it was only our first year of middle school.

We were short and little sixth grade girls, except Qamar. She was very tall. I was so proud of my team because even though I was nervous they were not, which boosted my confidence. They were the real reason we won. The announcement was the best surprise I've gotten in my life. We split the money into $33 and gave the leftover to Qamar. We owed so much to Sister Rasheeda, who helped us tremendously. We made her a thank you card to show her our appreciation after we won. I think it was our mathematical equation and chart that impressed our judge because we handmade ours using the equations we produced to find the time and distance of our experiment.

Additionally, after many observations from our display board and other winning projects, I found out the secret to winning a science fair, which many students might still be curious to find out. After winning this project, I took a break from science fairs and went into the world of robotics and engineering. After all, it was things like science fairs and scientific documentaries that led me to engineering.

Unfortunately, both Sister Kalimah and Sister Rasheeda had to move on with their lives and move to Chicago. Sister Rasheeda told us that she had to leave because her grandma had become very ill and she had to care for her. Obviously, as smart as we were, we knew that wasn't the reason because her husband Brother Rashad was still living in Milwaukee and teaching Arabic in Clara Mohammed. My friends claimed something happened in their personal life and they probably just divorced. As honest as she was I didn't understand why she was not being honest with us.

But then again, we were young and I guess we would've asked many questions about her personal life or perhaps she thought we would end up crying. She told the class that she would come back to visit us some day. That of course never happened. Besides our victory with the science fair project, the best memory I will always remember with Sister Rasheeda is the time we did a play written by her about our school's history. I played

Layla who was the teacher's pet and often tattletaled on the students for fun. I thought I would do great playing Layla because I was the teacher's pet in some of my years in Clara Mohammed. But then, after I read my script I realized she was also a tattletale and I didn't want to play someone who got people in trouble for amusement.

Then, I remembered it was just a play and enjoy being out of my comfort zone. Sister Rasheeda obviously played the teacher and did a splendid job. She had great enthusiasm as she always did. I still miss seeing her and Sister Kalimah. The school was thriving during their presence. Everyone loved them.

Things definitely changed when I became a seventh grader. Instead of being fun Zeynab as I've always been, I started to take school more serious than I should have. I started isolating myself from my friends. Not because I thought they were not good for me to be around, but because I was facing a difficult situation in my personal life. When I left for school every day all I could think about was family problems. Also, the thought of trying to be the top student in the class was eating up my brain.

Everything became a competition for me: finishing work first, most detailed writing, reading the most books, having the most right answers, etc. I was pretty much building up more stress than I already had. Overthinking excluded me from my friends. This led me to be very introverted. Ever since I was younger growing up in Africa, I've always been extroverted. I had tons of friends some of which were even older than me. I also loved going out. I was a very happy child. I loved company. I took studying to the farthest. During lunch, instead of eating I was reading biographies.

Eventually I lost appetite for eating because I did that every day. My weight dropped drastically, which was bad for my health because I was already skinnier than I should be. My mother tried to buy me medicine that would make me eat more and gain weight. But the medicine my mother gave me only made me go to sleep. The first time I took the medicine, which was in a tall orange bottle, I couldn't stop sleeping in class for three days. I stopped taking it after those few times. I told my mother jokingly that I would take it on nights that I have trouble falling asleep.

Part of the reason why I overstudied was that I felt like I had some sort of gift for helping others. At the time, I was also looking into careers that did just that. After careful observations all I could think of was politics. Almost everyone I knew who had been working in the community helping others were somehow involved in politics. For that reason, I started reading books on politics and politicians. I remember in seventh grade trying to check out *Politics For Dummies* at the Central Library. I knew such book would give me a great crash course to politics. I also started reading biographies of politicians and famous black leaders. I read about two biographies about President Obama. I thought he was a remarkable man. The fact that a black Kenyan man would later have a son who would become the first black man to lead the United States of America was truly an amazing thought to grasp. I remember when he was first elected. The whole black community from Somalis to black families in Africa and Europe were celebrating such unprecedented and exciting event.

On the day of President Obama's inauguration, classes were cancelled because the teachers and staff wanted to watch him take his oath and feel such proud moment in history. Rugs were placed in the entire cafeteria for the students in the entire school to sit on. There was a huge high-definition TV on the area of the cafeteria where Jummah prayer was held. We watched the inauguration for about two to three hours. At the time of the inauguration I was in fifth grade. The event was a great example for us students. This is when we really took the quote seriously that anything was possible if you put your mind to it. I was glad to see how happy many black children were including me because now, we had a reason to achieve our dreams.

At this point I was so fascinated in books and improving my writing skills that I somehow stopped talking to my friends. I felt like I was doing my parents a favor and pretty much taking education seriously as they've always told me. Though I was a straight A student everything got to me. I had a bad relationship with English class. I had an A in every class including Arabic except for English. I always got a B+ in English and that often annoyed me.

My parents were already glad I had outstanding grades, but I wanted to show them I could do better than that. I didn't understand why I was always getting a B+ in English. I was a great writer, I always carried a small dictionary, which I bought myself and read actively. Though it was complicated, I finally got an A+ in English including all my other classes in the last marking period of the school year. I still have no idea what I improved on to get an A+ in English. I already thought I was good at everything before.

Unfortunately, seventh grade was my last year as a student in Clara Mohammed. I made a choice to attend an MPS (Milwaukee Public

School) school. I made such decision thinking that MPS would have a more challenging and rigorous classes for me to take. At least that was my intention. But at the same time my family planned on moving back to Louisville, Kentucky. It was a constant thought for my parents. My father had settled in Louisville for at least a year and worked there making sure that when we moved back, we would have a house and school prepared for us. My father came to visit us in Milwaukee at least once a month. I thought it was a waste of gasoline because Louisville, Kentucky was eight hours from Milwaukee. By that summer we had already packed most of our things. There were many boxes of things stacked up in our kitchen. We were only waiting for my father to confirm that he had found a house. I wasn't happy about moving.

I fell in love with Milwaukee. I met so many people in Milwaukee from friends to mentors. I wasn't ready to leave. But then I knew I had no choice but to move. I had a great idea in which I could stay with my cousins and finish school in Milwaukee. Then, I realized my mother needed me in helping her to raise the kids and write all our bills and payments.

Life would only get complicated for my parents if I stayed in Milwaukee. So I told my parents I would move with them to Louisville. Next I started researching schools I could attend in Louisville. I became fascinated about a magnet high school in Louisville, which was the top school at the time. It was called DuPont High School. I wanted to make sure I went to a school that was known for its reputation. When I was attending Clara Mohammed, one of my cousins wanted me to attend Rufus King, which I considered for high school. Rufus King was the top school in Wisconsin at the time and was known for its rigorous International Baccalaureate (IB) program. I was very fascinated by the IB program as well and thought it was just what I needed. I've always been fascinated by global issues and learning more about them in order to bring peace and harmony in the world, and that's exactly what the IB program was about.

I realized that even though DuPont was also a great school, my heart was set for Rufus King in Milwaukee for high school. So that whole summer I had an internal debate about what I was going to do in terms of school. Luckily, my father had come back from Louisville for good and I no longer had to think about moving to Louisville. My mother had gotten really sick because she was pregnant with my brother Nasir. She was so sick that she had to have nurses come to our house every day. They gave her shots and connected IV bags to her arm. This was because she was not eating and drinking as much as she should have. She had so many illnesses including hypertension because of stress. We had to stay in Milwaukee because my mother wouldn't get the medical treatment she needed in Louisville. We knew this because living in Louisville was hard years before. There weren't many job opportunities for my parents and health insurance was hard to obtain. We didn't want my mother to suffer if we did indeed settled back in Louisville.

Even though I was happy to be staying in Milwaukee, I didn't want to see my mother suffer in such horrific situation. I was always concerned about her health. Since the nurses couldn't keep coming to my house every day to give my mother a shot, one of them trained me to give her shots on the belly and insert IV tubing in her hand. Every time I did such task, I thought about how painful it was for her. Oftentimes, I cried because I had to give her shots. Every time my mother's blood pressure decreased and her nausea went down, I was relieved and prayed to Allah that it stayed that way.

Part of the reason my mom stressed herself out so much was because she was thinking about her family in Somalia, Kenya, and Tanzania a lot. They depended on her for money. During the month of Ramadan our relatives needed money for food almost every week. My mother has to somehow give them money and think about how she should also feed us and buy us other necessities since she couldn't work after having babies. My father was making less money than her. They both worked for Goodwill, but their paycheck was not enough to pay bills, support our relatives in Africa, and take care of us. All the stress facing my parents caused me to stress as well. I often wished I had a job to support them, but I was not old enough to get any job. Also, my father said that it was not good for a student to work during school. It would cause them to fall behind. So, I was left to go through hardship.

My mother told some of her relatives (cousins) that she was sick and couldn't provide them with any money at the time, but they didn't understand where she was coming from and they kept calling for money anyway. As sympathetic as my mother was, she still sent them money hoping that they would stop asking for more money.

When school resumed my mind was always on my mother's health and how I could assure my parents of a better future. A future where they didn't have to work, a future in which I would be paying them for all the hardship they faced in raising us and all the chaos and dangers they faced as refugees—all the things that they never deserved. I did this just like I did in elementary by doing my best in school and making them proud, hoping to give them hope that the future would be brighter for them and for my siblings if I did my best to accomplish my goals and dreams.

In eighth grade year I couldn't get into the schools that I wanted to attend since they were already occupied, so I was placed in Bayview High school, which was a middle and a high school. It was definitely not the school I wanted to attend. The school was outstanding years before sometime in the 1900s, but this time it was known for its bad reputation. The first couple of weeks were okay, but the classes were bigger than I imagined them to be. There were about thirty to forty students in each class. In Clara Mohammed the biggest classes were only about twenty-two to twenty-five students. Classes in Bayview were too big for me. The worst part was that it was hard to get teacher's assistance on certain assignments.

Things did get out of hand at times. I was very good in history and loved history class, but things were hectic in my US history class in Bayview. The teacher was new. He just graduated from college with a history and a teaching degree. His name was Mr. Crawford. He was really skinny and tall. For a first impression I already felt bad for him because he was so bony. I thought he was facing some sort of health issue because he didn't have any muscles in his body. And when he was teaching it seemed like I and another student were the only ones paying attention in class, while everyone else kept talking to their friends in the middle of class. One morning, everything suddenly changed.

Two girls who didn't seem to like each other suddenly started to argue right in front of me. They then started fighting in front of the classroom where I was sitting. Mr. Crawford tried to break them up but one of them shoved him over toward the door. The teacher called one of the security guards outside who then called the principal, after his effort to break the girls up failed. When the principal came one of the girls kicked him in the private area. After many struggles more guards were called to get the girls. After they were taken out, the class started chatting about the incident while the teacher was in complete shock. This happened on the first month of his teaching career. I could see how terrified he looked. I felt bad for him that he had a horrible experience as a first-time teacher. He was really nice. He always tried to answer the questions I had to the best of his knowledge.

Later that afternoon another fight erupted in the cafeteria. This time there were ten fights. So many students were arrested for their involvement.

There were about five police cars. News stations such as WISN 12 News, CBS 58, and FOX 6 were there to report what had occurred. The teachers had warned us not to give news reporters any videos of the incidents, which many students had recorded. As I was walking to my bus at the end of the day, I was asked by a 12 News reporter if I knew about the incident. I couldn't lie, so I told her what happened as she was recording me. She then asked if I had footage of the incidents. I told her I didn't, but that one of my classmates did. When I got home I told my mom everything that happened, I even showed her the news report about it. She became worried. We both decided that it wasn't going to be the right school for me. The following week I went to visit the counselor. She was very nice and lovely. I told her I wanted to go to a different school. She helped me find a better school. On that same day she found that Westside Academy II was the only school available on the MPS website. She warned me that it was a charter school and that they required uniform. I was okay with that because I hated trying to find an outfit to wear every morning.

Ms. Young was very supportive of my decision. She could see I was a bright student and that I needed to attend a school with a better environment. She knew where I was coming from. It didn't take me a while to transfer. I started school at Westside two days later.

Something told me that this school was going to be great. My gut told me that I would be happy at Westside, and that's exactly what I took from the school. Westside wasn't diverse. It was literally all black, but it didn't matter to me because the students were very friendly and seemed to be interested in getting to know me. I was often the center of attention because I looked a little different, mainly because I wore a hijab on my head, but I was still treated like everyone else. On my first day, instead of feeling nervous, I felt a feeling of relief to be attending a quieter school. My homeroom teacher was Mrs. Koss, but we called her Ms. Drews. That was her maiden name. She got married that summer and the students were still used to calling her Ms. Drews. She was and still is a lovely person. She treated her students as if they were her own kids. She was the English teacher as well as our volleyball coach. All the other students would always wish they had her as a homeroom teacher because she was fun to be around. She always brought us treats. She held a tradition where she brought baked turkey, stuffing, and sweets every Thanksgiving. She bought it all with her own money.

On my third day of school at Westside I met a girl name Angel at the computer lab which we called the tech lab. She asked me who I was and what school I came from. Then, I asked her where she has been all day, if she was also a student of Ms. Drews. She told me about the program she was a part of in the school. The students called it the Washington Program. It was sort of an advance placement opportunity for students who had a MAP score of 330 or above. Seven students were chosen to take three high school courses at Washington High School for high school credits. Students took math, science, and English as freshmen. I would of course be the eighth student to enter the program. The high school students at Washington and the staff called us the Baby Eights.

Mr. Furniss, the technology teacher at Westside was in charge of making decisions like who would be accepted in the Washington Program. I heard that he was the founder of the program too. In order for me to be a part of the program, Mr. Furniss needed to see my seventh grade report card. He was quite impressed with all the As he saw on my report card. Meanwhile, I wanted to find out if I could be in the program right then and there. But he didn't tell me his final decision until two days later. Perhaps he was putting my information on the high school system during those two days.

I was very happy when he finally told me I was accepted into the program. Every morning we were expected to meet in the conference room to receive our bus tickets for our ride to Washington High. We had to walk from our school which was located in 36th in Lisbon to 40th in Lisbon to the bus stop to catch route 30. Then, we returned to school around 12:30 PM for lunch and gym. The rest of the time was for us to do homework or play educational games from the MPS website.

I believe it was on my first day of the program when I got to know Keturah, one of the students. She was a redhead and looked mixed. It was ironic because she wasn't mix. Both her mother and father were black and she looked just like them but was lighter. They were her biological parents. I didn't understand how she got red hair. Both of her parents had black hair. Her younger brother had the same situation she has, while her younger sister resembled her parents. I thought that was very cool. Keturah was very funny and a great writer. She wrote amazing poems that I wish she read out loud to students. She had a laugh that was contagious to me. Sometimes I didn't laugh because something was funny but because her laugh made me laugh.

Throughout the year, Keturah and I became close friends. We both even volunteered to organize the school library the summer we graduated eighth grade and also volunteered at the Milwaukee Art Museum. When we came from Washington, after doing our homework she would show me funny YouTube videos that we laughed about throughout the day.

We sat together pretty much in all our classes except our physical science class. All of the eighth graders were already sitting together and there was no chair left for me. So, I had to sit with the high school girls. I was okay with it because I could get work done quickly and not have to get distracted by others. However, I did talk to the high school students when we were doing lab work or when I was helping them with assignments. They often talked about their drama outside of school and their relationship life, which made me uncomfortable at times. But I always acted as if I wasn't listening in order to get work done. But they were nice except for the time when one of the male students asked me if African people ate dog food.

I, as well as all the other students, found it very rude. He was trying to be funny, but no one was laughing. The first thing that popped in my head was that I've never seen dogs in Africa and no African country makes dog food. Also, why anyone would want to eat dog food? It made me realize that people believe the things the media put in their mind about Africa rather than researching it themselves or asking a native African about the continent or countries within Africa.

I understood why I was a refugee. It wasn't because Kenya was poor; it was simply because the government and the United Nations had to use a vast area of Kenya where no one was living in order to create a refugee camp that would be a safe haven for people who were fleeing war and turmoil from their native country. Of course people like my family wouldn't have access to simple things other Kenyans and people all over the world had.

As a child I've never been targeted for my identity, whether it was because I was a Muslim or that I looked different. People have always known me for my character and my respect to them, but it does hurt me when I see others being judged or stereotyped without being known through direct communication.

One day at Washington, our class had a substitute in science class. The substitute teacher was a black woman. She asked me about my religion and the hijab I was wearing. She shared a story with me of her experience wearing the hijab. She told me that any time she wore a hijab men in the street respected her and had chivalry, but when she didn't wear hijab they would call her all types of rude words like whore and slut. I felt frustrated as she was telling me about her experience. I couldn't understand why anyone would disrespect her even if she wasn't wearing a hijab. There was no reason anyone should have treated her such way.

It wasn't a laughing matter to me. It reminded me of all the inequality and unjust treatment women and girls face around the world. It goes back to important global issues I would learn in my junior year of high school. I learned so much from *Half The Sky* written by Nicholas Kristoff and his wife Sheryl WuDunn. The book opened my eyes to many problems females face around the world that I hadn't known and issues that I knew a little about. One of the biggest issues the book spoke of was human trafficking and education.

I read three stories that talked about three girls' experience with human trafficking. One of the girls in the stories was looking for a job. A man at a store assured her she would find a job if she came to the location he told her to be at the next day. The girl of course didn't tell her parents she was leaving to find a job because she wanted to surprise her parents. They were poor. She planned on helping them out by getting a job that would pay her well.

When she arrived at the place, the man abducted her. She was taken from across the border from her home country. She would spend there until her adult life and have two children from her so-called customers. She was lashed and burned with a hot iron if she didn't make enough money. And if she tried to escape, she would get hot chilies inserted in her private part as punishment. In such deadly situation she couldn't care for her children. The brothel owners took them from her. If the child was a girl she would be raised to be a victim of human trafficking at a young age.

I watched a clip of the documentary relating to the book which had the same title as the book. It was very emotional to watch. I cried the entire time I was watching it. One of the clips was about a little girl who was very dedicated to getting a good education so she could be a lawyer and payback her mother for her support. The girl's mother was a victim of human trafficking. The abuse and damage she faced was visibly shown on her face. She had many scars and burns. The little girl knew about her mother's experience and knew that staying in school was the best way to keep her from also becoming a victim. I started crying even more when she said she wanted to give all the money she made as a lawyer to her mother, because that's also what I planned to do for my parents in the future as an engineer. The girl was a native of India, which is known for human trafficking. I was so happy to see how smart and ambitious she was. But the best part of all was that she had her mother's support every step of the way.

The other clip was about another Indian school girl who was only eleven but looked like she was nine years old. The little girl loved school. She was very smart and earned good grades, but one day out of the blue her mother decided that she didn't need to go to school anymore and stated that they would be moving back to their village because of the girl's grandfather's order. The owner of the school was worried. She knew that the girl's grandfather was not a good person. He sold his other two daughters to sex trafficking so that he could make money off it. The owner of the school knew that he was planning on selling his granddaughter as well. The school owner begged the little girl's mother not to take her back to the village several times. It didn't work.

The girl had no idea what was happening. The owner of the school provided her with a book bag that had her phone number on it just in case something horrible happened. The school owner did so by not telling the girl's mother about it. That way she could reach out for help and her mother wouldn't stop her from getting help. It was quite emotional for me because her mother wouldn't let her stay at the school which is where they lived and were getting food and medical care. I didn't understand what mother would want her daughter to be harmed even if it was by her own father's decision.

My first time hearing about the issue of human trafficking was at Washington High School in my English class. Our teacher Mr. Brendelhorst often showed us movies that dealt with different issues. Most of the movies we watched dealt with race relations—struggles that occurred during the civil rights era. But the movie about human trafficking was I believe the first movie we watched. I had no idea what was happening because I didn't think human trafficking was actually taking place within the static quo. There was a clip of a twelve-year-old girl who was at a market with her mother. When she left her mother for two minutes to look at a dress, a man came and kidnapped her along with other younger kids. They were all taken to a brothel while looking confused and terrified simultaneously.

Meanwhile, *Half the Sky* also talked about issues like Female Genital Mutilation (FGM) and education which I could relate to. I read that countries like Kenya, Somalia, Egypt, Senegal, and Yemen continue to practice FGM today. FGM is the cutting of organs surrounding a girl's private area. The procedure is done by cutting the labia and the clitoris. My native country of Somalia is notorious for such issue. Some Muslims believe that it is a religious act when in reality it's actually a myth. In Somali culture the procedure is supposed to prevent girls from having premarital sex and from running off with men. If a girl doesn't get mutilated she is seen as unchaste and dirty. This is of course a myth. My father refused for my siblings and I to be mutilated. He was very religious at the time and only people who knew a lot about the religion knew not to approve such act.

Meanwhile, all my aunts and cousins have been cut. For many years my mother warned us not to tell others we weren't cut. It was embarrassing in our culture. I didn't understand why. In fact the girls that have been cut were the ones who often had premarital sex and ran off with men. Girls like me were expected to do such thing. Plus, girls who experienced FGM dealt with problems such as excessive bleeding (hemorrhage), genital tissue swelling, urinary problems, tetanus, shock, maternal mortality, painful menstruation, and sexual problems.

It's funny to me that something that can be deadly is done because people assume it's a cultural or a religious requirement. FGM is usually associated with some Muslim countries which is very ironic because people started practicing FGM centuries after the Prophet Muhammad's death in Muslim countries. There's no evidence that it is a religious requirement. The practice also exists in Christian countries like Ethiopia as well, but still there is no religious evidence for such act to be done. I don't believe any religion advocates torture and cruelty.

I believe eighth grade year was when I really started to understand the world although I did hold campaigns about certain issues in sixth grade. It was in eighth grade when I wrote a newspaper article about how America could be improved by making major changes, but I never got to publish it. I wanted to publish the article through the *Milwaukee Journal Sentinel*. Things in my personal life and my mom's illness got worse. So, I wasn't able to make that happen. I still have copies of my article hoping that I will someday have an opportunity to share it with leaders in the United States.

I also had the idea to start a blog in eighth grade, but I didn't create one until freshman year in high school. I later began blogging. I called my blog *Informed* because that's exactly what it was supposed to do, inform others. Initially, I created it to inform youth about current issues locally and globally, but so far my audience have only been adults. As happy that I am that more and more adults love hearing about my opinions, I needed youth audiences since they're going to be tomorrow's leaders and will need to know about the issues currently affecting them. I've written about various issues from education, poverty, terrorism to political issues. I thought that was the best way to get my voice out in the world.

There are youth around my age group who have solutions to problems, but aren't sure how to get their words out. One way I thought I could achieve this was by blogging and attending local gatherings and discussions. One day while I was in the tech lab at Westside, I searched keywords like *change* and *youth*, hoping that it would lead me to some sort of organization that involved getting youth to speak about issues alongside city officials. Suddenly out of nowhere, the City of Milwaukee Youth Council came up. I then clicked on the link of its website which had all the details of what the council did and how work was achieved.

The council consisted of fifteen high school students ranging from the ages fourteen to eighteen. Each student was a representative of their home district similar to the aldermen and alderwomen who represented their home districts. I loved the fact that the students were seen as leaders of their community. I also loved that the students were able to speak about any issues that affected them in the council. It could be human trafficking, education, poverty, etc. That's all I needed to convince me to sign up for such well-formed council. So I did. I would have to apply several times for about two years due to misinformation on the website. I thought if I signed up in eighth grade I would have a chance of making in the council by the time I was a freshwoman in high school. Also because I was only going to be an eighth grader for four more months. Sadly, I wouldn't make it in the council until my sophomore year.

Meanwhile, when our graduation was near I was left to think about how much I was going to miss my friends and Westside Academy. I saw the school as the perfect school environment I wanted to be in, even though it wasn't as diverse as I prefer a school to be. Part of it was the small classroom size and the flexibility of our school schedule. I could get all my homework done in school and spend the rest of the day on the computer doing my own research or watching interesting videos on YouTube. I always tried to get my work done before I did anything else. That's how I ended up getting a 4.0 GPA at Washington High School that year. Part of it was because I studied sometimes when I was bored. I was very focused in eighth grade. Nothing could distract me from completing my school assignments.

However, I was always thinking about how I was going to miss the rest of the Baby Eights since we were all going to attend different high schools. I was to attend Rufus King, Angel and Devon would attend Milwaukee High School of the Arts, and the rest except for Darius would attend Washington High School. I never heard Darius speak of where he was going to go for high school. I was left to think about the great and amusing memories we had together. My best memories with them was the day we were chased by a dog. It was hilarious. I still laugh about it till this day.

I remember it was on a winter morning either sometime in December or January. Most likely in January only because winter is brutal during January in Wisconsin. We were all walking through an alley in front of the school on our way to the bus stop on 39th and Lisbon. Keturah and I started walking ahead of the group because they were taking too long. Out of nowhere a dog came from behind the house we were going to pass and started barking at us. His owner was out with him. I didn't understand why the dog was out early in the morning with so much snow on the ground. The dog started chasing us. I started running and that's when Angel and the rest started running. My terrified face made them realize something bad had occurred. Keturah on the other hand was walking normally and wasn't one bit scared. Devon jumped on a black car that was parked near the alley. We were lucky an alarm didn't go off and that its owner didn't see him jump on the car. We were all so frightened except for Keturah. We ran back in the school. I never ran that fast previously. When Jamonta (*Jamontay*) and the rest of the boys tried to tell Mr. Furniss what happened, Mr. Furniss looked at us like it wasn't a big deal and stated that we would perhaps be late to school. Mr. Furniss often acted like a parent toward us. He didn't have any children. If something were to happen to us in Washington, he was the person to be contacted.

The day the dog chased us also reminds me of the day we had to beg Mr. Furniss to drive us to Washington High School. It was very cold. The temperature was below zero. The snow was piled everywhere. Angel, Shanice, and the boys begged him several times to drive us to school in his car. We weren't going to leave unless he gave us a ride. Angel called it a boycott, which was funny to the rest of us. When Mr. Furniss finally agreed, the girls and I rode with Mr. Furniss while the boys rode in Ms. Walker's (the principal) car. The boys wanted to ride Mr. Furniss's car but Angel and Shanice asked first. Mr. Furniss often favored the girls because we worked harder.

Unfortunately, Mr. Furniss refused the next time we asked. That day was also really cold and the wind was blowing furiously. Our begging didn't work even when the boys constantly called his office phone. It was very funny to watch. The students enjoyed messing with Mr. Furniss even though it was a serious situation. It was usually Darius, Devon, Jamonta, Angel, Carlos, and Shanice who usually messed with Mr. Furniss. Keturah and I always watched and laughed in the background. One of my other favorite memories with the Baby Eights was when we were trying to get all our hours for National Junior Honor Society.

Most of my hours were spent helping teachers like Mrs. Richmond, the sixth grade math teacher and a fifth grade math teacher, grade papers. Already experiencing high school life, I understood how big of a help I've been to the teachers, because grading was obviously what they had to do at home. I would finish grading their papers for them at school. They didn't understand how happy it made me. I was getting a lot of hours from grading papers for them, while they were glad I was getting things done for them. It was like a mutualism relationship. We were both benefiting from each other. Angel and I also helped the secretary file and label papers. Hence, I was getting more hours from that as well because I stayed in the office filing and labeling papers even after it was closed.

It was really hard for me to say good-bye on the week of graduation because I finally felt like I belonged somewhere and was surrounded by people that made me laugh and didn't mind me being a little weird, different, and independent at times. Henceforth, I was looking forward to high school. I figured it would be even better than Westside, but a few years later, that would not be the case.

In our eighth grade graduation, we had two gentlemen come to talk to us. They came to talk to us about the shooting that took place in the Sikh Temple of Wisconsin. One of them seemed to be talking more about his life as a white supremacist. I didn't understand how their stories related to our graduation; I just remember being touched by what they had to say. Their stories inspired me to take action even though I wasn't sure what I was going to do right then and there.

I didn't know their names nor did I remember when they were introduced during the ceremony, but I looked up the name of their organization Serve2Unite which was on their shirts, as soon as I got home and read about them on their website. On the site I learned that the father of Pardeep Kaleka (the Indian speaker) was the president of the Sikh Temple and was killed by a white supremacist name Wade Michael Page. Page killed five other worshippers in the temple on August 5, 2012. I was saddened to read that Page killed such spiritual, innocent human beings just because he thought they were Muslims or looked threatening to him. I felt that I had to apologize to Pardeep as a Muslim for such tragedy. So I found an email on the website and showed my condolence. I also thanked Arno Michaelis, his partner who was a former skinhead for sharing his story, because it showed me that change is possible no matter what situation you are in.

I never thought in my life that someone so racist could suddenly be not racist until I met Arno. The day I met Arno I didn't believe he was ever a racist. He was funny and so kind. When I became a freshman at Rufus King, I invited him and Pardeep to come to our Interfaith Club meeting. Even though they said they would be there, I didn't think they would come. But surprisingly, they did. When I saw them walk in, I thought I was seeing things and almost fainted from excitement. At first, I was nervous to talk to them because I've never met them face to face. When they came in, Mrs. O'Keefe, my English teacher introduced them to us. They began to tell us their compelling stories about faith. I remember Mrs. O'Keefe getting emotional about Pardeep's story when he talked about his father's death. She made me cry as well. Mrs. O'Keefe was and still is a very emotional person. But that's just because she's compassionate and cares about a lot of issues, especially when it involved people being persecuted or killed for no reason.

Meanwhile, when Pardeep and Arno were done talking, we had a break in which we ate pizza and had refreshments. At that point, I was really trying to hide from them because I was really shy. I wasn't sure about what to say. I wasn't expecting their arrival and Mrs. O'Keefe hadn't told the group there would be guests coming until five minutes before Pardeep and Arno's arrival.

I tried to think of a way to meet them. I saw some of my friends talking to Arno, so I thought I had nothing to worry about and came in the conversation. As I was having a great time talking to Arno and my friends I thought I really needed to somehow meet Pardeep as well. I was really nervous about meeting Pardeep because I thought I had to be a fun person or perhaps cool to talk to him while Arno was very reserved and easy to talk to. My friends who were chatting with Pardeep were a bit cooler than me and could talk to anybody. But I knew if I came in their conversation, I would probably bore them instantly with my presence.

So after wandering around for about ten minutes, I took a risk and went to talk to Pardeep only because I didn't want him to think I didn't find him interesting like Arno. Plus, I asked them if they could come by my school someday. It was only fair to finally meet them. It would be weird inviting someone to a place and not talk to them. It just sounded very rude.

I came into the conversation while Pardeep and my friends were talking about Bollywood movies. Of course, I didn't know much about Bollywood movies because my parents didn't like us watching romantic movies. I used to watch Bollywood movies at Nurto and Isha's house when I was younger, but even though they were tragic love stories they weren't inappropriate. It sucked that all they did was watch Bollywood movies, because I loved watching PBS Kids shows and Cartoon Network, which they barely watched. Bollywood movies were kind of boring to me in my younger days. I had no idea what was going on in the movies. Love stories were just not my favorite shows or movies to watch even today.

Meanwhile, it seemed like Pardeep and my friends were having a great time talking about Bollywood movies. I pretended like I knew what was going on and laughed with them when something funny was said. Additionally, I didn't think Pardeep was intimidating after all. He was just as cool as Arno but with a different personality. Since then I've been in touch with them, attending events they held in the community, and at one point volunteered to do photography for them. I also try to help them with the annual Chardhi Kala Memorial Run and Walk 6K, which is a fundraising event that commemorates the lives of the Sikh Temple shooting victims.

Currently, Arno and Pardeep are one of the coolest people I know. There's no point of a party or an event without their presence. Frankly, they're the reason how I met even more incredible people in my life. I always told Par and Arno to make sure they invited me to every event they were hosting or attending relating to their work. One morning I got an email from Arno about an event that was being held at the Father Groppi Unity Bridge, which is a bridge connecting the north and south side of Milwaukee. The purpose of the event was to gather all the organizations in Milwaukee that promoted peace and violence prevention so that they could be a part of one big music video promoting unity. The music video was shot at the Father Groppi Bridge because bridges are seen as a symbol of unity. Plus, it was named after a civil rights activist, Father Groppi who fought for equality.

At first, getting to the event was hard. I took the city bus not knowing where I was headed or where to get off. I asked almost everyone I walked by where the bridge was located. I also called Arno several times. He answered his phone the first time but not the other three times. So, I had to keep walking until I saw a sign that said James E. Groppi Bridge. It was a very chilly day for a March weather. I was freezing by the time I got to my destination.

I saw a lady with an orange head scarf sitting on what looked like a beach chair. She had a table set out with clip boards and made sure people signed in. So, I signed in. She then asked me if I was a part of some of the organizations that were participating in the event such as Running Rebels and Urban Underground. I told her I was a part of Serve2Unite. She didn't know what the organization was so I had to tell her all about it. After I told her about the Sikh Temple shooting and how it related to Arno, she felt inspired and wanted to meet Arno and Pardeep right away.

She told me her name was Talibah Mateen and that she was a community organizer for Safe & Sound, which is an anticrime organization that works with youth and law enforcements to bring peace in Milwaukee communities. The music video hadn't started at the time. People spent the time until then to promote their organization. At one point I saw my fourth grade teacher, Brother David walk by wearing a black suit with a black hat holding a bunch of the Final Call newspapers. I greeted him. He gave me the greetings back and handed me a newspaper. I thought it was going to be a great reunion, but apparently he was very dedicated about the task he was fulfilling that day. I felt like I was excited for nothing. It seemed like he changed a lot. He was always a serious person but knew how to have fun back in fourth grade.

Meanwhile, while we were waiting for others to show up I told Ms. Mateen about everything I wanted to accomplish in life and what I wanted to do as an activist. My goals involved fighting for certain global issues. She gave me one of her best advice and told me to start locally. She told me that the mayor, the district attorney, and other politicians were going to be there and that I should meet them to see if they could help me with anything. Ms. Mateen said she would introduce me to them.

I thought she was joking. So many people told me that before. I had a feeling it wasn't going to happen. But as soon as the event started and cameras started rolling things began to happen. Those coming from the north and the south side merged and walked down to the bottom of the bridge, where the celebration would be held. Ms. Mateen asked me if I was ready to meet some politicians. All of a sudden, I started getting nervous and couldn't believe it was happening. I wasn't sure what I was supposed to say to them. Even though it was nerve-wracking I sucked it up and met them anyway.

First, I met the district attorney, John Chisholm and his son Ted. My first thought was, what does a district attorney even do? I've never heard of such position. I introduced myself to the D.A. and talked about my background, which Ms. Mateen urged me to do because I was too nervous to say anything. Then, he introduced me to his son who was a sophomore, but I assumed was a college student because he was so tall.

However, it was hard to start a conversation with Ted. We kept asking each other the same questions at the same time three times in a row. It got a little awkward. The only thing I remember from the entire conversation is that Ted was a sophomore in high school. I was so nervous I didn't remember anything I talked to him about. Since then Ted and I have remained connected. In addition to that, some of my family members and I attended Ted's high school graduation party since he was going to leave for college.

Meanwhile, Mayor Tom Barrett was about a few feet away from the D.A. Ms. Mateen walked me over to him and introduced me. Since I wasn't prepared to meet any politicians, I told the mayor the same thing I mentioned to the district attorney, which was basically my background as an immigrant from Kenya. I also mentioned to the mayor about my interest in violence prevention, especially gun violence. I told him I had a few ideas on how to decrease our city's homicide rate, which was drastically high. His friend Ms. Terry Perry, who was the director of the city's office of violence prevention, gave me her contact information so that I could get a hold of her as well. A few months later I scheduled a meeting with the mayor that July.

At the end of the event it started raining heavily. I was going to walk back home since I lived very close, but since the weather wasn't great Ms. Mateen offered to give me a ride. On our way to my house, Ms. Mateen gave me her business card and suggested I call her if I wanted to meet other people or needed help doing something. I didn't hesitate. As soon as I got home, I added her to my contact list in my email, since I didn't have a phone at the time. Since then, I contact her about anything—good news and sometimes even bad news. Ms. Mateen is always the first to know what

I'm up to before anyone else. The following month on April, Ms. Mateen invited me to a neighborhood cleanup which was hosted by the awesome, Andre Lee Ellis. Mr. Andre owns a few gardens in his neighborhood.

He created a program in which young black men work on the gardens during the summer as a paid internship to keep them off the streets. Mr. Andre is one of the hardest working men I've ever met. His goal was always to be a mentor to young African American men so that they could be successful in life. The young men are very obedient to him because Mr. Andre is a very serious guy. He is a father figure to the boys. He started an annual event where hundreds of the young men dress up in suit and tie and attend a large dinner at a fancy ballroom.

I was very impressed about the first one. It was very emotional for me. All the guys, especially the little ones looked adorable in their suits. They looked like soldiers walking down the street. I thought it was a symbolism of their future achievements and the obstacles they would conquer. I could see myself in their shoes in terms of coming a long way and facing hardship. I was so proud of Mr. Andre, the young men, and those in the community who contributed to the event.

Though I was so dedicated in my community activism work, I had other plans. That summer from June to August, I was in Marquette University's Upward Bound Math and Science program. The program was six weeks long and required students to stay on campus. There were two Upward Bound programs at Marquette University. The program I was in was geared toward students who wanted to pursue a career in math- and science-related fields, while the other one was for those interested in any other fields.

Most of the students including me were first generation future college students. I'm not sure about the situation of the other students. I, along with a few of my friends, took STEM courses in the morning. We took physics, trigonometry, and engineering. In the afternoon we took English and culture class. It was almost like attending school during the summer. We had to wake up early in the morning around 6 AM and had to be at the cafeteria for breakfast by 7 AM. Our entire day was based on a schedule. I didn't like that. I hated waking up early in the morning. Since, my roommate Hawa and I weren't morning people, we would put our alarm clock on snooze until our hall monitors knocked our door.

We were always the last ones to leave the residence hall. I still am the last person to leave a residence hall in every summer program I attend.

My favorite class in the Upward Bound program was engineering and the culture class.

In our engineering class each group was assigned to build a boat entirely out of duct tape. The motor and the wiring of the boat had to be adjusted in a way that it could receive the signal from the controller. The boat had a size limit. After weeks of building the boat, we had to test it. After constructing it, we had a competition. All the teams met in Marquette's gymnasium which had a pool. We competed to see whose boat reached the other corner the fastest without sinking.

Fortunately, our team won. The best part of the project was that we were using everything we learned from our science and math class to build the boat. The day after our competition we went canoeing at the Milwaukee River. It was a beautiful sunny day but a little windy. It was one of the scariest moments of my life. Each boat had to have three people in it. Unfortunately, my team members either never canoed or forgot how. Meanwhile, I was just terrified and assured everyone that I was likely to drown and die that day. Of course that didn't happen.

The other female member of our team, Delicia, and I literally screamed several times during our canoe ride. I on the other hand, was screaming and yelling the whole time. Razak, the other team member just laughed at us whenever we panicked, especially me. He seemed to be enjoying the whole experience. For him it was like relaxation I guess, which I didn't understand. I kept telling Delicia that I was going to do the same thing people did in the movies after getting off a cruise ship and kiss the ground several times. Unfortunately, our boat kept spinning several times not allowing us to move in the direction we wanted. That's when I really thought we were going to fall out of our boat and die.

Luckily, our math teacher showed us how we could get out of our situation. When we came back to our starting point and got off the boat, I was soaking wet. Maybe it was because I was sitting in the middle and water kept splashing at me more than anybody else. I attempted to kiss the ground as I said because I was so happy to get out of the canoe boat, but the ground was also wet. Since that day I vowed not to go canoeing ever again. Despite it being a little scary, I had a great experience. Now I know not to go on a cruise ship.

My other favorite class was our culture class. I don't remember its exact name. We mostly watched documentaries about different cultures in the class. The first documentary we watched was about three Ivorian boys who were given the opportunity to settle in the United States to play professional basketball and join the MBA. The documentary spoke of their financial struggle, not having their families to support them, school life, as well as just adapting to American culture.

The second documentary we watched was about the lives of Muslim families living in Dearborn, Michigan. I don't recall the purpose of the documentary, but I think it was to show that Arab Americans were no different from other Americans. I remember seeing how families in the documentary balanced having a normal American life while still practicing their faith. It was very fascinating to me. While watching the documentary I thought about how lucky people in Dearborn were, because they owned a lot of businesses and shops. As a person that loves fashion I thought about not having to travel to different states or order clothes from different countries just to obtain the latest Islamic or even modest dresses and skirts.

Also, not having to miss school to celebrate Eid. One of the more interesting scenes was when the Muslim young men in the football team had to practice for their games at night during Ramadan after breaking their fast so that they didn't pass out at practices during the day.

On the last day of our culture class, we had a small food festival. The food was sponsored by Immy's African Cuisine, which is a restaurant in Milwaukee. The food was very delicious. Some of it was similar to Somali cuisine such as the *samosas* and the rice. Although chicken peanut stew was new to me, it was very good. I learned so much from the culture class. It definitely taught me to be open-minded and meet people from different backgrounds and open up my horizon. As a person who loves learning new languages, it taught me that meeting new people is one of the best ways to learn a new language.

Unfortunately, because of family problems arising frequently, I could no longer participate in the Upward Bound program. My mother needed my assistance in helping her with my siblings. She also didn't like the fact that I wasn't at home with the family during Ramadan. I met a few cool students who eventually became my friends during the Upward Bound program. One of them is currently my best friend.

On our last week of the program in the summer of 2014, we toured colleges all week. We visited eight colleges from Wisconsin and Minnesota. It was great because I felt like I was on a road trip as a college student leaving my parents for college. We stayed at three different hotels that week since most of the colleges were nearby each other. After touring in the University of Minnesota in Duluth we ate dinner on a fancy boat. We ate seafood for dinner. Apparently, everyone complained about a stomach ache except for me after dinner. I guess the food had something that bothered everyone's stomach. When students had stomach aches and some were puking, I sat on my bed thinking what's going on with everyone. I remember during dinner most of the students were eating too much of the seafood, while the rest just had weird reactions an hour later.

One of my friends that I shared a bed with at one of the hotel puked in the middle of the night. We never found out why that was happening to the students, but I guessed that some of them were probably allergic to seafood. On our last night we went to the Mall of America for dinner and shopping. We first had dinner at Bubba Gump Shrimp which offered seafood as well. Luckily, no one complained of any aches and pains from its food. I ordered a rice dish with shrimp. It was my first time eating shrimp, but it didn't taste as delicious as people normally say it did. So, I ordered fries and chicken tenders. I never got to finish it since we had to leave. I had barely even started eating it. I felt like I wasted my food, but it also didn't look like I could take it with me though I should have asked. I regretted ordering my first dish. I felt bad that it was to be thrown out. Since I am an environmental supporter, I felt very guilty.

For the most part, I did enjoy the Marquette Upward Bound Math and Science program. I was able to do things I would never have an opportunity to do, especially dining at places I've never even heard of. At our trip to the University of Wisconsin-Superior, I learned that Arnold Schwarzenegger went to college there. That was interesting to me because I wondered why anyone would choose to go to college in Wisconsin, considering its brutal winters. It was funny that we were taken on a college tour to colleges none of us were interested in going to.

I was very saddened that I had to leave the program. I met so many friends. But it was for the better. My mother needed my help. By this time I had seven siblings: Malyun, Sahara, Abubakar, Fatuma, Aisha, Najma, and Nasir. My youngest siblings have always kept my mom in and out of the hospital. Nasir and Najma were born with asthma and eczema. Every season Najma's asthma at some point would always act up. Nasir on the other hand had both asthma and eczema including allergies. He is allergic to anything with nuts, fish, and soy. So pretty much any food you can think of since soy is pretty much in every food product. We always read the ingredients of every food we buy. This means my siblings and I can't enjoy the foods we like at home because my mother doesn't want my brother to cry for the things we eat, nor do we want to eat stuff he can't have in front of him. That would be unfair. Furthermore, my mother suffered the most during Najma and Nasir's pregnancies.

When my mother was pregnant with Najma, she had hypertension. The day she returned from the hospital after giving birth to Najma, my mother was sent back to the ER (emergency room) again that night. I was only eleven and I was left to care for a newborn baby since my father had to accompany my mother. Despite my age, my parents trusted me with Najma's care because they knew I was mature enough. Plus, we didn't live near any other family members so they had no choice. I don't think I would have trusted an eleven-year-old with a newborn baby if I was the parent. But knowing myself, I was very mature for my age.

As a child I always engaged in conversations with adults. I never really understood kids my age. Growing up in Kenya and until I was about eleven I simultaneously interacted with kids and adults. But as soon as I entered middle school, things changed. It definitely had nothing to do with puberty, because I hit puberty at a very young age, which was quite frightening to me. As far as I can recall growing up in Kentucky, my neighbors always spoke to me as an adult like them. When they joked around with the kids saying things like "I'm going to marry you to my son," which Malyun was told a lot, they would just ask me how I was doing like all the other adults in the neighborhood. I'm not sure if it was because I appeared to look very serious at times or I spoke very maturely.

However, I do remember my mother getting upset with me every time I snooped into a conversation with her and the neighbors. She would always tell me I could snoop when I was older. And I would always ask her, "What age would you consider me to be old enough to engage in your conversations?" She would sometimes say when I'm fifteen years old, but I never listened. I was very stubborn. My mom was the only one who had a problem with that. All the other adults thought I was very smart and wise. Until this day, I still don't understand how I managed to have so many friends and act like a kid and be taken seriously by adults. When I was attending Clara Mohammed school some of the staff would always tell me that they knew I would do something great in the future even though they had no idea what it would be. They could see I had a big curiosity and had passion for learning and helping others.

Surely enough they were right. I always knew I was different in some shape or form. One of my passions since I was young was always being able to address different global issues. Ever since I was twelve years old, I've always dreamed of speaking at the United Nations to speak about issues humanity isn't aware of or bringing obvious conflicts to rest. The conflict of Israel and Palestine has angered me so much. I don't understand why both countries are still fighting over something that has occurred decades ago. Why can't they both live in peace together? After all they're both descendants of Prophet Ibrahim (Abraham). The Jews are descendants of Isaaq (Isaak) and the Arabs are descendants of Ismail (Ishmael). I know for a fact that both brothers wouldn't accept this conflict between the two groups of people. They would be very upset with their people. Some of the people close to me argue that God gave the land to the Jews according to the Bible. From my perspective from the Qur'an, God gave the land to the Jews for protection from the pharaoh. God didn't say the land only belonged to the Jews. Plus, Palestinians are technically Jews. Being a Jew didn't only pertain to the religion. Palestinians are just Jews who are Muslims in terms of their faith. If you go to Israel and Palestine, you'll see that both are very similar.

People make stereotypes and say Jews have long nose. Well, most Arabs do too. This comes to show that they are related and have no reason to be fighting each other. I mean, why is it so hard to live in peace together? God puts us on Earth so that we can live together in harmony. He never said that people should separate themselves according to race or religion. It's us humans who make life so complicated when it's really not! What hurts me even more is how American politics plays a role in this. Democrats are considered to be pro-Palestine while Republicans are seen as pro-Israel. This only causes more separation and war. America was founded as a country that would unite other nations as a world police. According to America's political system, this is not evident.

One of the other matters that I would've brought up to the United Nations is more of a personal plea. Both of my grandmothers are living in the middle of nowhere in Somalia. They don't live near any cities. While the president of Somalia is supposed to be working for all of the people in Somalia, people like my grandmothers receive no government assistance. They live in the middle of the woods with no access to food and are in constant fear of being invaded by bandits. I have cousins who are seven years or younger growing up in such harsh environment. After paying the bills, most of the money that my parents earn goes to them. My parents and I are constantly praying for their health because one of my grandmas has serious asthma while the other suffers from hypertension.

Also, one of my little cousins has seizures. Every time my parents try to get my relatives from Somalia, I start to worry that bandits would capture them at the Kenyan border and slaughter them. This was the situation for some Somalis who tried to escape Somalia. One day in the winter of 2015, I caught my mom watching a boy get slaughtered by an armed Somali man. My brother Nasir always listens to Somali songs on my YouTube page and the frightening video somehow popped up in my feed. None of my siblings were shown the video. It was too graphic. The boy who was a teen was Somali. The boy kept pleading, "Please uncle, don't kill me." In Somali culture an adult male is referred to as uncle for respect. The boy was fleeing Somalia with a couple of older women and men who were his neighbors.

Despite his constant plea, he was slaughtered. I couldn't wrap my head around it. The boy calling him uncle while a knife is being pointed at him made me cry so much. I wondered how coldhearted you had to be to kill such respectful and innocent child. Another thing was that the man who killed him wasn't dressed up like an ISIS or Al- Qaeda member. He was dressed up like an average Somali man. This made me realize that anyone you know could be cruel without you even realizing.

Meanwhile, the rest of the people with the boy weren't left alone. They were gunned down. I didn't watch the rest of the video, but my mom told me about it since I was too afraid and emotional to watch it. But I heard the commotions in the video. My mom wanted me to see it so that I understood what she and others went through. I couldn't do it. I knew I would not go to sleep for weeks if we did.

That day I thought about how being dead was better than seeing all these things going on around the world. I thought about how lucky people in the Qur'anic and Biblical times were. I don't understand the world right now. I wish the president of Somalia was able to send help for people like my relatives living far away from civilization just to make sure they were okay and not left forgotten. Sometimes, I don't like revealing the exact location they live in, because I know Al- Shabaab or the crazy bandits would torture them. They remind me of the many people in poor countries around the world that are suffering in the wilderness, but aren't heard or seen. Sometimes I wish there was a way to track people who are suffering so that I could come and help them. This leads to why some people ask me why I care so much about others.

Well, some of us are just lucky to be born to have an instinct that drives them to help others in need. With me being very spiritual, I also act upon what I've learned from the Qur'an. The Qur'an including the Prophet Muhammad stated that we must help those that need our assistance, especially the poor and vulnerable. I live my life fulfilling that mission. Also, since the Prophet is my role model, I do my best to live his legacy. To me and most Muslims around the world, he was the perfect human being.

One of the other issues that have always stuck to me was poverty. I don't like seeing people suffer around the world due to war conflicts similar to what my parents faced as well as families in Syria and Iraq. Every year at the MAS (Muslim American Society) conventions in Milwaukee, a few representative of an organization called the United Muslim Relief come to recruit volunteers who are interested in caring for families in the poorest countries in Africa, Asia, and the Middle East. One of the contributions is that you can foster a child and send him or her some money for food, clothing, and supplies. This was something I've always wanted to do. In my case I wanted to foster three babies from Africa, Asia, and the Middle East just to be fair. I wanted to help the babies because they were more likely to die, especially newborns. And besides, they could be the ones that would rebuild their country when they grow up. I have faith and hope for children who grow up in conflicts. I know they will be the ones to look back and come back to restore their parents' homeland as I try to do.

On December 3, 2014, I along with fourteen other members of the City of Milwaukee Youth Council were inaugurated. It was my first year in the council. I was excited to finally get the opportunity to join this fascinating council that I've been trying to be a part of since eighth grade. It took great effort, perseverance, and persuasion to finally join. I couldn't wait to see the accomplishments the members and I would make.

Little did I know it was going to be very political. Every member represented their home or school district. My school district was District 2 while my home district was 15. Sadly, both districts were occupied. But since I constantly asked Mr. Owczarski, the city clerk that I didn't mind working in any district, I was assigned to District 9 and District 9 is located near Brown Deer, WI, which is a suburb of Milwaukee.

I didn't know how I was supposed to represent people living in Brown Deer when I lived in Milwaukee. I assured Mr. Owczarski that I would somehow work it out with Alderman Puente, who represented the district. Unfortunately, despite my constant request to meet with Alderman Puente for a year and a half every month, I was never able to meet with him. In my last email to him on January of 2016, I stated that I could not represent a district I knew nothing about. And if I couldn't meet with him to discuss issues facing residents who live in District 9, then I didn't feel like I was doing my job. I didn't join the council to put something on my resume. I wanted to take action and help people in the community, not come to City Hall twice a month for a meeting with no benefit to the community. Regrettably, that wasn't the only problem I ran into as a member of the youth council.

For the period of time I've been in the council, I felt that something was wrong or that I didn't fit in with the other members. One thing was true. I always thought that I was seen as too soft or very shy because I rarely spoke when we were discussing certain topics. And that was because I felt like most of the things we discussed had nothing to do with the issues I cared about. Plus, some members spoke so much I could never give my input on what we could discuss. The two issues I deeply cared about at the time and I still do is gun violence and poverty. However, I rarely remember any of those issues being a topic of discussion. I only remember being invited to a gun violence panel discussion with people from different states through the Joyce Foundation. I didn't see why I was still a member of the youth council if I wasn't doing something about the issues I cared about.

Second, I didn't think I was treated fairly at all. There were some members who never showed up to meetings, about three of them. I'm not sure why they would never show up considering the fact that the youth council was a commitment. One of our biggest problems was that we lacked attendance. There was never a day that we had ten, eleven, or even twelve members show up. At least two seats were vacant; it made sense that we could never have fourteen or fifteen members present. I was very committed and came to every meeting until I started driver's education class to get my permit. Since my classes were three weeks long, I missed two meetings. I always emailed Mr. Owczarski to let him know I had a class and couldn't come. This way he knew why I couldn't be present.

But in June, 2015 we had a CDBG (Community Development Block Grant) meeting in which we had to assess people representing different youth organizations and determine the three organizations that would receive the grants from the youth council. That same day, I made a commitment to attend another CDBG meeting with the aldermen at a different location. This one was for other nonprofit organizations. I was scheduled to speak as a youth representative for Safe & Sound, an anticrime organization in Milwaukee. So, I walked to Mr. Owczarski and told him that I had another meeting to go to. He then, told me that he would have to replace me due to my absences. I thought he was going insane or confusing me for someone else. I knew he wasn't telling me I've been absent for so long when some of the members only showed up to the inaugurations but not any of the meetings.

I became so upset. I was going to respond back to him and say something perhaps hurtful, but I didn't want to cause a disturbance and interrupt the guests who were doing their presentations. So I left with anger. Ms. Mateen was my ride to the next meeting. I told her what happened. She told me that it was all politics, which made sense to me. It made me realize that maybe the youth council was not for me. When it was time for me to speak at the second CDBG meeting, I tried to put a smile on my face as I had to make sure Safe & Sound was able to obtain the grant they needed to continue their amazing effort to prevent crime and create safe neighborhoods.

After my comments on how Safe & Sound impacted my life, I had time to meet some of the aldermen present. I didn't have time to meet all of them, but I met Alderman Joe Davis, who founded the City of Milwaukee Youth Council. In the short time I've known him, he has so much hope for young people and is optimistic that we will bring change in the city. When I met him at the CDBG meeting I mentioned to him that Mr. Owczarski was planning on replacing me for no good reason. He told me that there was no way Mr. Owczarski would do such thing. I was relieved, but I didn't know how Alderman Davis would know that for sure. He told me that Mr. Owczarski couldn't replace me from the council just because I missed two meetings due to driver's education. He also stated that it was vital for me to get my permit and that it wasn't a good reason for me to be replaced. I felt better when he stated such comments and told myself that I shouldn't be upset because Mr. Owczarski can't kick me out of the council just because of two absences. Likewise, he never explained to me about the ruling of absences when I first started. I didn't find out that we couldn't have more than six excused absences until a few months before I left.

For the following seven months I actively showed up to our youth council meetings. But the following winter on January 27, 2016 I decided to resign. I hated the political atmosphere in the council. Originally, I was in search of a council that dealt with bringing change and positivity in the city without any political affiliation. It took me a while to decide to quit, because I felt that things were going to change in the youth council soon, every time. But that wasn't the case. I remained patient for too long. I felt that I was only coming to meetings and talking about political-related agendas with no mention of the serious issues that were haunting our city. It was finally time for me to say good-bye and focus on issues that were more important to me such as gun violence, poverty, education, and human trafficking.

On February 20, 2016 I met an amazing, intelligent, fun-loving woman named Ms. Dana World-Patterson. She worked for the Human Trafficking Taskforce of Wisconsin. Human trafficking is a serious issue in which I always wanted to help to prevent. As a matter of fact Milwaukee is said to be the hub of human trafficking. I wasn't surprised about that because I remember one day while riding on the school bus, I saw a woman dressed up with tight clothing waiting for a car to pool up at six in the morning. I didn't know what the woman was doing until one of the girls on the bus stated that she was a prostitute.

Henceforth, I was invited to attend an event at the University of Wisconsin-Milwaukee for the coming of the French Minister of Justice Christiane Taubira. Ms. Nicole Palasz, the program coordinator for the university's world affairs office, sent me the invitation hoping that I would resonate to the remarks the minister would make. Ms. Dana was one of the guests who were invited. When she walked in we bumped to each other and introduced ourselves. She thought I was a very determined young lady so she asked me if I could start a new youth council with her. I was honored that she wanted me to create a council with her. I always thought of starting my own youth-driven organization and hoped that working with her would lead to a new youth organization rather than a council.

Despite that, we agreed to start a new youth council. I loved that she suggested we start a youth-driven council rather than just a new youth council. She knew that youth these days are very curious and have great ideas. She suggested that she would just advise the council rather than be a part of it. We agreed that our council would solely focus on eradicating human trafficking by targeting key factors such as poverty, lack of education, and gender-based violence. On March 20, 2016 Ms. Dana held a fashion show to show awareness on human trafficking. I and several other girls from other schools were among the models. Community members including our county executive Chris Abele were among the models as well as actual professional models. Thanks to Ms. Dana, my dreams were coming true. I got to model at an actual fashion show for the first time and founded a youth-driven council where youth are actually in charge and are fighting for issues that affect their city.

Lessons from Half the Sky and Other Global Issues

The following are issues that I believe are important within the global spectrum and need to be spoken about more often. The issues are ones that I've read from *Half the Sky* written by best-selling authors Nicholas Kristof and his wife Sheryl WuDunn. The points on immigration, terrorism, and bullying are from my personal experiences.

Maternal Mortality

According to the World Health Organization (WHO), maternal mortality is the death of a pregnant woman within forty-two days of her termination of pregnancy. A great amount of maternal mortality occurs in developing countries. More than half of these deaths occur in sub-Saharan Africa while a third of it occurs in South Asia. Approximately 830 women die from preventable causes to pregnancy daily. Maternal mortality is higher in women living in rural areas and poor communities.

In Half the Sky, the story of a woman named Prudence is told. Prudence was a twenty-four-year-old Cameroonian woman and a mother of three children. When she went into labor to deliver her fourth child by an untrained birth attendant it was discovered that her cervix was blocked, which meant that the baby couldn't come out. After three days of labor, the birth attendant decided to sit on Prudence's stomach and jump up and down. This eventually burst her uterus. She was then taken to the hospital on a motorcycle. The doctor that was seeking to treat Prudence realized that she needed a C-section. The doctor needed $100 to do the procedure, but Prudence's family insisted that they could only raise $20. The authors mention that if Prudence was a man, the family would've sold enough possession to raise $100.

After three days of being untreated the fetus died and began decaying, which slowly toxicated Prudence. Nicholas Kristof and his videographer,

Naka Nathaniel agreed to paying the rest of the $80 for the surgery. But three days after the surgery, Prudence was spitting blood and had complications breathing. Her family then decided to take her back to her village to die. She died there a few hours later.

According to Nicholas Kristof's research there were four major factors that contributed to Prudence's death.

Biology: Having a narrow pelvis makes giving birth very difficult. Today most women are lucky to have medium-sized pelvises that allow quick locomotion and permit them to survive childbirth. Head size contributes to the problem as well. The head of a human baby is bigger than the maternal birth canal, therefore it makes giving birth painful and challenging, while it's easier for other primates.

Lack of Education: An educated family would have enough finances to afford the medical cost of childbirth. They would have saved up some money for medical expenses for the delivery in case something goes wrong. Education and family planning allows families to accumulate savings. If Prudence had an educated birth attendant, she would have been careful of not jumping on her stomach.

Lack of Rural Health Systems: If rural areas of poor countries had better health care structure, pregnant women would have been treated as soon as their arrival. Countries like Cameroon would have powerful antibiotics available to treat infections. There would also be trained rural birth attendants.

Disregard for Women: In most part of the world, women die because they are seen as unimportant in society. In the 1920s, America had about the same rate of maternal mortality as poor parts of Africa today. In societies where women were given the opportunity to vote, their lives became more important. This led to women being provided with good healthcare.

Human Trafficking

Human trafficking—the modern-day form of slavery involving the coercion and fraud in commercial sex in which a person is forced to participate in sexual acts, victimizes 12.3 million people around the world. The average age of victims is twelve to fourteen years old. Some of them are runaway girls who've suffered sexual abuse as children. Many victims become romantically involved with someone who manipulates them into

221

prostitution. Others are given false promises of a job. In some parts of the world such as India, some are forced to sell sex by their parents or other family members. A UN report estimates about one million children are forced into prostitution annually and the total number of children prostituted could be as high as ten million. Between 14,500 and 17,500 people are trafficked into the United States each year.

Half the Sky tells a story of Meena Hasina, an Indian Muslim who was trafficked. Meena was only twelve years old when she was put into the horrifying business. This was of course five months before she even went into puberty. Her first customer was very wealthy. Meena fought and cried when she was forced to have sex with him. So the brothel owner by the name of Ainul beat her with a belt, sticks, and iron rods. Occasionally, she was also threatened to be killed with swords if she resisted again. But Meena constantly refused after four to five customers, which resulted into more beatings.

Finally, the brothel owners who were from the Nutt tribe, a low-caste tribe that controls the local sex trade, drugged her by pouring wine in her drink and got her entirely drunk. Then, one of the owners raped her. Without any medical help Meena gave birth to a baby girl months later. Ainul, the head brothel owner took the baby from her so that she wasn't breastfeeding. Customers didn't like girls who were breastfeeding. The baby was kept as a hostage in case she (Meena) decided to run away. Unfortunately, after a few years Meena's daughter would also be forced into prostitution.

Female Genital Mutilation

FGM is a procedure involving the partial or total removal of the female genitalia. FGM has no health benefits. It damages female genital tissue. It causes immediate and long-term complications. Immediate problems include fever, infections, urinary problems, shock, and genital tissue swelling. Long-term complications include childbirth complications, painful intercourse, and menstrual problems. More than two hundred million girls and women today experience female genital mutilation mainly in parts of Africa, the Middle East, and Asia.

Though FGM is a cultural practice rather than a religious one, many people practice it fearing that their daughters can't get married if they are not cut. In most cases, if females aren't cut they are seen as unchaste. The cutting is done to prevent sexual desires. In Somalia it's done so that a girl doesn't run away with a man without marriage.

Today, female genital mutilation is practiced by Muslims in Africa, though it is also practiced by Christians in Africa. It's not common in most Arab countries or other Islamic cultures. FGM is taken to the extreme in Sudan, Ethiopia, and Somalia. In these countries the entire genital area is cut off by cutting away the clitoris, labia, and all the external genital area. In Egypt, girls are commonly cut during their teenage years. In Yemen, girls are cut within two weeks of birth. And in Somalia, girls are cut between the ages of four to eight. Knives or razor blades are typically used to do the procedure.

When I was five years old I remember some of my friends being cut. They were cut as a group. They were lined up on the ground with their feet tied with ropes. After the cutting, they were to lie on the ground for days until they could start walking again. If they had to urinate, they had to urinate in such position. My sisters and I were fortunate enough to not be cut. My dad knew the act was wrong and was not permitted in Islam. Pretty much every female member of my extended family was cut. My mom would always tell me not to tell others that I wasn't cut as it is a shame in our culture if you weren't. But, I take it with pride because some of my relatives who were cut ran away with men anyway. I didn't see the point of the cutting. I wasn't cut and still I'm living with my parents. I didn't understand why those who did the cutting were causing so much pain to girls and women but didn't accomplish the point of the cutting.

Immigration

Syria's civil war is said to be the worst humanitarian crisis that ever occurred. More than eleven million people have been killed or forced to leave their homes. The conflict commenced when antigovernment demonstrations began in March of 2011 as part of the Arab Spring. Peaceful protest quickly soared after the government erupted into violence and rebels began fighting against the regime. After five years of the civil war, hundreds of thousands of civilians died. The United Nations estimates that 6.6 million people are internally displaced.

In October 2015, Russian airstrikes targeting ISIS in Syria killed at least two thousand civilians. Many Syrian refugees are currently living in Jordan and Lebanon. Hundreds of thousands of refugees are risking their lives and making dangerous trips by boat from Turkey to Greece, hoping to have a better life in Europe. Some unfortunately don't make it. In response to the humanitarian crisis, many countries made a commitment to take in Syrian families. Germany took in eight hundred thousand asylum seekers, France took in 24,000 refugees, Britain took twenty thousand Syrian refugees, and the United States took in 1,500 refugees. Other countries including Australia and Sweden are also accepting refugees.

However, due to the recent terrorist attacks in Europe and North America, a 2016 presidential candidate called for a ban on Muslims entering the United States if he becomes president, because of ISIS's location in Syria. He claimed that ISIS members are posing as refugees in order to enter the United States. This can obviously be prevented with high security checkpoints, but it does not make any sense to restrict thousands of families who are leaving their country for survival to suddenly be banned from a country that was built upon immigrants who also left their countries due to persecution and suppression. ISIS is not only terrorizing Syrian families but also the Yazidi people of northern Iraq. Recent reports by the BBC and other news agencies have described ISIS's torture and killings of Yazidis as an act of genocide. Many of them were killed or captured and enslaved. Yazidis follow an ancient religion ISIS regards as devil worship and use that as an excuse to torture and kill them.

Many of the Yazidi girls and women ISIS captures are forced to become sex slaves. According to the Human Rights Watch, twelve-year-old girls were said to have been raped by ISIS fighters. In September 2014, about 3,133 Yazidis have been kidnapped or killed. However, this number has risen to 5,324 in March of 2015. In other cases, women and girls were forced into marriages with ISIS fighters.

If a Yazidi woman was pregnant before her capture, her baby was killed. This way ISIS would rape the woman in order for her to be pregnant with an "Islamic baby." Young girls no matter what age they were are forced to have sex with ISIS members often violently. Many of these women and girls attempt to commit suicide in order to avoid rape, forced marriage, and forced practice of the religion of Islam. According to the Human Rights Watch, the females attempt to commit suicide by cutting their wrists with glass or razor, try to hang themselves, attempt to electrocute themselves in the bathroom, and drink poison. These are the horrendous issues that are taking place around the world. Despite all this there are people in the world who are trying to find ways to prevent people like the Yazidis to enter the United States and other developed countries due to fears of terrorism. What group doesn't commit terror around the world! Immigrants or not there will still be mass shootings and chaos, especially when you give people the permission to have guns. Oftentimes, politicians in the United States will claim that most mass shootings are done by people who come from immigrant families. However, if you look at mass shootings such as the Sandy Hooke shooting, Aurora movie theater shooting, the Sikh Temple shooting, etc., these are Caucasian men who are taking the lives of innocent people.

This is only part of the problem. Once these shootings take place these men are said to have mental illnesses. It might've been the case for the Sandy Hooke shooter, but not for all the other Caucasian men who also committed the same crime. When it's a so-called Muslim shooter or anyone with an Arab name, he is deemed to be a terrorist, which may be true but is also the same for Caucasian killers. If it's a black man, he basically deserved to die. I mean what kind of society do we live in! This is outrageous! Why do we look at our religion and race so much? Are we not all human beings? Is respect even in existence?

The Republican candidate for the 2016 presidential race in the United States also made a controversial statement about Mexicans. He stated, "When Mexico sends its people, they're not sending their best. They're sending people that have lots of problems, and they're bringing problems with us. They're bringing drugs. They're bringing crime. They're rapists. And some, I assume, are good people."

This is clearly a statement made by someone who has no awareness on the problems immigrants or refugees face. There will always be criminals in each society. Blaming a problem on a whole ethnic group is ridiculous. There are many reasons as to why Mexicans enter the United States. Among these problems include the incredibly high crime rate in Mexico, especially homicide rates; unemployment and poverty has increased exponentially in Mexico in recent years. In 2009, unemployment rose by 34.43 percent. And even those with jobs suffer with low wages, hence not being able to fully provide their families with needs.

Despite all these problems taking place in Mexico, people continue to talk about illegal immigrants as if they are a threat to humanity. It's understandable that they come in the United States illegally, but when you're fleeing for your life trying to escape from drug dealers and criminals, there's no time for a proper check. This does indeed give drug dealers an opportunity to come in the United States, but the majority of Mexicans coming in the United States left because they wanted a better life for themselves and their children. There are a few cases in which young children cross the border by themselves. Some of them are often orphans. With that said, why would anyone deport such group of people in a terrible situation? The obvious answer is someone who lacks knowledge of immigration. Stereotypes of immigrants whether they're Hispanics, Africans, or Asians need to be put to rest. We are all humans, and yes, we'll make mistakes sometimes but that's part of human nature. Build bridges not walls!

Bullying

It's very saddening to hear about all the suicides that have occurred among young people due to bullying these past few years. I might not be a victim of bullying, but there are youth out there who are already facing personal problems, whether it's psychologically or financially, and saying one rude thing to them will make their day even worse or even make them feel bad about themselves. The sad truth about potential suicide victims is that they often feel alone and have no one to talk to. There are two types of potential suicide victims: One type seem very happy about life and may even have a great social life, but hide their suicidal thoughts from family and friends, meaning they hide internal conflicts from others. The other type of potential suicide victims are typically seen as introverts. They are seen to be independent, soft spoken, and quite nervous.

Normally, they just want someone to speak to them. Someone they can tell all their problems and hopefully give them good advice. My biggest advice to students and adults has always been to talk to people who fall in this category. In a lot of situations, greeting them and asking them how they're doing makes their day. This type of people isn't being awkwardly quiet because they are antisocial. They are in need of assistance. I highly encourage talking to people who we deem to think are extremely shy and independent. You'll save someone's life.

According to studies, suicide is the third leading cause of death among young people. According to studies by Yale University, bully victims are two to nine times more likely to consider suicide than nonvictims. Warning signs of suicide can include:

- Signs of depression, not interacting with others, or trouble sleeping or eating
- Engaging in dangerous activities
- Stating that they can't handle things anymore
- Saying that things would be better without them
- Talking about death

Unfortunately, I experienced all these things, but I never thought about killing myself. I always thought of running to other family members that I thought would understand me. However, I've never been bullied. My situation was a bit different. I came from immigrant parents who don't know how to read or write. So, everything is my responsibility, especially as the oldest child. I am responsible for writing my family's monthly bills, school work, required after school activities, my activism work, chores at home, helping my siblings with school assignments, bathing my siblings, and translating for my parents at every appointment.

During my first two years of high school, I was often overwhelmed with my responsibilities. I went to school, and instead of trying to concentrate in class, I was always thinking about how much chores was waiting for me before I could do homework or practice for the tests and quizzes I had the following day. Sometimes I thought about running away to one of my aunts' house because I thought they would understand my problems. It didn't seem like my parents did no matter how many times I told them I was struggling due to the expectations they had for me.

My father who at one point stressed the importance of education would tell me to drop out of school if I couldn't handle life anymore. But I knew that's not what I wanted for myself, and I didn't want them to think that they sacrificed many things for us to come into America just so that I could quit school. I knew I wanted to graduate high school and eventually college; dropping out was never an option for me. I just wanted my parents to stop depending on me so much and learn to trust Malyun and Sahara for once. That never changed; they still depend on me a lot and I can't do anything about it. So, I went from a straight A student to an A and B student. I went into high school thinking I would get straight As, join many clubs, and hold student office positions. I then realized that with me being the oldest child of eight, that was unlikely. I dealt with my problems by writing them out on my journal. I kept a journal where I only wrote about my feelings when I had a bad day, which was almost every week. Sometimes I read verses from the Qur'an about hardship and the rights and duties to parents. From that I learned to look at the good things in life and what I was fortunate to have that others don't. As time went by, my depression was fading away. There are several things that make me feel down, but I'm a happier person now. Writing and my faith was my cure.

In terms of bullying, Abubakar, my eleven-year-old brother had experienced such cruel act. My siblings attended a school called *Milwaukee Math and Science Academy* (MMSA). It's a concept school or some say a charter school located in the Harambee area in Milwaukee. I signed my siblings up to the school in 2011 when I realized their previous school had a poor education system. It was also a private school. MMSA was a new school at the time. Because of the advertisement on the fliers we were given through the mail, my mother and I assumed that it was a good school. When Abubakar became a fourth grader in the fall of 2015 that's when problems arose. That November he was beaten by two classmates on the school bus.

According to my sisters and the other students on the bus, two of his classmates who were best friends attacked him. The bus driver didn't do anything to stop the students from beating him. My sister Sahara couldn't do anything about the situation because the bus driver would threaten to suspend her when she tried defending her brother. The driver himself was accused of reckless driving by the students. My siblings would always tell me and my mother that he had favoritism for the African American students and disrespected the African students. During the cold winter when the bus stopped at their stop, he wouldn't open the door until five minutes later. During those times the temperature was around below zero. My mom constantly complained to the school and the bus company, but nothing would be done. The bus driver still came back each day. Things escalated even more when my brother told us that the boys tried to put his head in the toilet once at school and that the driver punched him when he tried to defend himself from the boys on the bus. That week my brother had nightmares. He had nightmares about school months before, but we weren't aware until one day when he confessed to killing himself.

That's when my mom and I really got worried about his state of mind. We lectured him about not killing himself as that was a sin in Islam. We told him that Allah (God) would not be pleased with him if he did such thing. That time we hid everything he could possibly use to kill himself. I took extra precaution and had him sleep with me in case he decided to walk out in the middle of the night to grab a knife. He then told us that he was hearing voices in his head telling him that the monster (the two boys) were waiting outside for him. He also mentioned seeing weird creatures appear in his visions daily. In his next doctor's appointment, my mom told his doctor everything that was happening to him. The doctor referred him to a psychiatrist. After an evaluation, the psychiatrist stated that Abubakar would stay at the psychology center for two nights in a secure room for patients who are suicidal.

After leaving that facility, he was put in a daytime program, learning about how to cope with bullying, along with other kids who were dealing with bullying. During these transitions, he wasn't going to school by doctor's orders. He ended up missing two weeks of school. I couldn't believe all of this was happening to my brother. I could see why he was bullied. He's very quiet, shy, gaunt, and very smart for his age. He is highly artistic and knows a lot about cars. He loves engineering-related toys. Sometimes he would break his toy cars just to put them back together again. I thought the boys were probably jealous of his intelligence or might've just thought he was the easiest thing to mess with.

When Abubakar was attending daycare when he was younger, the teachers called him Smiley because he would never talk, but he would always smile. As a youngster he also didn't know how to interact with other kids. He was always playing with my sister Fatuma, who was like his twin. They were born the same day and month but different years. They are two years apart, but some people think they're twins because they're about the same height.

After his psychology sessions were over, the psychiatrist prescribed him an antidepressant medication. The community activists who were helping my mother to sue the school and the bus company told us that it was not a good idea that he take the medication. They told my mother and I that he was very smart and they were afraid the medication would sort of decrease his intelligence. So, my mom stopped him from taking the medication after a week.

After a while we tried to meet with the parents of my brother's bullies. The principal, who was not a very good principal and spoke only a little bit of English said that talking to the parents was a bad idea. However, my mother wanted justice for her son and demanded to get a meeting with the parents. When we finally had the meeting, the two parents decided to leave in the middle of the meeting shouting ridiculous comments as said by the activists. They didn't believe their sons caused any trouble toward my brother. We forgave the parents because both me and my mother knew that children act different when they are in school and with their parents. We didn't think they would possibly know how their sons behaved at school.

Meanwhile, my mother tried to sue the school for not punishing the boys for bullying and for punishing my brother who was the victim every time he tried to defend himself. We were also going to sue the bus company which was *Lakeside* for not firing the bus driver even till this day. He still drives one of the buses for MMSA today. I convinced my mom to forgive them and drop charges since we were taking my siblings out of the school anyway. Since then, my brother was back to his old curious self again. All of my siblings were placed in a better private school. The whole situation was very frustrating to me because my brother is one of the best things that ever happened to me. He's usually one of my siblings who would try to cheer me up when I'm down. He's a very happy person and his presence makes me happy. I appreciated everything my mom has done to help him get over bullying and suicidal thoughts. She was very determined and did above and beyond even though she herself was going through rough times. My mom and my brother are my motivation and joy each and every day. They shaped who I am today.

Color in the Justice System

You would think that life would get better for people of color after the civil rights era. Think again. Marks of injustice can still be traced in our current justice system. According to the Center for American Progress, 30 percent of the United States's population consists of people of color; they are also 60 percent of those imprisoned. One in every fifteen African American men are incarcerated. Racial profiling is also a huge problem in America. The Department of Justice reported that blacks and Hispanics were three times more likely to be searched during a traffic stop than white motorists. And during arrests African Americans are four times likely to encounter the use of force by police. Not only that, African American youth have higher juvenile incarceration rates and are more likely to be sentenced to adult prison. When convicted, black offenders get longer sentences than white offenders. The Sentencing Project reported that African Americans are 21 percent more likely to obtain mandatory-minimum sentences than white defendants and are 20 percent more likely to be sentenced to prison.

This problem is not far from our education system either. Many education reformers such as the ACLU (American Civil Liberties Union), the Advancement Project, and Burns Institute, state that oppressive school policies and restrictions have created a schoolhouse-to-jailhouse track for students. According to the Advancement Project, "The schoolhouse-to-jailhouse track is an education problem as much as it is a criminal justice problem. When students are pushed out of school through harsh disciplinary policies, their education is interrupted."

The organization proceeds to say, "For many students, harsh discipline is part of a vicious cycle. Students who are already struggling are more prone to misbehave out of frustration. When they do act out they are harshly punished, which in turn leads to further academic struggle and frustration. Stopping the schoolhouse-to-jailhouse track, thus not only promises to treat our children humanely and keep them out of prison, but it also promises to be a first step toward offering every child the opportunity to succeed in school and beyond." This is a broader reason why some minority students choose to drop out of school. Students in such group feel as if policies like the school-to-prison pipeline are established to target them, leading them to believe that they aren't guaranteed any success in life.

According to *Rethinking Schools*, the school-to-prison pipeline begins in deep social and economic inequalities, and has taken root in the historic shortcomings of schooling in this country. The civil and human rights movements of the 1960s and 1970s spurred an effort to "rethink schools" to make them responsive to the needs of all students, their families, and communities.

But according to an article from PBS's Tavis Smiley Reports, the school-to-prison pipeline is an epidemic that is plaguing schools across the nation. Far too often, students are suspended, expelled, or even arrested for minor offenses that leave visits to the principal's office a thing of the past. Statistics reflect that these policies neglect poverty or learning disabilities.

The report also indicates that students who are forced out of school for disruptive behavior are usually sent back to the origin of their angst and unhappiness—their home environments or their neighborhoods, which are filled with negative influence. Those who are forced out for smaller offenses become hardened, confused, embittered. Those who are unnecessarily forced out of school become stigmatized and fall behind in their studies; many eventually decide to drop out of school altogether, and many others commit crimes in their communities.

According to the ACLU, many of these students have learning disabilities or are experiencing poverty, abuse, or neglect, and would benefit from additional educational and counseling services. Instead, they are isolated, punished, and pushed out.

"Zero-tolerance" policies criminalize minor infractions of school rules, while cops in school lead to students being criminalized for behavior that should be handled inside the school. Students of color are especially vulnerable to push-out trends and the discriminatory application of discipline.

Reformers like the ACLU believe that children should be educated, not incarcerated. They are working to challenge numerous policies and practices within public school systems and the juvenile justice system that contribute to the school-to-prison pipeline.

The growth of the school-to-prison pipeline is part of a larger crisis. Since the 1970s, the US prison population has exploded from about 325,000 people to more than two million today. According to Michelle Alexander, author of *The New Jim Crow: Mass Incarceration in the Age of Color Blindness*, this is a phenomenon that cannot be explained by crime rates or drug use. According to Human Rights Watch (Punishment and Prejudice: Racial Disparities in the War on Drugs, 2000) although whites are more likely to violate drug laws than people of color, in some states black men have been admitted to prison on drug charges at rates twenty to fifty times greater than those of white men. Latinos, Native Americans, and other people of color are also imprisoned at rates far higher than their representation in the population. Once released, former prisoners are caught in a web of laws and regulations that make it difficult or impossible to secure jobs, education, housing, and public assistance—and often to vote or serve on juries. Alexander calls this permanent second-class citizenship a new form of segregation.

The impact of mass incarceration is devastating for children and youth. More than seven million children have a family member incarcerated, on probation, or on parole. Many of those children live with enormous stress, emotional plan, and uncertainty.

Kenya/ Somali Bantu refugees to be resettled to the U.S.A. / Arrival in Kakuma for processing. / UNHCR/ B. Press/ July 2002

Kenya/ Somali Bantu refugees to be resettled to U.S.A. / Leaving Ifo camp, Dadaab / UNHCR / B. Press / July 2002

Kenya / Somali Bantu refugees to be resettled to U.S.A. /
Mwingi Transit centre / UNHCR / B. Press / July 2002

Kenya / Somali Bantu refugees to be resettled to U.S.A. /
Dagahaley Camp, Dadaab / UNHCR / B. Press / July 2002

Kenya / Somali Bantu refugees to be resettled to U.S.A. /
Dagahaley Camp, Dadaab / UNHCR / B. Press / July 2002

Kenya / Somali Bantu refugees to be resettled to U.S.A. / Bus
transfer to Ifo camp, departure point from Kakuma, then U.S.A. /
Dagahaley Camp, Dadaab / UNHCR / B. Press / July 2002

Kenya / Somali Bantu refugees to be resettled to U.S.A. / Line up for
transfer to Kakuma / Dagahaley camp / UNHCR / B. Press / July 2002

Kenya / Somali Bantu Community / Kakuma ll
camp / UNHCR / B. Press / July 1999

Me (right) with one of the Juneteenth 2016 contestants

Ms. Terry Perry and I at the Youth Council inauguration in 2014

Westside's Serve 2 Unite Group at a Gun Violence Prevention Summit

Me taking the oath at the Youth Council inauguration

Ms. Dana World-Patterson, County Executive Chris Abele, and I

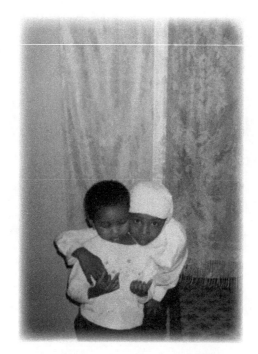

Me and my sister Sahara in 2005

Me at a soccer practice with my dad

My maternal grandmother in Tanzania (2015)

My Father (middle) with my great uncle (right) and his friend (left)

Malyun (back) and Sahara (front)

My dad with my brothers Abubakar (right) and Nasir (center)

My Siblings Abubakar, Sahara, and I

Sahara and my uncle Jamal

Me in our backyard in Louisville, Kentucky in 2005

Ms. Mateen and I

Me and my friend Ayanna along with Milwaukee Mayor Tom Barrett (2016)

My school picture from 2005 at Wilkerson

My sisters and I walking to our car heading to Qur'an class

My first grade picture

My parents (2005)

3-year old Sahara

My dad (left) and a friend in 1998

Malyun (2006)

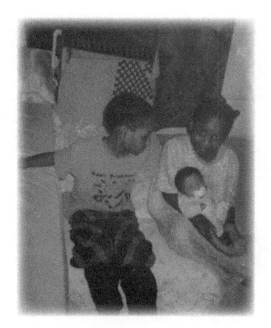

Malyun holding baby Fatuma as I watched

My second grade school picture

Giving my acceptance speech after winning Safe &
Sound's Youth Leadership Award (2015)

A portrait of Dictator Siad Barre drawn by Janice Vogt

Westside Acadamy's Baby Eights group: (left) Angel, Shanice, me,
Davon, Carlos, Keturah, and Jamonte (center).
Derriss is not pictured.

Timeline of Somalia

15,000–8000 BCE: The Laas Geel, one of the earliest known rock cultures in Africa, exists on the Somali Peninsula

3000–2000 BCE: Domestication of the camel in Somalia

1475 BCE: Queen Pharaoh Hatshepsut sends a trading voyage to Punt

615 CE: Prophet Muhammad and his entourage take refuge on the Horn

1500–1600: Portuguese traders land on the east coast of Africa and start intermittent power struggles with the Sultanate of Zanzibar for control of port cities and surrounding towns

1800: Many Bantu people from Malawi, Mozambique, and Tanzania were taken from the homes and sold as slaves in Somalia

1840: The British East India Company signs treaties with the Sultan of Tajura for unrestricted trading rights

1885: Italy seizes control of Massawe in Eritrea

1887: Britain reaches a final agreement with the local King Menelik and various tribal chiefs and draws a boundary with neighboring Ethiopia to form British Somaliland. Besides trading interests, the British Protectorate serves as a counterweight to the growing Italian influence in the key port city of neighboring Zanzibar.

1897–1907: Italy makes several agreements with tribal chiefs and the British to finally mark out the boundaries of a separate Italian Protectorate of Somaliland.

1908: The Italian Government assumes direct administration of Italian Somaliland, giving the territory a colonial status.

1934 Dec 5: Ethiopian and Italian troops clashed at the Ualual on disputed Somali-Ethiopian border.

1935 Feb 18: Rome reported sending troops to Italian Somalia.

1936: Following decades of expansionism, Italy captures Addis Ababa and Ethiopia to form the province of Italian East Africa.

1940 Jun: Italian troops drive out the British garrison and capture British Somaliland.

1941: British recapture British Somaliland and most of Italian Somaliland.

1947: Following Italy's defeat in World War II, Italy renounces all rights and titles to Italian Somaliland.

1950: The UN General Assembly adopts a resolution making Italian Somaliland a UN trust territory under Italian administrative control.

1941–1959: Meanwhile, British Somaliland sees a period of colonial development as the territory moves toward a gradual development of local institutions and self-government.

1960: British and Italian Somaliland gain independence and merge to form the United Republic of Somalia.

1969 Oct: Maj. Gen. Mohamed Siad Barre seized power in a coup. Democratically elected President Abdi Rashid Ali Shermarke is assassinated.

1970: Siad declares Somalia a socialist nation and undertakes literacy programs and planned economic development under the principles of "scientific socialism."

1972–1977: A period of persistent border clashes with Ethiopia for control of Ethiopia's Ogaden region, which also sees a severe drought in the region that leads to widespread starvation.

1974: Somalia and the Soviet Union sign a treaty of friendship. Somalia also joins the Arab League.

1977: Somalia invades the Ogaden region of Ethiopia.

1978: Following a gradual shifting of Soviet favor from Somalia to Ethiopia and the infusions of Soviet arms and Cuban troops to Ethiopia, Somali troops are pushed out of Ethiopian territory.

1978 Feb 7: Ethiopia mounted a counterattack against Somalia.

1978–1990: A period of growing cooperation and strategic alliance between Somalia and the West begins. The United States becomes Somalia's chief partner in defense and several Somali military officers are trained in US military schools

1981 Apr: A group of Isaaq emigres living in London formed the Somali National Movement (SNM), which subsequently became the strongest of Somalia's various insurgent movements. According to its spokesmen, the rebels wanted to overthrow Siad Barre's dictatorship.

1981 Oct: The Somali National Movement (SNM) rebels elected Ahmad Mahammad Culaid and Ahmad Ismail Abdi as chairman and secretary general, respectively, of the movement.

1981: Northern Somalia rebelled against Dictator Mohammed Siad Barre. A national civil war followed. During the civil war an estimated forty thousand people were killed and about four hundred thousand refugees fled to Ethiopia.

1981: China emerged as a major arms supplier to the Siad Barre regime in Somalia.

1982 Jan 2: The Somali National Movement (SNM) launched its first military operation against the Somali government, operating from Ethiopian bases.

1983 Feb: Siad Barre visited Northern Somalia in a campaign to discredit the SNM. Among other things, he ordered the release of numerous civil servants and businessmen who had been arrested for antigovernment activities, lifted the state of emergency, and announced an amnesty for Somali exiles who wanted to return home.

1991 Jan 27: Muhammad Siad Barre, the dictator of the Somali Democratic Republic since 1969, fled Mogadishu as rebels overran his palace and captured the Somali capital. Dictator Siad Barre was ousted and power fractured into some twenty-seven warring sides and Ali Mahdi Mohammed declared himself president.

1991: The northeast corner of the country declared itself the independent Republic of Somaliland.

1991: Thousands of Bantus fled Somalia for Kenya. In 1999 the United States designated this group of people as persecuted and eligible for resettlement in the United States.

1991–1992: Some 350,000 Somalis died from disease, starvation, and civil war.

1992 Aug 14: President Clinton ordered the Pentagon to begin emergency airlifts of food to Somalia which was suffering from severe famine and factional warfare.

1992: A UN arms embargo was imposed in Somalia.

1992–1994: Italian Warrant Officer Francesco Aloi kept a diary while in Somalia and documented instances of rape, torture, and other brutality against the Somalis

1993 Mar 16: Canadian soldiers in Somalia beat to death a local teenager, Shidane Arone, during their participation in the UN humanitarian efforts. An inquiry led to the disbanding of Canada's elite Canadian Airborne Regiment, greatly damaged the morale of the

Canadian Forces, and damaged both the domestic and international reputation of Canadian soldiers.

1993 Sep 9: About a hundred Somali gunmen and civilians were killed when US and Pakistani peacekeepers fired on Somalis attacking other peacekeepers.

1993 Oct 7: President Clinton ordered more troops, heavy armor, and naval firepower to Somalia, but also announced he would pull out all Americans by the end of March 1994.

1994 Mar 25: American troops completed their withdrawal from Somalia following a largely unsuccessful fifteen-month mission. Twenty thousand UN troops were left behind to keep the peace and facilitate "nation building."

1995 Feb 20: An American Marine, Sgt. Justin A. Harris, died in a helicopter crash during the evacuation of United Nations forces from Somalia.

1995 Mar 1: Somalia militiamen loyal to warlord Mohamed Farrah Aidid seized control of the Mogadishu airport after peacekeepers withdrew.

1995 Mar 2: The last UN peacekeepers in Somalia were evacuated.

1998 Dec 8: At least eighteen people were killed and thirty wounded in clashes between two rival clans in Baidoa

1999: In Somalia Hassan Sheikh Mohamud helped found the Somali Institute of Management and Administration Development to train administrators and technicians to help rebuild Somalia.

2000 Apr 25: In southwestern Somalia nearly four hundred people in famine-ridden villages were reported dead from cholera over the last two weeks

2000 Jul: Thousands of Somalis took to the streets of Mogadishu in support of a peace conference in Djibouti.

2000 Aug 13: Over two thousand Somali leaders gathered in Djibouti to form a central government with a new 225-member parliament. Somalia swore in legislators for its first central government after almost a decade of internecine warfare.

2000 Aug 26: Abdiqasim Salad Hassan, a former interior minister, won the presidential elections.

2002 Jan 3: The United States announced increased military operations in Somalia and prepared to send marines there. It was suspected that Al Qaeda fighters might attempt fleeing to Somalia.

2003 May 20: The first of more than 12,000 Somali Bantus awaiting resettlement set out for the United States, leaving at long last the refugee camps where most have lived for a decade.

2004 Oct 10: Members of Somalia's transitional parliament elected Col. Abdullahi Yusuf (70) as interim president.

2005 Feb 9: In Somalia, BBC journalist Kate Peyton was shot to death outside a Mogadishu hotel where she had interviewed some members of the interim parliament.

2005 May 3: An explosion erupted as Somalia's provisional prime minister was starting a speech, killing at least seven people, and causing an undetermined number of injuries at a government rally in Mogadishu's soccer stadium.

2005 May 14: Warlords began withdrawing thousands of militia fighters from the Somali capital in a bid to restore order after more than fifteen years of anarchy and civil war.

2005 Dec 25: In Somalia, warlords and civilians installed a council to govern Mogadishu, an action that further fragments the nation but could bring the capital under the control of a single group after fifteen years of anarchy.

2005 Dec 29: Drought was reported to have triggered extreme food shortages in the East African countries of Ethiopia, Kenya, and Somalia, putting millions of people at risk of famine as the lean dry season approaches.

2005: In Somalia, some three dozen Somalis formed a club of Islamists, soon dubbing themselves Shabaab (Arabic for youth).

2006 Jan 1: East African leaders said that millions of people in the region faced hunger because poor rains had affected vital crops and pasture. Burundi, Ethiopia, Kenya, Somalia, and Tanzania faced acute food shortages.

2006 Feb: In Somalia, a warlord alliance, the Alliance for the Restoration of Peace and Counter-Terrorism (ARPCT), was created with US support in a bid to curb the growing influence of the Islamic courts, hunt down the extremists they are accused of sheltering, and disrupt feared plans for new terrorist attacks

2006 Mar 21: The UN appealed for nearly $327 million in aid to help starving people in southern Somalia, which is suffering its worst drought in a decade.

2006 Jun 27: In Mogadishu, Somalia, members of an Islamic militia that controls most of southern Somalia battled for a clan-held checkpoint, killing five people before declaring victory.

2007 Dec 2: A Somali human rights group said violence in Mogadishu has killed 5,960 civilians this year.

2007: US military advisors began secretly operating in Somalia. This was only made public in 2014 as Washington planned to deepen its security assistance to help the country fend off threats by al Shabaab.

2008 Feb 3: In Somalia, a roadside bomb killed eight civilians and wounded nine others when it exploded near a minibus full of passengers in war-ravaged Mogadishu.

2008 Jul 13: A World Food Program contractor was gunned down in Somalia, the fifth agency worker to be killed that year.

2008 Sep 15: In Somalia, an African Union peacekeeper was killed in a roadside bomb explosion in Mogadishu, the second AU member to be killed in there in as many days.

2009 Jan 16: The UN Security Council unanimously adopted a resolution expressing its intention to establish a UN peacekeeping force in Somalia, but putting off a decision for several months in order to assess the volatile situation in the Horn of Africa nation.

2009 Jan 24:, In Somalia, seventeen people were killed in Mogadishu by a suicide car bomb targeting African Union peacekeepers. The dead included a police officer who tried to stop the suicide bomber's car. A gunfight between peacekeepers and insurgents followed and left five more dead

2009 Mar 19: Al-Qaeda chief Osama bin Laden urged Somali militants to overthrow the country's new president in a new Web audiotape; trying to torpedo a new push for peace in a lawless African nation where many fear al-Qaeda is gaining a foothold.

2009 Mar 20: The UN Security Council gave a stamp of approval to Somalia's new unity government and urged increased international aid to African Union (AU) peacekeepers trying to contain the violence in the lawless country.

2009 Jun 26: The UN refugee agency said that the bloody conflict in Somalia has created the world's largest refugee camp, with five hundred hungry and exhausted refugees pouring into a wind-swept camp in neighboring Kenya every day.

2009 Jul 20: In Somalia, Islamic insurgents with alleged links with al-Qaida looted two United Nations compounds in southern Somalia and announced they will ban three UN agencies from operating in areas the militants control.

2009 Sep 9: A Somali Islamic court cut off the hands of two men accused of theft and lashed another accused of rape.

2010 Jan 5: The UN food agency said it is stopping aid distribution to about one million people in southern Somalia because of attacks against staff and demands by armed groups that aid organizations remove women from their teams.

2010 Jan 31: In Ethiopia, UN Secretary-General Ban Ki-moon attended the AU's annual summit in Addis Ababa and again failed to pledge peacekeepers for Somalia. Ban Ki-moon criticized power-grabs in Africa in a speech to the continent's leaders as Libya's Muammar Gaddafi reluctantly handed over the presidency of the African Union to Malawian president Bingu wa Mutharika. The AU agreed to consider a Senegalese proposal to resettle Haiti's earthquake homeless and possibly create a state for them in Africa.

2010 Mar 10: A UN Security Council report said up to half the food aid in Somalia is being diverted to corrupt contractors, radical Islamic militants, and local UN workers.

2010 Apr 14: President Obama signed an executive order freezing the assets of Somali militias. The order could make it illegal for US ship owners to pay ransoms to Somali pirates.

2010 Jul 20: A Somali human rights group said at least fifty-three civilians were killed over the past week in clashes between government forces and Islamic militants.

2010 Sep 7: UN officials said fighting in Mogadishu has killed over 230 people in the past two weeks after al-Shabaab threatened a massive war against the government.

2011 Jul 20:, The United Nations said it faces a $4.3 billion shortfall in helping the fifty million people worldwide in need of emergency food, shelter, and other humanitarian aid. The UN declared famine in two regions of southern Somalia.

2011 Jul 21: In Somalia, al-Shabaab spokesman Sheikh Ali Mohamud Rage said al-Shabaab won't allow banned aid workers into the areas it controls. He called the UN's declaration of famine in parts of Somalia politically motivated and pure propaganda. Al-Shabaab rebels in Balad abducted and detained Asha Osman Aqiil, a newly appointed woman minister, while she was on her way to take up office in Mogadishu

2012 Feb 18: Somalia's disparate leaders agreed on the basic structure of a new parliament and government to replace the fragile transitional body that has failed to bring peace to the war-torn country. The accord proposed a parliamentary system for anarchic Somalia, with both Puntland and Galmudug recognized as states within a federal system.

2012 Sep 10: Hassan Sheikh Mohamud, a university professor and dean is elected president of Somalia.

2013 Apr 29: Nicholas Kay is appointed by the United Nations Secretary-General Ban Ki-moon as the new UN Special Representative for Somalia.

2013 Jun 3: Established May 2, 2013 by the UN Security Council, UNSOM was launched in order to support the Federal Government of Somalia's agenda of peace, security, and nation-building and help the country move toward free and fair elections in 2016.

2013 Dec 21: Somalia's parliament approved as the new prime minister Abdiweli Sheikh Ahmed, a political newcomer and economist who faces tough challenges in the war-torn nation.

2013: James Fergusson authored *The World's Most Dangerous Place: Inside the Outlaw State of Somalia.*

2014 Jan 26: In southern Somalia, a US missile strike killed Ahmed Mohamed Amey, a chemicals expert also known as Isku Dhuuq. He was a senior al Shabaab commander who had masterminded suicide attacks by the al Qaeda-linked militant group.

2014 Feb 18: Human Rights Watch said Saudi Arabian authorities have deported more than 12,000 migrants held under "appalling conditions" back to their native Somalia. The International Organization for Migration said the Somali government expects Saudi Arabia to deport another thirty thousand people in the coming weeks

2014 Mar 3: Uganda said it will send about four hundred extra troops to Somalia to protect UN personnel in Mogadishu.

2014 Apr 7: In Somalia, two men working for the United Nations were shot dead at Galkayo airport. Former British police officer Simon Davis (57) and his French colleague, researcher Clement Gorrissen (28), were working on links between money transfer systems and piracy.

2014 Jun 11: UNICEF reported that Somalia is suffering an outbreak of measles with 1,350 suspected cases reported in March and April.

2014 Jun 18: In Somalia, a doctor and a nurse were killed and seven others wounded when a car bomb exploded at a hospital in Mogadishu.

2014 Jun 30: China said it will reopen its embassy in Mogadishu twenty-three years after evacuating its diplomats as Somalia plunged into civil war.

2015 Apr 3: At least 147, mostly students, have been killed in an assault by al-Shabaab militants on a university in northeastern Kenya.

2015 Feb 24: President Obama nominated Katherine Dhanani, a long-time diplomat with deep experience of African affairs ambassador of Somalia; she's the first ambassador to Somalia since 1991

2015 May 6: Secretary of State, John Kerry became the first US secretary of state to visit Somalia.

2016 Jan 15: A massive siege broke out at an African Union base in El Adde killing at least 120 Kenyan soldiers.

2016 Feb 5: Al- Shabaab captured Merca, but is driven out of the city four days later.

2016 Feb 24: Somali police arrest a senior Al- Shabaab member in a hotel in Mogadishu.

2016 Mar 8: American airstrikes on Al- Shabaab camp in Somalia kills about 150 militants who had gathered for a graduation ceremony.

Bibliography

Half the Sky by Nicholas Kristof and Sheryl WuDunn

Fact Monster. *"Somalia"* June 2015
http://www.factmonster.com/country/somalia.html

U.S. Department of State. *"U.S. Relations With Somalia"* June 15, 2015
http://www.state.gov/r/pa/ei/bgn/2863.html

Lehman, Dan Van and Eno, Omar *"The Somali Bantu: Their History and Culture"* February 2003
http://www.hartfordinfo.org/issues/wsd/immigrants/somali_bantu.pdf

Minority Rights Group International. *"Somalia Overview"* May 2011
http://www.minorityrights.org/4511/somalia/bantu.html

Bridging Refugee Youth & Children's Services. *"Somali Bantu Refugees: Cultural Considerations for Social Service Providers"*
http://www.brycs.org/documents/upload/SBantu-Service-Considerations.pdf

Horizons for Refugee Families. *"Somali Bantu: Their History"*
http://refugeehorizons.org/on-refugees/somali-bantu/history/

Nations Encyclopedia. *"Somalia: Country Overview"*
http://www.nationsencyclopedia.com/economies/Africa/Somalia.html

Mohamoud, Mohamed Hagi. *"Somaliland: The Political Formation of the Somali Republic"* http://www.somalilandpress.com/somaliland-political-formation-somali-republic/

Wazigua Community Organization of Central New York. *"History and Discrimination of the Bantus"* http://cnywazigua.org/history.html

Centers for Disease Control and Prevention. *"Chapter 2. Overview of Somali Culture"* http://www.cdc.gov/tb/publications/guidestoolkits/ethnographicguides/somalia/chapters/chapter2.pdf

Zapata, Mollie. *"Somalia: Colonialism to Independence to Dictatorship, 1840-1976"* Jan 31, 2012 http://www.enoughproject.org/blogs/somalia-colonialism-independence-dictatorship-1840-1976

Infoplease. *"Somalia"* http://www.infoplease.com/encyclopedia/world/somalia-history.html

UNHCR The UN Refugee Agency. *"Finding a Home on Ancestral Land: Somali Bantu Refugees Gaining Citizenship in Tanzania"* http://www.unhcr.org/4c4444266.pdf

Baki Press. *"The Ethnic Origin of the Somali People and Clan System"* December 15, 2013 https://bakipress.wordpress.com/2013/12/15/the-ethnic-origin-of-the-somali-people-and-clan-system/

Samatar, Abdi Ismail. *"Origins of the Somali Famine"* August 16, 2011 http://www.newsday.com/opinion/oped/origins-of-the-somalia-famine-1.3100205

Berkley Center for Religion, Peace & World Affairs. *"Somalia: Islam and Colonialism"* http://berkleycenter.georgetown.edu/essays/somalia-islam-and-colonialism

Ray, Nivedita. *"Rise of Islamic Forces in Somalia"* April 2006 http://www.idsa.in/strategicanalysis/RiseofIslamicForcesinSomalia_nray_0406.html

Lewis, Toby. *"Somali Cultural Profile"*
https://ethnomed.org/culture/somali/somali-cultural-profile
(Society)

Country Studies. *"Islam in the Colonial Era and After"*
http://countrystudies.us/somalia/49.htm
(Society)

Permanent Socialism. *"Siad Barre's Regime, The Cold War, And The Civil War, Draft"* May 15, 2013
https://permanentsocialism.wordpress.com/2013/05/15/siad-barres-regime-the-cold-war-and-the-civil-war-draft/
(Independence to the Civil War)

United Nations. *"Somalia- UNOSOM II Background"*
http://www.un.org/en/peacekeeping/missions/past/unosom2backgr1.html

The Center For Justice & Accountability. *"Somalia: Colonial Legacy"*
http://www.cja.org/article.php?id=436
(Colonial Times)

Wise, Rob. Center For Strategic & International Studies. *"Al Shabaab"* July 2011
http://csis.org/files/publication/110715_Wise_AlShabaab_AQAM%20Futures%20Case%20Study_WEB.pdf
(The Rise of Terror)

BBC Africa. *"Kenya Attack: 147 Dead In Garissa University Assault"* April 3, 2015
http://www.bbc.com/news/world-africa-32169080
(The Rise of Terror)

BBC Africa. *"Who Are Somalia's Al-Shabaab?"* April 3, 2015
http://www.bbc.com/news/world-africa-15336689
(The Rise of Terror)

Poverties: Research For Social & Economic Development. *"Poverty & Famine In Somalia The Root Causes"* March 2013 http://www.poverties.org/famine-in-somalia.html **(Refugee Crisis)**

National Somali Bantu Project. *"Religion"* http://www.bantusupport.pdx.edu/daily_life/religion.php **(The History of the Somali Bantu)**

Ahmed, Ali. Jimale. *(1995) The Invention of Somalia*. Lawrenceville, NJ: The Red Sea Press, Inc. (pgs: 1–19) **(The History of Somalia)**

Bryden, Matt. *(2013) Somalia Redux?*. Lanham, MD: Rowan & Littlefield. (pgs: 1-14) **(A New Era)**

Afyare Abdi Elmi and Dr. Abdullahi Barise. *The Somali Conflict: Root causes, obstacles, and peace-building strategies.* **(A New Era)**

file:///C:/Users/Guest/Downloads/Chapter4%20(2).pdf

MO. "Somali president discusses his achievements and challenges ahead." *Mareeg*. September 12, 2014. http://www.mareeg.com/somali-president-discusses-his-achievements-and-challenges-ahead/ **(A New Era)**

"Somalia 'determined' to improve on human rights situation." *Horseed Media*. March 4, 2015. http://horseedmedia.net/2015/03/04/somalia-determined-to-improve-on-human-rights-situation/

"Somali President Message to Al-Shabaab After Hotel Attack." *CCTV Africa*. http://cctv-africa.com/2015/07/27/somali-president-message-to-al-shabaab-after-hotel-attack/

(The Rise of Terror)

Eilperin, Juliet and Sieff, Kevin. "Obama commits U.S. to intensified fight against terrorists in East Africa." *The Washington Post.* July 25, 2015. http://www.washingtonpost.com/politics/us-to-expand-support-in-kenya-somalia-for-counterterrorism-operations/2015/07/25/b6f386f0-3210-11e5-97ae-30a30cca95d7_story.html
(The Rise of Terror)

Felbab-Brown, Vanda. "How Reconstruction Stalled—And What to do About It." *Foreign Affairs.* June 23, 2015. Saving Somalia (Again). https://www.foreignaffairs.com/articles/somalia/2015-06-23/saving-somalia-again

Ahren Schaefer and Andrew Black. "Clan and Conflict in Somalia: Al-Shabaab and the Myth of Transcending Clan Politics." *The Jamestown Foundation.* November 4, 2011. http://www.jamestown.org/single/?tx_ttnews%5Btt_news%5D=38628#.VcZJ8yvF9rb
(Somali Clan System)

"Somali Culture and Belief." *Blogspot. Focus On Africa.* http://focusonafrika.blogspot.com/p/sports.html

"Somalia." *Every Culture.* 2006. http://www.everyculture.com/Sa-Th/Somalia.html

Knott, John. "UK: Somalia: Clan Rivalry, Military Conflict, And The Financial And Human Cost of Piracy." *Mondaq.* March 17, 2009. http://www.mondaq.com/x/76272/Marine+Shipping/Somalia+Clan+Rivalry+Military+Conflict+And+The+Financial+And+Human+Cost+Of+Piracy
(Somali Clan System)

"2015 UNHCR country operations profile- Somalia." *UNHCR The UN Refugee Agency.* 2015. http://www.unhcr.org/pages/49e483ad6.html

Omar Nor and Jason Hanna. "12 killed in Al-Shabaab attack on Somali education ministry." CNN. April 14, 2015. http://edition.cnn.com/2015/04/14/africa/somalia-violence/

(The Rise Of Terror)

"Origins, Migrations, And Settlement." *Country Studies.* http://countrystudies.us/somalia/3.htm

Besteman L., Catherine. "Genocide in Somalia's Jubba Valley and Somali Bantu Refugees in the U.S." *Crisis In the Horn of Africa.* April 9, 2007. http://hornofafrica.ssrc.org/Besteman/

"Refugees in the US: One Family's Story." *National Geographic.* October 28, 2010. http://news.nationalgeographic.com/news/2003/06/0620_030620_banturefugees_2.html

Goffe, Leslie. "New life in US for Somali Bantus." *BBC News.* August 13, 2004. http://news.bbc.co.uk/2/hi/africa/3559298.stm

"Somali Bantus gain Tanzanian citizenship in their ancestral land." *UNHCR The UN Refugee Agency.* June 3, 2009. http://www.unhcr.org/4a28cd886.html

"Somali Bantus begin first stage of journey to United States." *UNHCR The UN Refugee Agency.* July 2, 2002. http://www.unhcr.org/3d2194174.html

"Somali Bantus prepare for life in America." *UNHCR The UN Refugee Agency.* August 1, 2002. http://www.unhcr.org/3d493a2f5.html

"Life in a refugee Camp." *Somali Bantu Community Development Council of Denver.* 2011. http://www.sbcdcden.org/the-somali-bantu/refugee-camp-life

"Somalia: The Real Causes of Famine." *Global Relief Somali Foundation.* 2011. http://www.grsf.no/newsroom/news/somalia-the-real-causes-of-famine

"Bantu." *Nashville Public Television.* No date. http://ndn.wnpt.org/documentaries/somali/bantu/

The Editors of Encyclopedia Britannica. "Horn of Africa." Encyclopedia Britannica. http://www.britannica.com/place/Horn-of-Africa

Horn of Africa. "*Crisis In The Horn of Africa.*" http://hornofafrica.ssrc.org/ (Overview: The Horn of Africa)

Njoku, Raphael C. *The History of Somalia*. Santa Barbara: Greenwood, 2013. (pgs. 52 and 62-65)

Mengisteab, Kidane. *The Horn of Africa*. Cambridge: Polity Press, 2014. (pgs. 1,2,16,17, and 25)
I.M. Lewis pg. 11

"Clan and Conflict in Somalia: Al-Shabaab and the Myth of." The Jamestown Foundation. N.p., n.d. Web. 02 July 2016.

Council on Foreign Relations. Council on Foreign Relations, n.d. Web. 02 July 2016.

"Bullying and Suicide - Bullying Statistics." *Bullying Statistics*. N.p., 07 July 2015. Web. 02 July 2016.

"Donald Trump Immigration Plan: The Specifics." *CNN*. Cable News Network, n.d. Web. 02 July 2016.

"Iraq: ISIS Escapees Describe Systematic Rape." Human Rights Watch. N.p., 14 Apr. 2015. Web. 02 July 2016.

"Geography AS Notes." *Mexico to USA Migration*. N.p., n.d. Web. 02 July 2016.

"The Top 10 Most Startling Facts About People of Color and Criminal Justice in the United States." *Name*. N.p., n.d. Web. 02 July 2016.

"Locating the School-to-Prison Pipeline." *American Civil Liberties Union*. N.p., n.d. Web. 02 July 2016.

"Fact Sheet: How Bad Is the School-to-Prison Pipeline?" *PBS*. PBS, n.d. Web. 02 July 2016.

"Editorial Stop the School-to-Prison Pipeline." *Editorial Stop the School-to-Prison Pipeline.* N.p., n.d. Web. 02 July 2016.

"The School-to-Prison Pipeline." *Teaching Tolerance.* N.p., n.d. Web. 02 July 2016.

"Female Genital Mutilation." *World Health Organization.* N.p., n.d. Web. 02 July 2016.
"Maternal Mortality." *World Health Organization.* N.p., n.d. Web. 02 July 2016.

"Quick Facts: What You Need to Know about the Syria Crisis." *Mercy Corps.* N.p., 16 June 2016. Web. 02 July 2016.

http://lltd.educ.ubc.ca/media/dadaab-camps/
file:///C:/Users/Guest/Downloads/HagaderaCampProfile_DadaabKenya
August2015.pdf
(Hagadera)

http://reliefweb.int/sites/reliefweb.int/files/resources/DagahaleyCamp
Profile_DadaabKenyaAugust2015.pdf
(Dagahaley)

file:///C:/Users/Guest/Downloads/IfoCampProfile_DadaabKenya
August2015%20(1).pdf
(Ifo)

file:///C:/Users/Guest/Downloads/Ifo2CampProfile_DadaabKenya
August2015.pdf
(Ifo 2)

http://www.un.org/en/peacekeeping/missions/past/unosomi.htm

CPSIA information can be obtained
at www.ICGtesting.com
Printed in the USA
LVHW01s2330200118
563321LV00001B/104/P